Praise for *A Charmed Life*

"As she struggles to reconcile love and shame in this courageous memoir, Campbell offers a fascinating glimpse into the nuanced snobberies of the British aristocracy . . . a page-turner set among moats, drawbridges, and portcullises both real and metaphorical."

—*Vogue*

"A haunting memoir."

—*OK! Magazine*

"Liza Campbell . . . has written a rip-roaring exposé that tells it as it was . . . This is a fascinating and tragic family story, and so well written."

—*The Roanoke Times*

"This beautifully written nonfiction book is full of Scottish history from a completely personal point of view, told in a way that is eminently readable."

—Tama Janowitz, author of
Slaves of New York and *Area Code 212*

"The writing is so ingratiating that the reader quickly likes the writer and feels enormous empathy for her life with such a strange and even dangerous father."

—*Deseret News*

A Charmed Life

A Charmed Life

Growing Up in Macbeth's Castle

Liza Campbell

Thomas Dunne Books
St. Martin's Griffin
New York

THOMAS DUNNE BOOKS.
An imprint of St. Martin's Press.

A CHARMED LIFE. Copyright © 2006 by Liza Campbell. All rights reserved. Printed in the United States of America. For information, address St. Martin's Press, 175 Fifth Avenue, New York, N.Y. 10010.

www.thomasdunnebooks.com
www.stmartins.com

The author and publisher are grateful for permission to reproduce the following: lines from *The Common Reader* by Virginia Woolf, published by Hogarth Press/Vintage, reprinted by permission of The Random House Group Ltd; lines from *Doubtful Partners* by Fiona Pitt-Kethley, first published by Arcadia Books, 1996; lines from *Do Androids Dream of Electric Sheep?* by Philip K. Dick are reproduced by permission of Victor Gollancz, a division of The Orion Publishing Group; lines from *The Crack Up* by F. Scott Fitzgerald are reproduced by permission of Penguin UK; lines from *Blood Meridian* by Cormac McCarthy are reproduced by permission of Macmillan UK; lines from *Unfortunate Coincidence* by Dorothy Parker are reproduced by permission of Duckworth Publishers. The publishers have made every reasonable effort to contact the copyright owners of the extracts and illustrations reproduced in this book. In the few cases where they have been unsuccessful they invite copyright holders to contact them direct.

The Library of Congress has catalogued the hardcover edition as follows:

Campbell, Liza.
        A charmed life : growing up in Macbeth's castle / Liza Campbell.—1st U.S. ed.
            p. cm.
        ISBN-13: 978-0-312-37477-8
        ISBN-10: 0-312-37477-1
        1. Campbell, Liza. 2. Campbell family. 3. Cawdor Castle (Scotland). 4. Aristocracy (Social class)—Scotland—Biography.   I. Title.

DA758.3.C25 C36 2007
941.1'58085092—dc22   2007022657
[B]

ISBN-13: 978-0-312-38496-8 (pbk.)
ISBN-10: 0-312-38496-3 (pbk.)

First published in Great Britain under the title *Title Deeds*
by Doubleday, a division of Transworld Publishers

10   9   8   7   6   5   4

To Storm and Atticus

Thanes of Cawdor

1st
Donald
d. 1295

2nd
William
(the donkey dreamer)

3rd
William
(built the central keep)

4th
Andrew
(murdered by Sir
Gervaise de Rait)
d. 1405

5th
Donald
(hereditary sheriff of Nairn)
d. 1442

6th
William
(Crown Chamberlain, further
fortified Cawdor in 1454)
d. 1468

7th
William
(resigned estates in favour of
his son)
d. 1503

.8th
John
(m. Isabel Rose of Kilravock)
d. 1498

9th
Muriel
(kidnapped and forced into
marriage with Sir John
Campbell of Argyll)
d. 1575

10th
Archibald
(predeceased his mother)
d. 1551

11th
John
(murdered in an Argyll plot)
d. 1591

12th
Sir John
(built Cawdor Kirk)
d. 1642

13th
Colin
(died at Glasgow University)
d. 1647

14th
John 'the Fiar'
MP, d. 1654

15th
Sir Hugh
(MP, m. Lady Henrietta Stuart of Darnaway, made large additions to Cawdor)
d. 1716

16th
Sir Alexander
(MP, Lord of the Admiralty & Treasury; m. Elizabeth Lort of Stackpole)
d. 1697

17th
Pryse
(MP, the tartan wearer)
d. 1768

18th
'Joyless' John
(m. Mary Pryse)
d. 1770

19th
John
(MP, defeated the French at Fishguard, 1st Baron Cawdor; m. Lady Caroline Howard)
d. 1821

20th
John Frederick
(MP, 2nd Baron, 1st Earl)
d. 1860

21st
John Frederick Vaughan
(MP, 2nd Earl)
d. 1898

22nd
Frederick Archibald
(MP, 1st Lord of the Admiralty, 3rd Earl)
d. 1911

23rd
Hugh
(4th Earl, m. Joan Thynne, contracted syphilis)
d. 1914

24th
John 'Jack'
(5th Earl, m. 1. Wilma Vickers 2. Elizabeth, Lady Gordon Cumming)
d. 1970

25th
Hugh John Vaughan
(6th Earl, m. 1. Cathryn Hinde 2. Angelika Lazansky)
d. 1990

26th
Colin Robert Vaughan
b. 1963
(m. Lady Isabella Stanhope)

The Campbells of Cawdor

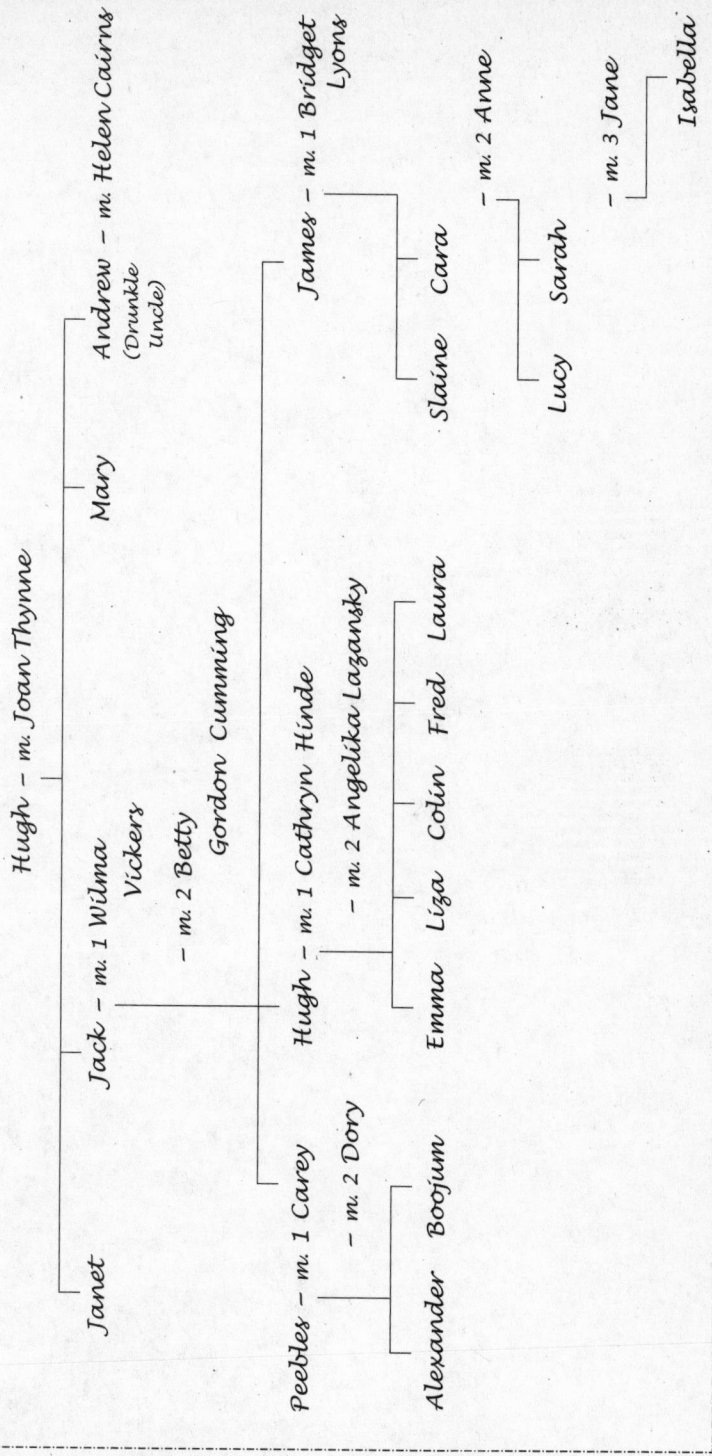

Hugh – m. Joan Thynne

Janet

Jack – m. 1 Wilma Vickers
– m. 2 Betty Gordon Cumming

Mary

Andrew – m. Helen Cairns (Drunkle Uncle)

Peebles – m. 1 Carey
– m. 2 Dory

Alexander   Boojum

Hugh – m. 1 Cathryn Hinde
– m. 2 Angelika Lazansky

Emma   Liza   Colin   Fred   Laura

James – m. 1 Bridget Lyons

Slaine   Cara

– m. 2 Anne

Lucy   Sarah

– m. 3 Jane

Isabella

A Charmed Life

Prologue

Many suffer from the incurable disease of writing, and it
becomes chronic in their sick minds.

Juvenal

IN MY FAMILY, WE WRITE NOTES, TEXTS, EMAILS, LETTERS,
diaries, articles, columns. My childhood was punctuated by
long spells away from home, and the pining for it was both
intensified and assuaged by the steady flow of letters. The
high point of any school day was to see the corner of an
envelope protruding from my pigeonhole. The love I felt
for my parents was only ever stumblingly expressed right at
the end of letters that laboriously recorded rounders match
results and what stationery I needed. Their love and my
love existed in a silent, inky world. We were brought up
proficient in the art of talking about what we thought, but
not in the messier art of how we felt. The vacuum was

filled by a love of facts. As long as we knew every tributary of the Congo, who cared if we were emotional pygmies?

The reason why we found it so much easier to express ourselves in writing than in speech can be traced back to a sexual misadventure in Edwardian times. It so traumatized our great-grandmother Joan that she brought up her children while resorting only occasionally to conversation.

In 1914, her husband, my great-grandfather Hugh, died at the age of forty-three after contracting syphilis in Japan. He spent the years leading up to his death in a sanatorium, rarely visited by his family – a non-person. The perceived shame of these circumstances was too much for his widow, and at home, Joan's life had become a mirror of his. She withdrew from the world, tremulous and mute, never mentioning her husband again. My grandfather Jack was fourteen when his father died and thereafter the family lived in a beige atmosphere of unspoken hurts, his mother a flitting wraith. If Joan wished to communicate with him, she would push a message under his door. Sometimes when she was feeling particularly taciturn she would scribble a note to him, or his three siblings, while sharing the same table. Every evening, supper started the moment the clock struck eight. The chink of spoon against bowl was often the only sound to accompany the rasp of the hall clock pendulum. At the tug of a bell-pull, a new course would arrive, and then another, until this lumbering nightly ritual was concluded at precisely ten to nine, in silence. It would not tax a trainee psychologist to work out that my grandfather grew up a poor communicator. Jack used letters as the main form of familial traffic, and when his son, my father Hugh – named in memory of his disgraced and forgotten grandparent – wanted to express his emotions to us, he picked up a pen.

Because I write articles for a living, there has been for some time a shadow in the corner, a murmuring voice, an inner pressure to produce something more, something longer. But what? Every time I began to write fiction – and there are many efforts now filed away on top of various cupboards – the characters and the plot kept coming back to the same old story and I would stop. Whenever I started up again, the story was lying in wait for me. Finally, I resolved to stop sidestepping and tell it, and then, with luck, have done with it. If my two brothers and two sisters sat down and wrote their version of events, the reader would have five markedly different accounts. We all saw different things and viewed the same things differently. We reacted differently and were treated differently. My story is only one slender wedge of the pie.

I sent a couple of chapters to a writer friend. He said I must 'work out my angle'.

'It's a morality tale,' I said.

'No, it's not,' Milo replied. 'The protagonist doesn't get his comeuppance.'

I was stumped. He offered some alternatives. Was the story looking back into history to see how the past informed the present? Sort of. Was it about how a child finds its way through a confusing family labyrinth? Sort of. Was the book about a modern woman in a medieval set of circumstances? Partially. 'You must go away and think and be able to say, "Yes!" not, "Sort of." And,' he added, 'you must also find "your sentence".' Milo explained that all books could be distilled into a single sentence or phrase. For example, Hemingway's *Old Man and the Sea* is 'pensioner loses fish'. *The Great Gatsby* is 'he was a parvenu, you know'. The Bible is 'piety: the paradox', thanks to the Old Testament condensing to 'an eye for an eye' and the New to 'turn the other cheek'. 'You must be sure of your underlying sentence,' he said. 'Everything should emanate from that. If the reader senses a firm foundation, they will trust digressions, but if they sense confusion, they will lose confidence in why they are reading.'

I went home and mulled over his advice, and although I really wished that his suggestions would fit, they fitted only up to a point. I was at the very beginning and already stuck. My only strategy in similar situations is to clear my mind as best I can and *not* think. Then, pling! Yes, I was trying to understand my past; yes, I wondered whether, if I plaited all the threads into one, I might find connections I had previously missed; yes, it was the story of a child who lived in a fairly unusual family setting where the past always sat alongside the present like a fat friend on the sofa. But the answer, the totally honest answer, was for a reckoning. My story has at its centre a protagonist who never got his come-uppance. It was this that drove me. I couldn't right the wrong, but I could write the wrong. So, what was my sentence? I think perhaps it is 'Papa was odd, but I got even.'

By the end of this book, I hope to have worked out who the hell my father was and what triggered his decline, and to have traced some of the consequences of his unfathomable behaviour.

Chapter 1

We owe respect to the living; the dead we owe only truth.

Voltaire

WHEN THE INVERNESS FLIGHT TOOK OFF FROM HEATHROW, London was experiencing the kind of June evening that encourages girls to stroll the streets in their tiniest finery. An hour later, the plane reached the Grampian Mountains and began its descent towards the southern shore of the Moray Firth. The polish of distant water winked in fierce Morse. Treeless moorland melted into geometric forestry patterns, and where the dense blocks of trees ended, the rolling coastal plains of wheat and pasture began. Solstice had only just passed, and this far north the summer dusk lingers until well after ten o'clock.

On this particular evening, the plane took a slight, un-announced diversion. Fifteen miles to the east of Inverness,

Cawdor stands out like a grey, stone fist. The plane banked over the battlements, dipped its wings, and then continued on its final approach to the airport. This silent act of respect was for my father, Hugh John Vaughan Cawdor: his body lay in the hold. As a family home, Cawdor Castle has the romantic cachet of being one of the few addresses featured in a Shakespeare play that can also be found on an AA road map.

The plan was for the undertakers to take my father's coffin from the airport to the house and leave it overnight in the Tree Room at the base of the tower. The walls of the room are bare stone and it is normally empty, aside from a dilapidated old chest and the trunk of an ancient, lifeless tree. This is the remains of a holly tree around which the castle walls were built. It died when the completion of the vaulted ceiling finally deprived it of sunlight. Holly trees, like rowans, are pagan symbols in Scotland and were planted to ward off witches. Many houses will have one planted in their gardens. Perhaps burying the tree within the house was just taking superstition to its logical conclusion.

The explanation as to why there should be a small tree preserved in the belly of Cawdor dates back to 1310, when William, the 2nd Thane of Cawdor, received a royal charter from Robert the Bruce to build a bigger fortification than his current castle, which guarded a boggy ford. Thane William's first task was to study the surrounding district and find a location of improved strength, but in an unorthodox and seldom imitated move, he left this decision up to a donkey. William had had a vivid dream in which he was visited by a host of angels. They told him that he should place all his worldly goods in a chest and strap it to the back of a donkey; he must then allow it to wander freely all day and mark where it chose to rest for the night. If he built the castle on that spot, they said, it would prosper for ever. And who was he to doubt the word of angels? He followed their instructions. The donkey had been born without a gift for martial strategy, however, so the site it chose was unremarkable. The holly tree is where it lay down.* I am conscious as I retell this slightly batty legend that I do so as fact. When my teacher spoke about family trees, I didn't realize it was only a figure of speech. I assumed there were trees in the cellars of people's houses everywhere.

To a child, that crooked trunk in a bare dungeon looked like irrefutable proof of the story's truth, just as the castle walls placed us at the centre of Shakespeare's *Macbeth*. In 'the Scottish play', as it is superstitiously referred to by thesps, when King Duncan rewards his loyal kinsman Macbeth with the title of Thane of Cawdor, it sets Macbeth on a path of treachery. For those dreaming in English classes, before he hears of his new honour, three witches

---

*When I write about the holly at Cawdor, it sounds like we always knew that that is what the tree was. In fact, until about ten years before my father died everyone knew it as 'the hawthorn'. This information had been passed down by word of mouth for hundreds of years, but then my father got a small chunk of the bark analysed and its true identity was revealed. In a family of people brought up to be the museum guides of our own past this was a seismic shock on the scale of learning that Jesus's real name was Gerard. I once read (in *King Arthur* by Andrew Matthews) that 'a legend starts off as a true story, but as the story is told over and over again, it gets mixed up in our hopes and dreams. Some things are missed out, and new things are added along the way, and in the end facts and imagination run into one another until it is impossible to tell which is which.' And that sounds about right for me.

accost him as he walks across the Blasted Heath and greet him as Thane of Glamis, Thane of Cawdor and King of Scotland, although only the first title is rightfully his. Then messengers arrive with word that King Duncan has given Macbeth the second title of the hags' prediction, and he concludes that their words chart the course of his future. At home, his wife, a red-haired beauty with an icy ambition, whips on Macbeth's transformation from hero to monster. She welcomes Duncan to Cawdor, and incites her husband to murder as their guest sleeps. The couple's ruthlessness takes its toll and together they drift into the arena of the mentally unwell. With a mounting death toll, Macbeth is troubled by visions of ghosts, and Lady Macbeth develops a standard example of obsessive-compulsive disorder, until the tragedy reaches its climax at the final battle.

The house we lived in wasn't built until three hundred years after King Duncan's death but Shakespeare hadn't let facts get in the way of a good story, and furthermore, Duncan had not been killed in his sleep at all. The historically correct version of events was that Macbeth had been born with an equal claim to the Scottish throne. He raised an army against Duncan, who was killed in battle when they clashed at the nearby town of Forres. Macbeth took the throne using a perfectly legitimate method of the time; a quarter of a century later William the Conqueror took the English crown in much the same way when he killed King Harold at Hastings. Even more surprisingly, given the lasting slur of the play, Macbeth was a popular king. He made a pilgrimage to Rome that lasted, literally, for years, without being overthrown in his absence. When he died, in the year before the Battle of Hastings, he was buried on the holy island of Iona alongside previous kings – a privilege denied usurpers. My family were always quick to point out the error of Shakespeare's ways, yet saw nothing odd in donkeys and angels and claiming descent from the stubbornly fictional swan knight Lohengrin.

I felt proud to come from such an ancient, myth-wreathed place, but mostly I took all these imaginary and historical details for granted. Visitors showed far more interest in the Macbeth connection than we did, and would gaze intently at the Victorian charcoal drawings of the three witches drawn directly onto the plaster walls of the library. There was a life-size sketch of Macbeth with flying hair and a pleasingly demented look in his eyes. Best of all, hidden behind an arras, was a drawing of a dagger dripping with blood.

The knowledge I had of my ancestors stretched back so far into the past that they vanished from sight around the roots of a shrivelled tree. And now, twenty-one generations later, it was my father's turn to join them.

Hugh was the 25th Thane of Cawdor. When my grand-parents' first-born child was a girl, the family held its collective breath for two years, when they heaved a primo-genital sigh of relief. On the day of my father's birth, a huge bonfire was lit on the highest local point, to salute the safe arrival of the next heir to Cawdor. Estate workers kept the beacon stoked throughout the September night and flames leapt to such a height that they could be seen from the Black Isle, twelve miles to the north, across the wide, dark waters of the Moray Firth. Tonight, sixty years later, the same hill was once more a blazing beacon, closing my father's life in fiery symmetry.

But the wonderful, charismatic, affectionate father I had known had died a decade before this. If I pulled out a rusty drawer of memories I could see that there were many things to celebrate: his wit, his encyclopaedic knowledge (especially of trees), his twinkly kindness, his generosity and his love of us. But he had changed so much. None of these recollections matched the final incarnation. For the last ten years of his life he had stopped being able to express warmth; he could only do anger, and it frightened me – which, naturally, pissed him off.

On paper he really did not have a lot to be pissed off about. Hugh had been born an exceptionally lucky man. The instant he successfully sucked in his first independent breath of air, he became the next in line to an abundance of gifts: two stately homes, four ruined castles of beauty rather than use, a hundred thousand acres in two separate parcels of land. The main estate was in Scotland, with Cawdor at its centre; the second was in Wales, around a house called Stackpole. The land interests included arable and dairy farms, timber and commercially grown flowers. There was shooting on the moorland and fishing on the rivers that flowed through the two estates. Hugh was the heir to beautiful French furniture, Chinese ornaments, Flemish tapestries, Persian carpets, a library full of rare books, family portraits, Italian landscapes, sculptures and a great deal of money invested in shares, cared for by expensive stockbrokers and grandee solicitors. His sole qualification for all this extraordinary privilege was to be born. These possessions were in his care, but not strictly his. He was one link in a custodial chain that had handed a unique legacy down from father to son for the previous six hundred years.

As the plane taxied to a halt the local undertaker – dark-suited, solemn, with black rock-a-billy hair – walked across the tarmac to oversee the transfer of the body from air to land. My sister Laura had been on the flight, and she watched through the plate-glass wall of the arrivals hall as four baggage handlers in day-glo jackets emerged from the hold and struggled awkwardly with the coffin, a large orange rucksack balanced incongruously on the lid. The undertaker swiped the bag off, snapped at the men, then tenderly wiped away the blemish of this impropriety with his handkerchief. The coffin was heaved onto a flatbed trolley. It jiggled jauntily as it trundled behind a forklift truck that took it to the hearse, parked at the furthest corner of the departures lounge.

I only know these things because I was told about them. At the time, I was four thousand miles away with my husband and children, on the Indonesian island of Sumba, walking at toddler pace along a jungle path near a remote camp that was our new home. If the sandflies weren't about, I was planning to look for butterflies where a small stream emerged from the edge of the jungle and had dug a miniature delta across the beach before entering the sea. My children were aged one and two, so I could just about manage them in papooses strapped fore and aft and still have a hand free for the butterfly net. It isn't until you start hunting butterflies that their mazy flight takes on new meaning. What looks like purposeless fluttering is in fact

11

extremely wily defence tactics. Willie, my husband, in his capacity as the camp's marine manager, was out at sea checking the marker buoys on a new dive site.

'Liza! Liza!' The camp manager came running down the path towards me waving a fax. He handed it over, adding quickly, 'I'm so very sorry,' before retreating a few paces. The printout was from my youngest brother, and it read:

After a week in hospital trying to fight off blood poisoning, Pa died peacefully, on June 20th. Emma, Laura, and Angelika were with him. Colin and I were in Norway. We returned a day too late. No signal in the effing fjords. Angelika wants to press ahead with the funeral, which will be at Pluscarden on June 23rd. Hurry back. God bless, love Fred.

I looked at my watch. It was the 23rd. Suddenly it was oppressively cold in the heat. A strange moan floated by that I vaguely recognized as coming from my own throat. The manager backed away looking unsettled. Sobs seemed to collide and crash through my whole body. The children looked at me in horror and instantly joined in with a chorus of terrified wails – grief trapped in reflecting arcs. My father had been dying for a whole week. We were remote, sure, but we had a two-way radio and faxes were forwarded to us via an office in Bali. Why had no messages reached me? I was shattered. I had been living in far corners of the world, but I had never meant to be beyond reach; yet, plainly, that is what I was. It was clear from

Fred's fax that even my sister Emma had made it back from her home in Africa. And why was Pa being buried at Pluscarden? The family church stood in the village, a stone's throw from Cawdor; Pluscarden was a monastery twenty-five miles away.

Pa had only recently been diagnosed with cancer. It had started innocuously enough. It had been only six months since he had taken to his bed with something initially diagnosed as flu. He wrote me a letter in which he complained of being bored, saying that he couldn't find anything written with any pith. The only thing that had caught his eye was the odd fact that Boudicca's grave was thought to be 'underneath platform 8 at King's Cross station'.

When the flu developed into pneumonia, his doctor sent him to a specialist. He rang to tell me about the cancer before Christmas, when Willie and I were still living in England. He said the news had been 'like receiving registered post': once you sign for it, you can't pretend it never came. Despite being very asthmatic, my father had been an ardent smoker throughout his adult life. He had chain-smoked since his early teens, graduating from single Woodbines bummed off the gamekeepers to catering packs of Rothmans. Later, when my stepmother Angelika insisted that he give up, he compromised with cigars which he surreptitiously inhaled. He saw it as a clever cheat, but who he thought was being cheated was a little ambiguous.

When we left for Sumba two months later, it was in my mind, but only in the most abstract of ways, that perhaps I would never see my father again. I adamantly believed that he would survive another year. It would have to be another year because, subconsciously, I could only envisage him dying during the winter. It suited his character. Not now, at the peak of a British summer. It made zero sense, and barely three seasons had passed from detection to death. Of course, we none of us know our sell-by dates and the timing is an inexact science, unless you are at the business end of a lethal weapon. The best we can hope for is that our dying will be comforted and not alone. Missing the instant of death is not unusual, but at least my stepmother Angelika and my two sisters Emma and Laura had been there. Like me, neither of my brothers Colin and Fred had made it to his bedside in time either. Soon after, Emma said she thought it was a good thing, saying, 'Death is women's work. Like birth.' But to miss the burial? I could never, ever have imagined that I would miss my own father's funeral.

I stumbled towards our cabin in a daze. Word had spread. The workmen in the camp stared at me shyly, but no-one said a word. I tried to quieten the children, but they would not be quietened. Nothing in my manner reassured them. My pink swimsuit and sarong seemed suddenly to throb with incongruous cheer. How strange, I thought. Here I am, half a world away from any ceremony, and my first impulse is to find something black to wear. I rifled through our sea-chest. Rats had nibbled a vertical cross-section of our clothes. I hated this co-habitation with the rats. Our bed was two singles pushed together and the rats used the central gulley made by the wooden bed frames as a nocturnal highway. I could hear them scuttling up and down it; once I woke up to find one squatting nonchalantly on my chest. The rats had no fear of us and I worried that they would eventually find a way into the children's cots and bite them. The closest thing to suitable mourning clothes was a dark blue dress that the rats had missed. I put it on and settled down on our doorstep to scan the sea for a sign of Willie's boat returning. Storm and Atticus began to play with a line of ants, and a while later I spotted the boat's hull, a pale smear just below the horizon. I gathered up the children, fed them an early lunch of noodles, bathed them in turn in a bucket to cool them, and stroked their foreheads until they slept.

Up in the shadows of our thatch a new gecko started up its racket. The geckos on Sumba were enormous and made deafening clicks and sounds like the 'he he he' of mirthless laughter. The crashing of surf made it hard to sleep, but the geckos made it harder still, and eventually Willie borrowed an air rifle from the camp manager. The offending gecko was directly over our bed when Willie shot it through the neck. Its head fell back, one suction-padded foot fell away, then another, and then a third; but the last foot kept its grip and the corpse hung there, dripping blood onto our mosquito net, until days later, when Willie finally scrambled up the roof beams and knocked it down. The new gecko took up residency the following evening. So far, life on Sumba had been more slog than adventure. There were no friends for thousands of miles, no-one to laugh with and downsize little ordeals like the geckocide.

I sat back down on the steps and waited another hour before the boat finally chugged to shore. All the time I was very quiet, very still, but my entire nervous system was humming like a faulty reactor. My thoughts kept returning to the fact that I did not know the identity of the huge tree that shaded our hut, and how Pa would have sagged his knees and clapped his hand to his forehead in mock despair at my woeful lack of local knowledge. And now he was dead. I walked down to the beach and told Willie my news. I hugged him, then clung, then reverted to hugging, and finally let go. The crewman Mo, who had had a Jesuit upbringing, stood beside us and sang 'Vaya con Dios' in a beautiful bass. These were the first two people who had fully responded to what had happened and I felt misery and gratitude.

Deep breath. OK, so I wasn't going to get to the funeral. I must mark it in some other way. While I had fretted about the tree and waited for Willie's return, a sketchy plan had formulated in my head. First, I needed to go into Waikabubak to try and put a call through back home. Secondly, I wanted to launch my Balinese kite off the hill above the camp and cast it free to fly away on the wind. Lastly, I wanted to buy a lot of candles and light them in tribute. My father had died at the age of sixty. I had never thought of sixty as young before, but it was. It was no age.

The small town of Waikabubak was only twelve miles from the camp, but the track was so rutted it took nearly an hour to get there. Still, being eight hours ahead of GMT meant I had time in hand. I went into the telephone exchange. It was a bare room with peeling plaster, a faded poster advertising Komodo dragons, and a bored-looking

clerk sitting behind a metal grille. I gave her the number
and waited in a small phone booth on the far side of the
room. I did not feel at all hopeful. A few moments later
the clerk called and told me to pick up the receiver. The
number was ringing. Someone picked it up.

'Hello,' I said.

'Hello,' came a tinny echo.

'It's Liza.'

'It's Liza!'

Another voice, not an echo this time, cut in. 'I'll get
Emma!' it called back, as if shouting down a garden hose
stuffed with socks. And then Emma came on; then Laura;
then Fred; and, lastly, Colin. They told me as much as they
could. It was hard to hear, but such a great, great comfort
to actually speak to them.

'What time is it there?' I asked.

'About half six in the morning.'

'I'm sorry to get you out of bed.'

'You didn't.'

They'd been up all night by the bonfire. They had holed
up with the keepers who were tending the beacon. Drams
were pressed on them as the men reminisced fondly about
Pa. The whisky sent stabbing warmth down their gullets
and the kindly talk soothed. Toasts were drunk and then
some more, and then another bottle appeared. Some time
later they were all lying on their backs away from the ferocious heat of the fire, watching the trajectory of chosen
sparks against a grey and pink herringbone sky slowly
darkening to blue. Many of the keepers, past sixty themselves, lamented the dreadful shame of their boss's

premature death and drank the health of Colin, the new young Thane.

'When is the funeral your time?'

'What?'

'How long before the funeral?'

'Four and a half hours.'

'OK, I'll do something then too.'

'Good idea. We'll be thinking of you here.'

I learned that Pa had been responding well to the treatment. So well, in fact, that Angelika thought it would be a treat for them both to go to a party given by some friends of hers in Paris. While there, Hugh developed a cold sore, probably the first one of his life. His immune system was so shot that by the time he and Angelika flew back to London it had developed into septicaemia. When Laura arrived at the hospital Pa had an oxygen mask on and she could hear his lungs bubbling. He was very agitated. Each time he managed to catch enough breath, he would ask her where Colin was.

Lonely and unsure of how critical the situation was, Laura tried to contact us all. She had no luck with our brothers, who were away together on an architectural study trip in Norway. Nor did she have any luck with me. But Emma was at her home in a suburb of Nairobi and her telephone, for once, was working. Laura was apologetic: 'It could be a false alarm, but I think maybe you should come.' So Emma flew to London and arrived at the hospital two days before he died. As soon as he saw her, Pa looked terrified. Why would his eldest daughter have flown in from Kenya unless it was a crisis? Spotting the expression in his eyes, she quickly remarked that wasn't it lucky she was by pure chance in London to see possible schools for her son Jack? By then, Pa was so weak he could not respond; the last words he had managed to utter had been to ask for Colin. Emma and Laura kept each other company when not taking it in turns to sit with Angelika by his bed. Whenever they felt tears welling up, they left the room and wept in the passage.

Hugh rallied fractionally and, although he could not speak, he mimed to them that he wanted a pen. But when they put it in his hand, he could hardly hold it. There was something he desperately wanted to communicate. He spent an age trying to write something. Eventually, painfully, he managed to form four spidery letters: A, L, N, and W. It had taken him half an hour and he was exhausted. Was it an acronym? An anagram of 'lawn'? After lots of questions and lateral guesses they finally realized the word he was aiming for was 'Alnwick'. He wanted to know if the Percy family from Alnwick in Northumberland had replied to an invitation he had sent them for a party to celebrate White's Club's three hundredth anniversary later in the summer. 'It's good he thinks he'll be going to it – he must believe he'll get to the other side of this,' Laura said, trying to reassure herself as much as she was trying to reassure Emma. Emma wasn't so hopeful because he rolled his eyes at her and drew a knife-like finger across his throat. She noticed that he no longer looked at them. All his concentration was on the nurses: his eyes followed them around the room as they checked the monitors and the various tubes penetrating his body. Only they interested him; only they could help. He gazed after each of them in terror and expectation.

Laura spoke about the weather outside the hospital being incongruously sublime, although each day she found herself wearing sombre clothes 'like a funeral parlour maid'. She and Emma took a break from the sterile vigil at the hospital and went for a walk in Regent's Park. On their way back, Laura bought Pa a bunch of oversized sunflowers, but when she got to his room, she lost her nerve. Perhaps he would find the flowers ridiculous, cartoonish. Scorn was something he could deliver as easily in a tiny gesture as with words. She ended up giving the bouquet to a staff nurse, and when she rejoined Emma at his bedside they sang him his favourite song from *Butch Cassidy and the Sundance Kid*:

Did you ever hear tell of sweet Betsy from Pike?
Who crossed the wide prairie with old Uncle Ike,
With two yoke of cattle and one spotted hog,
A tall Shanghai rooster and a large yellow dog.
Singin' toora-li, loora-li, loora-li, ay . . .

On day five Pa's kidneys collapsed. The intensive care team sprang into action and the doctors managed to stabilize his condition. Once the crisis had passed, the consultants gathered around his bed to discuss Hugh's progress. While they talked, my sisters nipped to a local café to fuel up on some half-decent coffee. When they returned everything had changed. Pa was in a coma. It looked as if the doctors had decided they could not go on bump-starting his body; that the fight was, effectively, over. His monitors blipped away softly, his life winding down. Pa died at noon the following day. Father's Day.

While Emma and Laura had been spending their days at the hospital, our mother had been set the task of tracking down her other three absent children. She had had no luck, and by the last day she had resorted to calling the Indonesian embassy, the Norwegian high commission, and even the police in the relevant countries, but to no avail. The last time our brothers had spoken to Pa, less than a week before, he was heading off to Paris in high spirits, so it was only by chance that Colin happened to ring our mother while he and Fred waited for their plane out of Oslo. Ma had heard nothing from Emma and Laura at the hospital, but feared her ex-husband might now be very close to death. She decided not to say anything, but told Colin to ring the hospital as quickly as possible.

Laura and Emma drove out to Heathrow to meet the Oslo flight and take their brothers back to see Pa's body before it left the hospital. Fred, for reasons known only to himself, had taken his kilt with him to Norway. On the return journey he had had trouble shutting his case and ended up wearing the kilt. Any composure Emma and Laura had dissolved the moment they caught sight of him, white with misery, striding towards them wearing our family tartan. It was so unexpected, so incongruous, yet it added a poignancy that perfectly fitted this family upheaval.

'Why is the funeral going ahead so soon?' I asked.

'I don't know.'

'It's only three days since he died!'

Even if I had been told the instant it had happened, this timetable would never have allowed me to reach Cawdor in time – even if every single flight co-ordinated seamlessly. First, there was the bumpy crawl from our camp to Waikabubak, then it was a four-hour bus ride to Waingapu, the capital of Sumba, then a two-hour plane ride to Bali, and then seventeen hours from Bali to London that included a mandatory stopover in Singapore and a further flight up to Scotland.

'None of us know whether we're coming or going. It's been completely surreal.'

'Why is the funeral happening at Pluscarden?' I asked.

'He became a Catholic on his deathbed.'

'You are kidding!'

'Nope. How strange is that?'

How strange indeed. Both Hugh and his father before him had been rabidly anti-Catholic. I had always assumed this loathing was a remnant from times long past, when Scottish politics and affiliations divided down religious lines. Most of the families to the east of us were, like us, Presbyterian, while to the west we abutted the very big, very Catholic Fraser clan. Border folk hold their differences higher than those in the hinterland, but Pa's antipathy to 'left footers' went so far as shunning any socializing with the Frasers, even though neither he nor Jack was remotely devout. They attended the Presbyterian kirk to show their faces and pay lip service, but Hugh showed all the signs of being, if not an atheist, then a steadfast agnostic. It was not until we formed firm teenage friendships with young Frasers that Pa finally relented and allowed us to invite them over and offer them the first Cawdor Campbell hospitality in generations.

'I'm coming back!' I called out.

'There's no point! Half of us leave here tonight after the funeral and the rest tomorrow.'

'I'm coming back anyway. I can't just stay on here as if—'

'What's that humming? Your voice has gone crackly . . . Liza . . . Hello?' With much clicking and whirring, the line went dead. My head jerked back from Scotland to Sumba.

I had been sitting in the Waikabubak telephone exchange for nearly an hour, and suddenly it felt stifling. I stood up and moved closer to the window, stretching the telephone cable as far as it would go. On the road I could see a small dust-devil, red from the soil, whirling towards the boardwalk outside the Chinese-owned hardware store. I gently replaced the telephone on its cradle and then sat back down on the chair for a little while longer. The operator looked at her watch and calculated my bill. My ear ached, everything ached, my pulse felt bruised.

On the way home from Waikabubak we passed a white-washed church standing in a banana grove. I asked Willie to stop the car. I wanted to pray, or to try to, but when I got there the interior was a building site and a group of rowdy children were running up and down a large pile of sand beside a concrete table that served as the altar. As I walked up the aisle, they crowded around me, laughing and shouting *'Salamat pagi!'*– 'Good day!' I left, got back in the car and leaned my head against the side window. We drove home in silence.

Our sunset was the time of the funeral in England, and the children were tucked up in their beds once more. Willie and I climbed to the top of the hill above our cabin, from where there were beautiful views over the reef. Venus was in the western sky, and extraordinary little patches of rainbow called Newtonian prisms were visible at the edge of the backlit clouds. I had never seen these before Sumba, nor have I since. The kite was in the form of a bird of paradise, with multi-coloured streamers for a tail. I wanted it to soar away until it vanished in the distance, but the wind kept gusting, then promptly dropping, and the kite nosedived into the ground again and again. Eventually I had to admit defeat. I moved on to the candle idea and pulled handfuls of tea-lights out of a basket I had brought along. I arranged them into two back-to-back Cs, which symbolized our family names of Campbell and Cawdor. Every time I lit the last few candles, the wind, which I now wished to stay becalmed, did the opposite and began to gust. The flames blew out repeatedly until the lighter packed up. My ceremony had been a washout, totally unsatisfactory. In fact, it was pathetic. It would have been better to mark the funeral quietly in our cabin rather than with these futile gestures on the hill.

We headed back down and I told Willie that I needed to go home for a week, maybe ten days.

My father's grave was still covered in flowers when I finally saw it. I added my wreath to the pile and sat there in the sunshine, unsure what to do next. Emma had told me as much as she could about the funeral. Trays of champagne

24

and whisky had been served as the mourners gradually assembled in the drive outside Cawdor. Regulation black was interspersed with the tartan of men's kilts. In an apt end to my father's earthly existence, the gathering swiftly developed into an impromptu party. The funeral was well behind schedule by the time the undertakers finally managed to convince everyone to get into their cars and leave. In a bid to make up time, the lead hearse sped along the winding route at rally pace. Behind it was strung a sinuous cortège of four-wheel-drive cars in hot pursuit, breath-test failures to a man.

I sat in the grass and looked across the field beyond my father's grave. The graveyard he had chosen was old and full, so he lay alone, outside its walls. I realized, suddenly, that after the initial physical impact of overwhelming grief, a tiny spark of ambivalence had guttered into life. Part of me felt vertiginous from loss; but part of me felt thankful that this intimidating central figure in my life was gone. The family had a chance of a fresh start.

I searched out the anonymous posy of cream roses my mother had asked to be put on the grave, and placed it beside mine. Aside from wanting to enter the Catholic Church, Pa had apparently expressed a dying wish that our mother keep away from the funeral. It seemed unnecessarily cruel of him: my mother had been married to him for twenty years and had done nothing meaner than believe that she could love him back to sanity. I read some of the notes on the other flowers. There was one from our Gordon Cumming cousins, one from John Stewart the headkeeper and his wife, one from Hugh's brother-in-law Peebles, one from the Percys. Reading these moving messages reminded me of the monumental effort he had made to write 'Alnwick'. Not 'I love you', or 'There's something I need to tell you', or even 'This train ain't going nowhere', just social fussing. It was so lamentably . . . shallow. Almost an hour of effort to get across his last communication in this life: are the Percys coming to dinner? Bloody hell. I hope I don't die with 'There's a terrific offer on asparagus spears at the supermarket' on my lips.

I drove over to Pluscarden to keep an appointment with the monk who had converted my father. I struggled to express my confusion about his religious switch to this polite stranger who had dedicated his life to God and who had flown down to a London hospital in order to take a dying man into the Catholic fold. He described the process of conversion. I asked him whether my father had made a confession. 'Oh no,' he said, and paused. 'No, that is not necessary, in the extreme circumstances of . . . such . . . gravity.' I left Pluscarden with a queasy feeling about my father's conversion to Catholicism. My sisters had told me he could not talk, and later he lay unconscious. Certainly, from what they said about how scared and surprised he had been in hospital, he had not been anticipating his own imminent demise. At what stage had he suddenly decided to change his faith? How could he indicate his request when he could write only A, L, N and W? His mind had appeared to be fixated on a party rather than the possibility of purgatory. Was it possible that these Catholics were so eager to claim another soul? The conversion happened without either of my sisters' knowledge and the monk was nowhere to be seen as my father's life ebbed away to the subaqueous blips of hospital machines. Angelika has always maintained that it was entirely at his own volition, and as I had ceased to understand the knotty workings of my father's mind over the years, that might be perfectly true. He was a man who had kept some pretty huge secrets and displayed giddying contradictions. Maybe, just maybe, he had had a last-minute panic and wanted to ensure that the lift button was pressed for Up, rather than Down.

I flew south to London and met up with my brothers and sisters. We grew up with the same parents in the same castle, but in many ways we each had a moat around us. Sometimes when visitors came they would say, 'You are such lucky children. It's a fairytale life you live.' And I knew they were right. We were indeed incredibly lucky. We lived in the greatest comfort, roamed freely, and had parents whom we adored. Our mother would make a picnic, bundle us into the car and turn our trip into an adventure by letting us take it in turn to choose which way we went at each junction. Our father made us laugh until our sides ached, and filled our dolls' house with chic, ultra-modern furniture he had made from stiff white card. It *was* a fairytale upbringing. But fairytales can be dark, and I had no way of telling either a stranger or a friend what was going on. The abnormal became ordinary. When life became frightening on a nightly basis, I just blindly hoped that it would all somehow sort itself out for the best.

After my father's death, something strange and unexpected

happened to us as a family. We had been so united in our feelings of anxiety around our father, but now that he was gone it was hard for us to reach each other. The only thing we could be sure of being in one mind about was that we all had the same lyrics stuck on the brain for months after his death. It was a song by Louis Prima called 'Just A Gigolo', about growing old and commenting on the emptiness of his life.

But whatever vulnerability I felt at losing a parent, there was also that sense of deliverance, growing now since I'd first felt it at his graveside. His angry presence no longer loomed. The noisy silences of his moods were over. The power he once wielded had gone. By the time he died we were all wrung out. As a father he had provided us with an emotional rollercoaster ride, and however much any of us wanted to get off, none of us could. I was wrong, though. The sense of release within the muddle of grief was short-lived, and it vanished altogether when I discovered that there was a grand finale from beyond the grave. None of us had any idea that he had concealed a dirty bomb, timed to detonate only after his death.

In December, as we prepared our move out to Indonesia, I had snatched a weekend on my own at Cawdor during a lull in the packing. When I arrived, Pa was sitting in 'his' chair to the left of the fireplace in the Tower Room, surrounded by precarious piles of books on all sides. He was wearing his ubiquitous black polo-neck jersey, plough brown corduroy trousers, a belt with the family crest on it, yellow socks and Gucci loafers. His compact hair was looking a little greyer, but even though he had begun chemotherapy, it still looked as if he would need a poker to force a parting. I leaned down to kiss him; he turned and gave me his ear – always a bad sign. He remained in a filthy mood throughout my stay. How do you say goodbye to a dying man? I had no idea. The mention of anyone's name seemed to trigger fresh fury. Of Emma, he said, 'She's been sneaking around her room like a rat in the attic. *Rummaging*. I think she's stealing.'

'But she was in her own room, Pa! You've just said so yourself.' Emma had been at Cawdor the week before me. She had told me when she got south that she had been searching for the letters he had sent to her at school. I felt shy about letting him know exactly what Emma had been doing; I thought it might sound like a premature memento mori. Instead I said, 'When we spoke, she told me she'd been searching out her old school diaries. Does that help?'

'No it does not, especially when I hear rumours that Colin has plans for your mother to return to live up here.' This was madness.

'Where on earth did you hear that?' I said. 'Ma is perfectly happy in London! She has no intention of coming back north, and even if she did, what business is it of yours?'

The day dragged by. My father was in a door-slamming frame of mind and conversations were like wading up a cul-de-sac full of cold porridge. After lunch on the second day I excused myself, borrowed a car, and drove over to Jane Stuart's house. Jane and her husband had been family friends through both my father's marriages. I found her with some cut branches in the garden.

29

'How lovely to see you, Liza!' she said in her slow twang of the American South. 'I didn't know you were up here.'

'Yes, I . . .' But I got no further before bursting into tears. I described the mood at Cawdor and how my father was so full of venom that I felt utterly cowed. I had always imagined that if I knew I was dying, the world would have a desperate preciousness – that birdsong would be sharper, colours more vivid – and I'd want to tell everyone I loved exactly that. Pa seemed to be experiencing the polar opposite and I had no idea how to respond.

Jane led me into her kitchen. She made tea, and when I was all talked out she said, 'You might think that you'd feel those things, and maybe you would, but maybe you might also feel frightened and angry. No-one, but no-one, in my experience, is more tormented than your father. It can't help but spill over and splash folk from time to time.' This was fresh news to me. My father was so busy throwing verbal grenades around it hadn't occurred to me they might be exploding inside him too. Jane went on. 'Here's my advice. He's probably not at his best right now; he's on steroid medication, which makes people extremely aggressive. Remember, it doesn't matter one bit what he says, just tell him what you need to say. If you don't, you'll always regret it.' I had been wrong-footed by his paranoid ramblings and it was a relief to have someone slice through to what actually mattered.

I returned to Cawdor in time for dinner. On the walls of the dining room hang a series of tapestries depicting the adventures of Don Quixote. The candlelight gave them a warm glow that singularly failed to match the atmosphere.

My father was completely drunk. His mouth was a purple hole, and Angelika was standing behind his chair hand-feeding him morsels of food. It was something she had done throughout their marriage, but this time he spat them back out onto his plate after a couple of chews like a petulant old baby. The excited barks of their four Jack Russells broke up this ghastly scene and Angelika swept out of the room. Doors opened and shut. We could hear her in the courtyard shouting the dogs' names repeatedly. She rejoined us a few minutes later. 'Those damn animals have been hunting again. Looks like they caught a young rabbit.' Then she vanished again. I could hear her next door, in the flower room this time. When she reappeared, she had put on a calf-length coat trimmed with mink. 'Will you say I would like tisane served in the Tower Room?' she said, and turned on her heel.

As soon as we had finished eating, I went off and watched television on my own. Pa stayed on drinking alone in the dining room. Later, I heard him climbing the stairs to the little sitting room where I had holed up, but a thump, a curse, and then a tinkle of breaking glass on stone gave me time to make a swift exit out of the far door.

In the morning, I packed and called a taxi. My father offered to drive me, but I could see the extent of his hangover and I couldn't face his driving or the cigar he had just lit. We stood rather awkwardly in the drive as the taxi driver placed my suitcase in the boot of his car. In a flash, I knew how to say goodbye, and it was incredibly simple. I hooked my father's little finger with mine. 'I love you with all my heart, Pa.'

31

There was a long pause. He looked at his shoes. I looked at his shoes. He looked up at me. I returned his gaze. His puffy eyes narrowed.

'Oh, don't be so *boring*,' he hissed, and turned on his heel.

I turned to wave as the taxi set off down the drive, but he was slouching into the house. He didn't look back. I could not conceive of the bleakness of the hole in which his soul must have been squatting that day. I didn't want to embarrass the taxi driver, or myself, so I tried not to blink and rifled purposefully in my bag for the duration of our journey. All the wise advice Jane had given me was forgotten now, and years passed before I could feel compassionate towards my father for his reaction.

When I got back to London there was a message on my answering machine from him. 'Oh, I wish you could have stayed longer. Now I miss you, and apropos of nothing, I suggest you look up the derivation of "samphire". Laura arrived tonight. Thought she'd bring her new beau, but she tells me he has set sail for Nineveh on a quinquereme. Better go . . .'

Ah, the joys of the answering machine, the spoken letter: emotions expressed at one remove. Listening to his disembodied voice speaking to me as I sat on the sofa going through the mail made me sad. It was as if our last conversation, the whole weekend even, had been either blanked or reinvented. I didn't know it then, but the weekend had been not only the last time I would see him but the last time I would ever stay at Cawdor. In fact, it was the last time I would go home without paying for a visitor ticket for the next ten years.

32

Chapter 2

Life for both sexes is arduous, difficult, a perpetual struggle. More than anything perhaps, creatures of illusion as we are, it calls for confidence in oneself. Without self-confidence we are babes in the cradle.

Virginia Woolf, *The Common Reader*

ONCE UPON A TIME IN SCOTLAND, IT MUST HAVE BEEN unimaginable that feuds and obsessive cattle rustling would one day be seen as finite cultural tics. Treachery, clan warfare and shifting allegiances were like oats and whisky to the populace. There was scant expectation of people reaching the biblical objective of three score years and ten. Even during peaceful periods, a premature death came easily: a bone fracture, a tooth abscess; the unhygienic attentions of a doctor. There was the pox, the palsy, religious persecution and its cousin, superstition. While Cawdor was under construction, the Spanish inquisition was in full swing,

America would lie undiscovered for another century, the Hundred Years War was being intermittently waged, Plantagenets were on the throne of England and the Black Death was sweeping across Europe.

If asked to draw an imaginary flower, in general children come up with something that roughly resembles a gerbera. If a child were asked to draw a castle, they'd probably come up with something that looked like Cawdor. Like all medieval castles, it is essentially a colossal bunker in a traditional sandcastle style. The front is protected by a dry moat, and at the rear the building merges into a rocky outcrop. Battlements, drawbridge, bartizans, portcullis, etc. were all designed to say 'Fuck off!' with some conviction. Other castles that fell short of this mission statement lie in various states of dilapidation all over the kingdom. When I was little, my favourite ruin was Castle Campbell. Sacked by Cromwell, it stood in the parish of Dolour on top of Gloom hill and two small rivers passed on either side of it: one was called Sorrow, the other Care.

The fertile plain where Cawdor stands is an example in microcosm of Scottish life through the ages. Within a twenty-mile radius there are a dozen surviving castles and as many ruins – all testament to hundreds of fractious years when, if you were not with someone, then by definition you were fatally against them. Even with the protection of castle walls, enemies would make every effort to destroy you by lobbing decomposing animals over the battlements in the hope of starting a plague. And to think their descendants now loan each other their lawnmowers.

Our oldest forebears would have no problem recognizing the Cawdor of today. They might be pleasantly surprised to note a few restrained decorative flourishes, like the enlargement of arrow slits into windows. The only time there was any extensive refurbishment was in 1684 when Britain was going through a 'mini' ice age. It was a time when winter Frost Fairs were held on the Thames. The Thane wanted to make the house as warm as possible for his nine children, a chaplain, a butler, a gentleman's gentleman, a cook with an assistant, a porter, two footmen, two gentlewomen, a coachman, a chambermaid, three stablewomen and a dairymaid. His biggest innovation was to incorporate the main staircase into the body of the house so that it was no longer a refreshing outdoor climb to the upper floors. He also draped the walls in tapestries and built a massive fireplace in the great hall. The stone chimneybreast was carved with the family crest of a stag's head and the family motto 'Be Mindful' underneath.

At the opposite end of the drawing room is a minstrels' gallery reached by a concealed staircase. The space is cramped and narrow and the taller musicians would have had to stoop while they entertained with pipe and fiddle. I would clamber up there to get a bird's-eye view of my parents chatting with their guests by the fire at the far end, and I used to wonder whether any of those old musicians would have ever given credence to a soothsayer if she had whispered to them that by the twentieth century, minstrels would be pulling in some of the highest wage packets on the planet.

One of the reasons so much of the house remained unchanged over the years was that, for generations, the family had spent the majority of their year in Wales or London and had only ventured north in the warmer summer months. The years of the Second World War were the first in two centuries that the Campbells had returned to live at their principal home full time. For in 1939, the War Office requisitioned a large chunk of the Welsh estate close to Stackpole and turned it into a bombing range. The local hamlet of Castlemartin was evacuated and blasted to ruins. The army set up artillery batteries on the cliff tops to practise firing missiles at offshore targets and notified my grandparents that troops would be billeted in the house. My grandmother Wilma retreated to Scotland with Hugh and his older sister, Carey. The north of Scotland was one of the places least touched by the war, but even though they lived some way beyond the back of beyond, Wilma worried that the Luftwaffe might spitefully select Cawdor as a random target, and she ran into trouble with the Home Guard for persistently flying a Red Cross flag from the top of the tower.

As the Germans swept across Europe, invasion seemed only a matter of dwindling time. My grandmother had always been an avid Francophile and spent her time composing poems of dubious merit in praise of the Resistance and her hero, General de Gaulle. Wilma was not a great fan of rural simplicity, and to her the French embodied a refinement that was sorely lacking in wartime Scotland. Later, she became convinced that once the Germans had seized Britain it would be left to Scandinavian fishermen to cross the North Sea and rescue the family from the shores of the Moray Firth. In preparation for this inevitability, she rehearsed Hugh and Carey until they could belt out the Norwegian national anthem in piping voices:

Ja, vi elsker dette landet,
som det stiger frem,
furet, værbitt, over vannet,
med de tusen hjem.
Elsker, elsker det og tenker
På vår far og mor
Og den saganatt som senker
Drømme på vår jord,
Og den saganatt som senker
Senker drømme på vår jord.

Yes, we love this country
Which rises up,
Rugged and weathered, above the sea,
With its thousands of homes.
Love it, love it and think
About our mothers and fathers
And the saga of past ages
That sends dreams to our earth,
And the saga of past ages
That sends dreams, sends dreams to our earth.

Singing it would be a token of their thanks and appreciation when they were hiding under herring nets in the hull of a trawler, heading for exile in Stavanger.

When the war was over, the army left Stackpole but held on to much of the land they had seized. When my grandfather was decommissioned, rather than pack up and return to Wales, he settled with his young family at Cawdor, only visiting Stackpole for holidays. A reverse of the long-held living arrangements.

My grandparents' marriage was as brittle as a biscuit. Wilma was beautiful, but hopelessly spoiled. Her father, Vincent Vickers, was a rich, eccentric industrialist who had resigned his post as Governor of the Bank of England in protest at the continuation of the fixing of sterling to the gold standard. To illustrate this point, he used a gold bar as a doorstop where, he said, it was more usefully employed. He was devastated when his young wife died a year after the birth of Wilma, and she became the miniature substitute of his lost love. He doted on his only child; no gift or indulgence was ever refused. Even after Vincent remarried and started a second family, Wilma remained gazing at the world from pedestal height and it was considered a special privilege for her young stepsisters to gather around her dressing table before dinner to watch her brushing her fashionably bobbed hair and dabbing her long neck with eau de cologne.

Jack Cawdor's childhood, or lack of one, had left him stilted, formal and shy. After the First World War, he spent the rest of his twenties far away from his silent mother and society as a whole. In 1924, he set off with Frank Kingdon-Ward on an expedition to Tibet. Kingdon-Ward, a botanist, was diverted by every sprig and tuft that they passed. Exasperated by their deathly slow progress, Jack wrote, 'It drives me clean daft to walk behind him ... if ever I travel again, I'll make damned sure it's not with a botanist. They are always stopping to gape at weeds.' In a placatory gesture, when Kingdon-Ward came across a previously unclassified iris, he named the plant after his young companion and gave him some bulbs to plant at Cawdor. Its descendants, a cluster of dishevelled yellow flowers, can still be seen, huddled against a wall in a corner of the garden. The objective of their voyage was to discover the hidden falls of the Tsangpo gorge, which no Westerner had ever seen. Tibetan folklore spoke of a mystical water-fall over a hundred feet high in a virtual Shangri-La. The walls of the twisting gorge were perilously sheer, but Jack and Kingdon-Ward managed to penetrate far enough to discover two new falls, though both fell short of the one they had hoped to find. They named one Rainbow and the other Takin, after a wild sheep they had shot there, but were unable to pierce a route further.

On his return, Jack met Wilma Vickers, and although she would have been far more impressed by attendance at the Sorbonne than by years spent clambering over barren mountain ranges, they became engaged. By now, even Vincent realized that his daughter had become a rather impossible young woman, and he checked to see whether his prospective son-in-law was absolutely sure he knew what size of handful he was taking on. Jack assured Vincent that he did, and married her in 1929.

He might not have known then what Vincent was anxious about, but Jack soon got the picture. When Wilma sat down to play a tune to assembled guests at Stackpole, if they dared talk, she would slam the piano shut and flounce from the room. Wilma was clever and artistic, but her lack of any country sense drove Jack mad. If they crossed a field, she would invariably try to open the gate by its hinges. As far as Wilma was concerned, only barbarians automatically knew how gates swung. The French would never trouble themselves with agricultural trivia, and neither would she. All that the couple really had in common was a virulent loathing of Catholicism.

Aunt Carey was born in 1930, a week before Jack turned thirty, and Hugh followed in 1932. Wilma had no mother, Jack had no father; neither of them had a template for their parental roles. The Cawdors muddled along together, but the relationship was strained from the start, and it deteriorated dramatically after their car hurtled into a telegraph pole outside Swindon. Like his son after him, Jack had a propensity to divert from the road with casual disregard for health and safety. Jack's face was smashed up and for years afterwards he suffered excruciating headaches. Doctors were unable to help, and Jack's children grew up in the shadow of his carbon moods. Hugh found solace in the nursery with his nanny, Miss Dunkerley. When the children had to go through to the drawing room they learned that keeping their relationship on a very formal footing lowered the chances of inciting an outburst. X-rays finally revealed a splinter of skull bone pressing into the top of Jack's brain. An operation relieved the pressure, but it did not seal the fault lines that ran through the marriage.

Ten years after Hugh's birth, Wilma got pregnant again in an attempt to fill the emotional pothole. When the new baby, James, was born, both parents adored him, but his arrival did not solve their problems; instead they vied with each other for his affections. The Cawdors resolved to stay together until their youngest son was 'old enough', and in the meantime they maintained separate lives within the castle walls – an arrangement Jack had long been familiar with, thanks to the habits of his mother Joan. Not so Wilma. For her, the loneliness of their estrangement was alleviated only by long hours at the piano and extensive poetic outpourings. If her own muse wandered off, she would read volume after volume of verse, pencilling copious annotations in the margins. She lived far, far away in an iambic pentametric world of love and loss, and chain-smoked all the while, a long, elegant cigarette holder clenched between her teeth. For Wilma, no inhalation of oxygen was complete without nicotine content. There was ochre staining on her teeth, fingertips, the front of her hair, and even on the piano keys. When Wilma and her husband did meet up, she frequently fled in tears. During one encounter, Jack stamped so viciously on her foot with his steel-capped hobnail boot that he broke her toe. In her loneliness, Wilma would report Jack's crimes to her two older children. This practice had the diametrically opposite effect to the one she desired. She found no partisans, and Hugh in particular began to despise her. He had until then found Jack unreachable, but now a rudimentary bond was forged as they stood in an unspoken alignment against Wilma.

When Jack and she finally divorced, Wilma went off to live alone in Somerset, a county randomly selected, where she had no friends. As soon as his first wife was gone, my grandfather married for a second time. Betty Gordon Cumming was a very busy local widow whose only son William had long been Hugh's best friend. After her first husband died, leaving her with three young children to bring up, and before settling exclusively for Jack, she entertained him and two other local lairds with such metronomic regularity that they were known as Breakfast, Lunch and Dinner. One of these was the Earl of Moray, who lived at Darnaway, a castle not far from the Blasted Heath where Macbeth's witches lurked. One day, in a fit of sudden and inexplicable madness, the Earl of Moray took a sword and docked the stone tails off two handsomely carved lions that flanked his front door steps. Then he strode into his bedroom and shot himself. Betty, who had been in the adjoining bathroom, heard the explosion and rushed in to find his mutilated corpse. People said that out of her trio of lovers, Moray had been the favourite, but Betty never spoke of her feelings, and after his death she took a pragmatic view and married Jack, the richer of the two remaining lairds.

Competition with his two rivals may have intensified his ardour, but what really appealed to Jack was that Betty was the antithesis of Wilma. She was a far less interesting woman, but she was tough and self-reliant. She may have had a tongue that could clip hedges, but she was crisp and efficient – a homemaker. While Wilma's idea of looking after guests was playing a fugue on the piano and giving her opinions on Rimbaud, Betty saw to it that they were shown to their bedrooms and that there were flowers and bath towels when they got there.

Betty's competence gave her the domestic clout to modernize Cawdor. She rebelled against Jack's tolerance of the cold that extended indoors as well as out, had all the upstairs fireplaces blocked up, and introduced modish 'log fire effect' heaters with crinkly red cellophane backdrops. While Jack's first wife had exquisite taste, his second's was slightly suspect, but after she had redecorated the guest bedrooms, her interest in updating other aspects, like the kitchen, ran out of steam. She had little interest in food. In those days, the kitchen at Cawdor was at the furthest end of the house. Everything was wheeled the length of a football pitch on hospital trolleys. This guaranteed that the food arrived in the dining room at ambient temperature. The cook had never really spread her imaginative wings since the days of war rationing. Menus were very plain – barley broth, boiled beef, braised cabbage, the dread haggis. Not that Betty cared: she had no sense of smell, little sense of taste, and the appetite of a gerbil. When there were no guests to entertain, rather than sit down for lunch, Betty far preferred to be out taking cuttings from the herbaceous borders, with an apple to eat and *The Archers* for company.

She was an accomplished gardener and threw her energies into the large walled gardens that lay on either side of the house. The lower garden that had been made from parts of the old curtain wall was filled with rows of runner beans, onions and artichokes, and tomatoes grew under low glass frames. Under vast sheets of netting lay fraises de bois, gooseberry bushes and raspberry canes, and along the inside walls were espaliers of red- and black-currants. Betty added flowerbeds of gladioli and pin-cushion fat dahlias for use in the house. In the top garden, she laid out four large oval rose-beds in the fashion of the time: lurid, thorny atolls, each within a lagoon of woodchips and a reef of horse manure. Wilma had been a talented gardener too, but she wafted rather than weeded. Afternoons would slip by with secateurs in one hand, a trug in the other, with Wilma reciting poems and absent-mindedly snipping at a few tiger lily stems. Her successor could prune and tie an entire rose tunnel in the same amount of time.

Betty was also something of an expert knitter and was only interested in making things that required at least four needles working in tandem. When she came to live at Cawdor she became a one-woman production line of ornately decorated kilt socks. My grandfather would have been the envy of a sock fetishist, with a never-ending supply in every shade of the spectrum. She got Jack – a man with ultra-conservative dress habits – wearing, from the knee down, turquoise, cyclamen, cadmium, bright purple and palest mint.

My father had a classic establishment education: Eton (where he failed to flourish outside the shooting team) was followed by Magdalen College, Oxford. He was at Oxford at the same time as his sister Carey and neither breathed a sober breath for the entire duration of their stay – a time that was curtailed for Hugh when he was sent down before graduating for a resplendent lack of work. He went on to the agricultural college at Cirencester, where they taught him the bones of land management. He dodged National Service and qualified as a chartered surveyor. At some point, slightly behind schedule, he had an educational epiphany. He became a zealous autodidact and immersed himself in books and encyclopedias. He was artistic: he could draw, he had beautiful handwriting, and he had an academic fascination with the English language, architecture and anything to do with trees. When the government came up with the chirpy slogan 'Plant a Tree in '73', my father took pride in planting a million. If only all his passions could have been this wholesome.

Whatever the range of Hugh's personal interests, as was the case for the twenty-four thanes who preceded him, Cawdor and Stackpole were always going to be the main focus of his life. Pa inherited Stackpole and the Welsh estates in 1957, upon his marriage to our mother, Cathryn Hinde. Cath was the middle daughter of an army general, blonde, slender and blue-eyed. She was in the British ski team and doubled for Vivien Leigh in the ski scenes of an atrocious B movie called *The Deep Blue Sea*; but it was the actress Joan Fontaine whom she more closely resembled. The similarity was so uncanny, it always made watching the movie *Rebecca* a rather unnerving experience.

My grandfather Jack had desperately stiff communications with his children, and when my mother was first a guest at Cawdor she was amazed to hear Hugh and Carey working out the topics for discussion with their father over the forthcoming meal. Usually they talked about one local matter and then debated something current from the newspapers. This stilted form of interaction extended to all aspects of their relationship. When the gift of the Welsh estates was handed over to Hugh, it was without instruction. Jack assumed that his son would have an innate understanding; after all, no-one had told Jack how to go about the running of the place and he had still been a schoolboy when he inherited the whole thing. His own father's decline in the seclusion of a sanatorium had left Jack fatherless for years before the fact. Having had no guiding hand, he had no idea how to be one himself.

A year after their wedding, Ma was in the final stages of her first pregnancy when they were summoned to Scotland from Wales. My grandfather Jack wanted her to give birth to the male heir of the next generation at Cawdor. The baby turned out to be my sister, Emma. Perhaps there was a concealed gasp, but her gender was accepted with good grace and there was a muted celebration.

Eighteen months after my sister's arrival, my parents repeated their pilgrimage to Cawdor for the birth of their next child. There was no precedent, or even mental preparation, for a second daughter. My birth was greeted with undisguised consternation. Jack was up a ladder in the garden when he learned the news. While digesting the bulletin he lost his balance and fell into a flowerbed, breaking an ankle. From his hospital bed in Inverness, he sent a message to my father. Devoid of congratulations, it simply said, 'Call the baby Elizabeth or Carolyn.' (These were the proper names of his second wife, Betty, and his daughter, Carey.) In an effort to appease Jack for this second chromosomal faux pas, my parents complied and I was christened Elizabeth.

It was not until years later that I learned what turmoil my birth had caused. After it, my mother bought a pile of self-help books with titles like *How to Conceive a Baby Boy* and *Conception: Sex Determination Made Simple*. She followed salt-free, low-potassium diets, followed by high-potassium, salt-filled diets, in a desperate bid to ensure a boy-child. Three years later and pregnant once more, my mother put her foot down and stayed in Wales for the birth. She could not cope with yet another pre-natal trek to Cawdor with the possibility of a traumatic aftermath. Instead of the new heir arriving into an ancient four-poster, my brother Colin was born in the rather less charismatic surroundings of Carmarthen hospital. She did the same for the births of Fred and Laura. After umpteen Campbell births at Cawdor over the centuries, mine may prove to be the last.

Chapter 3

I said to Heart, 'How goes it?' Heart replied, 'Right as a
Ribstone Pippin!' But it lied.

Hilaire Belloc

WHEN EMMA AND I WERE VERY YOUNG, OUR PARENTS LIVED
at Stackpole. The house stood near the sea in
Pembrokeshire. The coastline there is made up of coves
and caves and limestone cliffs pierced by swallow holes that
boom like gigantic didgeridoos when the surf hits them at
high tide. Erosion of the limestone had produced any
number of spindly, natural arches. Surely, it was these flying buttresses of nature that inspired medieval cathedral
designers. In some places the arches have collapsed, leaving
freestanding stacks out at sea where puffins nest.

We lived a gentle afternoon's stroll away from St Bride's
Head. The cliff there had a steep flight of steps that led
down to a minuscule chapel perched limpet-like above the

waves. The interior was bare but for two benches carved from the rock. It was where sailors had prayed before they left home, where families mourned them when they didn't come back, and where the wreckers waved their lanterns from the unglazed windows, luring unwary ships on a moonless night.

I have few authentic memories of living at Stackpole, but one stands out, implanted by a photograph. In the picture I am sitting on a cannon, looking a little wistful, holding a balloon on a stick, and wearing a smocked dress for my third birthday party. The cannon was one of a pair that flanked the carriage porch at the entrance to the house. Once there had been half a dozen or more positioned around the terrace, but over the centuries, twittish forebears had failed to resist the urge to shove them down the precipitous slope into the lake. One by one, the cannons had hurtled down to sink into the deep, lily-tangled silt with an almighty splash.

The house stood on a promontory above a series of immense lily ponds, half a mile from the sea. An eight-arched bridge with elegant balustrades spanned the water. It led to a vetch-sprinkled warren dotted with ash trees, all wind-blasted into sloping topiary, and beyond them to Barafundle bay. A high wall enclosed the beach and kept it private for the family. As at St Bride's Head, there was a flight of flagstone steps down the cliff, built to make it easier for Victorian ladies in their long, hooped dresses. On clear days we could see Lundy Island and the coast of north Devon beyond.

Whenever he joined us at Barafundle, Hugh spent hours constructing sand-volcanoes, but it was never apparent whether they were for him or us. Clumsy fingers were not allowed near the building site. We would be sent off to collect sea grass and dry twigs. When we had found enough fuel, it was packed into the tunnel at the base of the conical chimney and lit with the hot embers from his cigarette. Smoke would suddenly belch satisfactorily out of the volcano's 'crater'. I assumed that we would be eating smoky sandwiches and sandy bananas on this beach for ever. I would have been happy to, but our stay at Stackpole was brief. No-one had bothered to tell us that not only were we Highlanders, but our exodus to the north of Scotland was inevitable and merely a matter of time.

The Stackpole estate came into our family through the marriage of Sir Alexander Campbell to a Welsh heiress in 1689. Like many love matches, the union came about by the slimmest of chances. So inadvertent was their meeting that it fuelled the couple's sense that some divine power had not merely pulled strings, but had hauled on bloody great hawsers – as if Cupid's arrow had become a heat-seeking Sidewinder on their hearts' behalf.

In those days, travelling overland to London from the Highlands was an arduous journey of seven hundred miles down the spine of the kingdom. Consider these: the Grampians and the Cairngorm mountains, the hills of Lammermuir and Lauderdale, the forests of Strathord and Redesdale, and the North Yorkshire moors. The names may conjure up bucolic idylls, but in reality it was league after lonely league of bumpy tracks that took a traveller only as far south as York Minster. Aside from the invisible risks from those who might spray their fellow stagecoach inmates with consumptive spittle, a seventeenth-century demographic would have shown these remote areas to be encrusted with brigands. Although a further distance, it was considered quicker and safer to go south by sea from the west coast. Accordingly, when Sir Alexander was called upon to attend to business matters in London, he crossed the Highlands along the natural corridor of Loch Ness and set sail from Fort William.

The journey went without incident until a ferocious gale blew up as his boat navigated the Irish Sea. After near catastrophe off St Bride's Head, the crew was forced to put into Milford Haven for repairs. While the sailors replaced caulking and patched damaged sails, Alexander sought accommodation. Knowing his stopover could be lengthy, he sent word to a fellow student from his university days, requesting temporary lodging. Sir Gilbert Lort lived near Fishguard, a little way along the coast from Milford Haven. He welcomed this impromptu visit from an old friend and Alexander duly arrived to stay at Stackpole. The visit became somewhat extended after he was introduced to Gilbert's only sister, Elizabeth. When Alexander finally resumed his journey to London, he despatched his business with all haste and returned to Wales, where he proposed and they were married. His brother-in-law never married, and when he died suddenly it was without heirs of his own. The Lort estate went to Elizabeth, and thus passed into Campbell hands.

A second, even more auspicious Welsh marriage followed. Alexander and Elizabeth had a son known as

'Joyless' John, but despite his unpromising nickname he found himself an even richer heiress, Mary Pryse. Her dowry added thousands of acres of Carmarthenshire and Cardiganshire to the Pembrokeshire estate. The family's landownership swelled to more than a hundred thousand acres in combination with the Campbell Scottish lands. This afforded, among other things, the creation of an opulent new Stackpole from the bones of the old Norman manor. Wales might be a country in need of a roof, but Scotland is a country that needs not only a roof but urgent attention to its central heating. Their new estates and the weather gradually drew the Campbells south.

Stackpole remained unchanged after Joyless John's renovation until things got rather out of control when the Victorians came along. The family indulged their wealth on feverish building projects. With a rivalrous eye on a neighbouring house undergoing similar enlargement, they started to heap wings and frontages onto Stackpole, until the previous structure was all but submerged.

When the Victorian Campbells had finished with Stackpole, with cash and energy to spare they went to work on another pile they owned in Carmarthenshire called Gelli Ayr (the name is pronounced to rhyme with 'deathly pyre'). The house had been owned by the head of the Vaughan family until 1810, when he, as Hugh put it, 'spitefully bequeathed it to his best friend, John Campbell of Cawdor'. The Vaughan family disputed the will for thirteen years, but with no success, which must have been bitterly frustrating because once the Campbells had finished embellishing it with gargoyles Gelli Ayr ended up large, long, and in an unpromising dark granite, like a feeble homage to St Pancras station. No-one was pleased with the result and it was scarcely used. The one happy outcome of this misbegotten building venture was that Cawdor remained fairly free from their meddling.

With their wanton additions to Stackpole, the Victorians had created Stygian courtyards where the abundant Welsh rain made it easy for damp to take hold. Later, the soldiers billeted there during the Second World War supplemented their rations by cultivating tomatoes on the flat roofs, causing further damage and rot. In the swirl of excitement of being the master of all he surveyed in Wales, my father decided to refashion Stackpole into a more manageable size when I was about three years old. He applied for a grant to strip away the extraneous Victoriana, but it was turned down. In a fit of caprice, he ordered in a demolition crew. Stackpole was flattened. Worse, he sold the rubble as foundations for Milford Haven Oil Refinery, a hideous monolith that now blots the Pembrokeshire skyline for miles around. The wrecking ball went back to the stockyard, but metaphorically it never left. Hugh not only had a destructive streak, but he had fallen for the great myth – that a destructive streak was romantic. Towards the end of his life the path he had carved underwent a road-widening scheme.

Stackpole had been in our family for almost three hundred years. My grandfather Jack, whose childhood home it was, never uttered a word to his son about its abrupt end. When my father had finished, the old stable block with its clock tower was all that remained, along with a plaque set into the ground on the terrace where the cannons once stood. The inscription reads:

The Stackpole Estate was cared for
by the Cawdor Campbells
from 1721–1972.

The words always put me in mind of a conversation I once had with some Kenyan park rangers who were telling me about an elephant poacher they had recently captured. When I asked what had happened to him, they said, 'Oh, he died in our care.'

With Stackpole reduced to its component parts and the gothic sprawl of Gelli Ayr on a long lease to a farming college, my father needed to provide a new family home. The house he built was called Golden Grove, the English translation of Gelli Ayr, and it stood on a hill on the opposite side of the valley from its Welsh namesake.

Golden Grove had an elegant interior thanks to mahogany doors and marble fireplaces ripped from Stackpole, but outside it had a Lego-like quality, with columns that were both ostentatious and slightly measly. The outstanding impression on arrival was of a giant brick shoebox. But this box was our home, and I loved, loved, loved it. It overlooked the serpentine curves and oxbow lakes of the River Towy. The landscapes were breath-taking. To the east was the ruin of Dynevor Castle; to the south-west, Paxton's Tower was a turreted outline on the horizon; and due west, on a neat, tussocky knoll near the river, were the ruined walls of Dryslwyn Castle. These were our views, but the fields and woods that swept down to the little bridge that crossed the Towy made up our immediate universe.

Initially, the most pressing problem of my childhood was not my bad old dad – he only had a walk-on part during my early years – it was that I wasn't sure where my sister ended and I began. Emma was eighteen months older than me. For half of the year she was two years older, but six months later, Aesop-like, I narrowed the gap to one. Her hair was thick, dark, and kept in a bob, while mine was fine and blonde and seldom cut. She had a right hook; I was a southpaw. Emma was bold, whereas I was timid. My interior world was suffused by anxious monologues rather than calming muzak, while hers seemed to be filled with exhortations to war. Emma looked like our father, while I looked like my mother, and our temperaments seemed to mirror theirs. When cross, I fell silent and sulked. There didn't seem to be room for any other reaction because Emma was prone to wild tantrums at the least provocation. It was as if she was beholden to some arbitrary inner code that, when accidentally contravened, drove her to express herself with untrammelled savagery. It was thrilling to witness, but it baffled my mother and myriad nannies who passed, sometimes slowly, sometimes at top speed, through our lives. The spark could be anything, but was most often clothing. A dress she had been happy to wear one day became the object of the most violent loathing the next. I had pretty passive wardrobe habits – dressing was a matter of course that I didn't question – but with Emma, it was like throwing matches at a munitions dump. For a long time we were rather proud to think we were unruly enough to drive so many nannies off, but when it transpired that Hugh came into their rooms as a matter of course, we realized that there were factors beyond Emma's irascibility.

My mother Cath had wanted her first child to share her elder sister E's birthday, 14 March. She jumped up and down in a bid to induce labour, but Emma resisted. My mother finally got things going after knocking back a bottle of castor oil. But Emma's birth had nothing whatsoever to do with castor oil. It was obvious to me that there was a cosmic logic to my sister's arrival on 15 March. It is the Ides of March, the only day of the year that comes with the prefix 'Beware!'

I longed to find a connection of equal glamour for my own birthday, 24 September. I was envious of all those significant dates like Valentine's Day, Halloween and winter solstice. It was only a small consolation that it wasn't called September Fool's Day. But why not 'Subtle September 24th'? Or 'Moody September 24th'? Then I learned about sex. I was overjoyed to discover, after calculating with a stringently exact nine-month gestation period, that in order to conceive me my parents had had slightly disgusting but undoubtedly devout and sacred congress on Jesus's birthday. An embarrassing number of years later I was crushed to discover that thanks to a grasp of numeracy which it would be boastful to describe as remedial, I had somehow overlooked that Christmas Day actually falls on 25 December. It meant that my parents had had slightly disgusting and no doubt perfunctory post-present-wrapping sex while covered in stray bits of sellotape one goddamn day too soon. It was no goddamn good to me at all.

I adored my sister. She, in turn, loathed me. My admiration for her manifested itself as slavish aping that drove her round the bend. We lived on flimsy truces. Our customary amber status went red at least once a day. And then there were the terrible occasions when my mother lost her head and thought it would be charming to dress us identically. This pushed us to battle stations. Automatically. Always. The top floor of the house had a long, cork-covered passage. Emma would look at her dress and then look at mine. Her lips would pucker. Seconds later I would be knocked to the floor and dragged along the length of the passage by my hair. By the time we hit the stairs we'd be going at a fair lick. I went down them headfirst so many times that one of my front milk teeth died and turned black. She was a primal force. Emma knew where she began and ended. She didn't care where I began, and the most satisfying outcome would be for my end to be at the bottom of a deep pit.

To be fair, I could be a pain in the arse, and Emma wasn't the only one who found me exasperating. The worst incident happened when, at the age of five, I bullied a girl called Hannah who sat next to me at Miss Gibbons's. I can't remember any details other than that it involved demanding sixpence while menacing her with a rubber. After school I went home and spent my time digging up worms for dissection, and clean forgot the quarrel. After school Hannah went home and reported me to her parents.

The next morning Miss Gibbons called me to her study. Whatever I came up with clearly did not wash because when we were called to assembly she ordered me to join her on the dais in front of the entire school. Through the window to our left I could see a man afloat on the Towy far below. He was circling downstream in a coracle, like an upturned ladybird. Miss Spencer, the deputy head, gave me a sharp prod and reminded me in a whisper to pay attention. My ears began to grow hot, and I knew I had done something truly awful when Miss Gibbons pointed her ruler at me and said, 'School! This. Is what. A black sheep looks like!' I was unfamiliar with the idiom and it amazed me. I liked lambs, especially the black ones, but I could only think, 'Look like a sheep? I do not!' I was sent home with an advisory note for my parents to punish me further if they saw fit. My father read it and looked at me sternly. 'Don't lie, don't cheat, and be loyal,' he said, before picking me up and kissing me on the ear. As he did, I whispered plaintively, 'They said I was a black lamb,' and he laughed until the tears trickled out of the corner of his eye and he had to put me down to blow his nose with his big spotted handkerchief.

'Am I?' I persisted.

'No! Not unless you betray the people you love. Only that can turn you into a black sheep.'

'And if I am a black lamb then you are a black ram.'

By now my childish pedantry had begun to bore him, and he said, 'Surely it must be time for your sheep dip. Let's go and find your mother.'

It was to be expected that Emma surge ahead in terms of

mastering childhood skills, but because our age gap was so small, every now and again I hit a milestone first. These rare feats were met with panicked whispers. I was not to breathe a word about learning to tie my shoelaces and must never let on that I could tell the time. Otherwise who knows what Emma would do? I realized that the grown-ups were just as alarmed by Emma as I was. Achievements must be veiled, but, unclear as to exactly what qualified for secrecy, I decided that pretty well everything was safer stashed beneath a bushel. There came a point, much later on, when we were all keeping secrets from one another, and for the most part they were the same ones.

Even though we were two of five children by the end of my parents' hectic nine-year breeding programme, Emma and I viewed ourselves as distinct from the others. We lumped our three younger siblings together as an amorphous cluster, referred to as 'the Smalls'. We were unaware at the time that there was a further subdivision within the Smalls. Years later it transpired that Colin, the next one down from me, had been an island adrift in the middle of the family. I was three years older than him, while Fred was three years younger. Fred and Laura were even more tightly jammed up against each other than Emma and me. I failed to notice Colin's isolation partly because I was too busy losing battles against Emma and partly because I hardly ever saw him properly. His solemn daily habit was to get a tissue and carefully separate the layers until he held a single membrane. He would then wander about for the rest of the day with the tissue stuck to his face by nasal suction. He kept his head tilted slightly back to keep the 'pockie' in place while he exhaled. He was able to see enough through the diaphanous gauze to navigate, but was faceless and silent to the rest of us. It was as if a snoozing sunbather had turned into a trundling zombie. Perhaps one explanation for Colin's behaviour was that he had undiagnosed tinnitus. The private conclusion he reached, at the age of five, was that the constant rustlings in his head were his thought processes, and although they were abstract, their noise constantly preoccupied him.

Fred was silent until he was nearly four, except for two words: 'hopper', which meant any building or container, and 'unhuhuh', which covered everything else, but as a rule meant 'tractor'. His nickname was Fredbox. This caused him problems when he first went to school as he assumed his surname was Box. The teacher was equally sure that he was a Campbell, but Fred would have none of it. He was so doggedly sure that the teacher eventually called Cath to double check that she hadn't divorced my father, married a Mr Box, and then divorced him to remarry my father. Our mother explained the nickname to the teacher, who explained it to Fred, but it cut no ice with him. Fred would only answer to Box.

As a baby, Laura contracted an obscure illness and suffered an extreme, almost fatal reaction to medicine she had been prescribed. Her skin fell off as if she had chemical burns. She and my mother lived for months and months in Cardiff hospital as she wavered on the threshold of death. On the few occasions we were allowed to visit, she lay still and saucer-eyed, too emaciated to shut her eyes, with every vein visible, like an Ordnance Survey map. She was too weak even to support her blankets, so a wire cage enclosed her wasted body, its stomach with the hard, swollen look of starvation. Cath's life went on hold and we saw little of her. Laura was saved by huge doses of cortisone, administered less in confidence than in desperation. It was another year before she regained her strength. The short-term side effect of the treatment was a downy covering of hair from forehead to feet. The long-term effect left her stone deaf in her right ear, and with a constitution that saw itself as a welcoming committee for every passing virus.

It was not until I was eleven that I began to register the younger three as individuals, but by that time I had been away at boarding school for four years and I only met them in the holidays.

My parents had a peculiar social life in Wales, where there were virtually no other young couples around. Guests were relations and imports rather than neighbours. Aunt Carey and her husband Uncle Peebles were frequent guests, stopping off on their way to and from London with their children Boojum and Alexander and their dog Potting Shed. They lived in a pretty house that had been in the grounds of Stackpole at the edge of the warren; now it was just at the edge of the warren. Carey had met Peebles at Oxford, where he would wander through the quads in a top hat with a pet mouse that ran round the brim. He was German, very tall, very droll and marvellously noble-looking. When I appeared with a runny nose and rheumy eyes to kiss him hello, instead of saying 'Are you ill?' he would say, 'Dear child, I suspect you are prey to some fell disease. Try not to pass it to Potting Shed, he is already in an autumnal humour.' Aunt Carey and Pa adored each other and they sat and drank and cackled over what Aunt Carey called 'effluent society'; they both smoked so much a pall of smoke hung over the entire library.

Our cousins were both pale, rather serious, and flaming redheads like Aunt Carey. Boojum's hair fell in a heavy apricot-coloured curtain, while Alexander's and Carey's had the colouring of iron oxide. Boojum wasn't her real name, which was Hero; the nickname was inspired by the final line of 'The Hunting of the Snark'. Alexander was the same age as Colin, but instead of playing he spent most of his visits at loggerheads with his father over whether the Cenomanian subdivision was part of the late or early Cretaceous period, and much else. When cajoled into joining us outdoors, Alexander would come reluctantly, and only if we were prepared to build a decent replica of the Ho Chi Minh Trail in the sandpit. Both children would frequently baffle us with their exchanges. 'Hither my Boojum and tell to us why you look so effulgent today,' Alexander would say. And she would bat him off: 'Alexander! Stop it and leave me alone. You know I am propelled into a bombazine gloom by the loss of my book.'

'What book, pray, Boojalisse?'

'The one on meteorites.'

The only other guests to come with a metronomic regularity were Uncle Bill and 'Uncle George'. Uncle Bill was my mother's older brother. He had contracted meningitis as a toddler in Egypt and it had left him with a child's mind in a burly adult body. He had a head full of wonder and brass-band music. We could hear him as he marched up and down his bedroom for hours. Bill worshipped Hugh. My father, who was normally intolerant of fools, adored him in return and spent hours explaining how things worked and helping Bill spell words he found difficult.

Uncle George was not our real uncle, or any relation at all, but a middle-aged man who would rent out his flat in London for months at a time, then call up people like my parents and say that he was 'on his way' from the Cloudsley-Shovells in Bath to the Webbs in Cardiganshire and might he 'stop off for a couple of days' on his way between the two? Only once he had secured an invitation with us did he call up the Webbs and say, 'I'm staying at Golden Grove on my way to the Leylands in Cheshire. Might I stop off with you?' And so it would go on, until he had belayed his way around the country. My mother said Uncle George wasn't married because he had 'never got over' a girl in his youth. It was her stock explanation for any man who was unmarried. Gayness did not light up on her mental dashboard.

My father would often make known his impatience with people solely motivated by social ambition, while in fact providing an easy target for one of the most avid. Uncle George was a nightmare: snobbish, waspish and un-predictable in everything except that he would be staying double the length of time he had initially proposed. His sharpest critiques were directed at the people he had just come from. 'It's all very well inviting the Bishop of Worcester to lunch – at least his knowledge of opera compensates for his leftie views – but it was a total faux pas to have that cheap Littlefair woman. Total slattern. She has made it her business to fuck everyone – pardon my French, girls; run along, and don't you listen to your old Uncle George – everyone I tell you, from Genesis to Deuteronomy! And yet she's still not bagged a husband! You have to laugh. My dear, I'm afraid I cannot. Abide. A social climber. She didn't even know how to pronounce chablis properly! Did you say champagne, Hugh? I say, yes please, raaath-err! A splash of bubbly would be diviiiine.' And he would excitedly clack his false teeth together. When the time came to extend his stay, he would start, 'Cath, did I tell you that Hermione Webb rang? When? Oh. It must have been ... while you were ... out.' And pizzicato now: 'She said she had a frightful, um, lumbago, and might I come, uh, aftertheweekend, uh, ratherthan-tomorrow ... such a bind. You don't mind d'you, Cath? Darling?' Eyes bulging with sudden nerves, then relaxing again as his board was guaranteed for a further three days. 'Girls, come over here! You look diviiiine in those Spanish dresses; now, do the flamenco for your Uncle George. What d'you mean no? Dance, I tell you!' Still I refused, and he grabbed me as I tried to run off. He held me in a tight avuncular squeeze, laughing a cloud of halitosis, and I swiped him with my castanet. He retaliated by biting me 'affectionately' on the stomach, but because he misjudged the thickness of my ruffles and wasn't fully in command of his dentures or his temper, he left a weal that turned into a grey-yellow bruise.

Uncle George became my sworn enemy.

*

Like our parents, we too had a dearth of normal childhood friendships. We were the posh lot on top of the hill, separated from our neighbours by the meaningless titles we children didn't even know were our prefixes. It was a mutual stand-off: my parents would have welcomed other children, but other children brought their parents with them, towards whom they were reflexively resistant. Those parents, in turn, didn't want to risk being seen as brown-nosing by having the toffs' scab-covered kids over to play. It didn't matter. We were always busy building some den or other and I was never aware that we were isolated, until I heard about other people's childhoods and watched my own children's.

Sweetly ignorant of every adult dynamic, we had a childhood in Wales of diminutive rural adventures. Although we were loosely segregated from our parents, if something thrilling happened during the day, we were not excluded. One of my most vivid childhood memories is of my father rushing into the nursery in the middle of lunch one day and saying, 'Come quickly! You can have your ice cream later!' It was very avant-garde not to have to finish up the food on our plates (a trial that could extend indefinitely into the afternoon if it was liver or spinach). Edith, the cook, was overseeing our eating in the absence of a nanny, since the last one had suddenly packed her bags and left. 'We're going to see a glider that's crashed by the river!'

Emma rushed from the table, knocking over her chair in excitement, but I was a little more apprehensive. Were we being bundled into the car to go and see a mangled corpse?

My father didn't say, so I stared at my lap as we turned into the watermeadow on the far side of the river. There was no blood and no body. The glider had only a cracked nose cone and a bent wing, and a slightly dazed pilot wandered about as Wylo and Zachariah, the estate carpenters, Father Cinelli, the vicar from our church, his daughter Rebecca and the postman all gawped at him.

As we stood there, my father turned to us. 'Why didn't it blow up when it crashed?' He always asked us questions like this.

'Because he'd run out of petrol?' I suggested.

'No,' he said.

'Did it hit the water and wet the engine before it landed?' I tried again.

'Because he was just damn flipping lucky?' said Emma.

'No! Because a glider glides, it has no engine. You have a brain the size of—'

'An iron filing. I *know*!'

If it had no engine then I couldn't understand why he thought it might blow up, but he got snappy if we went on and on asking questions, and besides, Father Cinelli had just come over. Father Cinelli was an Italian-American who had come to our church on a pastoral switch with Reverend Bowen, a very dull man who had taken his rainy Welsh message to Father Cinelli's parish in Cincinnati. There was no doubt in anyone's mind that we had got the long straw. Father Cinelli was a marvel. He was happy to shout and laugh and clap in the pulpit with such un-inhibited enthusiasm, it was contagious. Rebecca, his teenage daughter, was the most beautiful human being on this earth in my opinion, and years after the Cinellis had left us I begged my mother, unsuccessfully, to call our new baby sister Rebecca, instead of Laura, in her honour.

'Hey there, gang! Will you be coming to church this Sunday, Lord Hugh?'

'Lord Hugh' was not the right address. My father stiffened imperceptibly. He would never dream of saying anything to Father Cinelli because he was American and was not to know that in the arcane world of title rules, using the title alongside the Christian name and calling him 'Lord Hugh' implied that Pa was the younger son of a duke.

'Of course we'll be there,' my father said.

'Can I get you to read the first lesson? It's the Pharisees.'

'My pleasure.'

Father Cinelli beamed, and then turned his attention to us. 'Will you be coming to Yankee Doodle Sunday schoodle, girls? You betcha battam dallar you will!' he answered for us.

'How's Martha?' Emma asked.

The previous Sunday had taken a dramatic turn when Martha Lampeter fell to the floor screaming during the last chorus of 'Lord of the Dance'. There was a great kerfuffle, and Martha, pale as a seagull, was led out of the church wailing, 'My eyes! My eyes! They're burning!' It was very shocking. Were we witnessing a religious phenomenon, or was it arson? When Emma and I discussed the mysterious episode in the car on the way back home we agreed that neither of us had seen any sign of flames. We felt a bit cheated.

'Martha's much better!' Father Cinelli replied. 'She has a pair of pink glasses now. She looks real perdy. We should all be sure to tell her that.'

During Father Cinelli's tenure, the congregation swelled and swelled. Then suddenly he was gone, and the return of the piglet form of Reverend Bowen sent our theological enthusiasms into freefall.

Every day Emma and I, armed with small aluminium churns, were sent to fetch milk from the farm at the bottom of the drive. We liked to run down the hill windmilling the pails around our heads because the return was always slow to avoid slopping, and we had the cattle-grid to negotiate. We would clamber up the farmyard gate that smelled of creosote and watch Mrs Thomas, the farmer's wife, jacket belted with orange twine, whistling instructions to her collies. As she brought her herd into the yard, all mooing and mounting one another, their steaming haunches jostled our legs. Sometimes a slobbery nose would rub a slick of drool across our wellies, as if the world's largest slug had just come gliding by. Once the cattle had all passed, we would hop down and snake our way through their steamy pats, up past the silage pit and the hay bales to the milking parlour. Whenever calves were penned there, we would stick our hands through the bars and let a sandpapery tongue vacuum up our fingers.

Sometimes we would be invited into the house to have tea with Old Mrs Thomas. It would take a few minutes to get accustomed to the darkness of the place; any light entering the room had to penetrate a lattice of geraniums cluttering every windowsill. The floor had speckled lino, which was strange for a sitting room. I concluded it must be because the Thomases always came home with mud on their boots. Actually there was one rug, small, circular and red, but it sat in the corner, under the television.

Old Mrs Thomas could always be found in the same place, sitting by the fire in a wing-backed chair with an antimacassar draped over its back. She had a pretty face, soft and wrinkled. Her long white hair was held off her face by a dark ribbon. She wore a flowery housecoat, caramel tights made out of some sort of lagging, and, to my fascination, fluffy slippers during the day. It all seemed very exotic, especially when she put on an apron and disappeared off to make tea. We never had tea at home. They even had sugar lumps, something else we never saw. If we were quick enough with our spoons after she'd handed over the cup, we could fish out a cube and eat it before it disintegrated into hot, sweet slurry. Old Mrs Thomas would settle the tray down and serve up, asking, 'How many lumps, *bach* [dear]?'

'Five, please.'

'All right then, but only if you ask in Welsh.'

'*Pidwa*, please, Mrs Thomas.'

'You've only asked for four, *bach*. It's *Pimp* if you want five.'

At home, children drinking tea was a bit common; lumps of sugar were definitely common; so were pastries and antimacassars; and hair oil was the bitter end. Anything genteel was odious. To my father, a knife was a tool and a weapon and should be grasped as such. There

69

was no greater crime than to approach your cutlet as if writing a letter. A napkin was for brusquely swiping food from the face, not for dabbing at it with one finger dressed up as a ghost. Sticking your little finger out when holding a cup was frowned upon. So were chewing gum, poodles, alsatians, corgis, cats, trifle, custard, the words Mum, Dad, phone, partake, cheers, cheerio, bye-bye, coo-ee, super, by the by, don't mind if I do, dwelling, garment and fabric, the names Vernon and Paul, plus Essex, Kent and the Midlands, monkey puzzles and most ornamental conifers, any talk of money, and the colour mauve. Anything from Japan was cheap, plastic and inevitably dreadful. (Plastic, like elastic and drastic, rhymed with yardstick.) Nobody said any of these things explicitly; the unwritten guidelines sank in by osmosis – except for sticking my finger out while holding a cup. Even though I would be teased and scolded whenever I was spotted doing it, my little six-year-old finger just seemed to operate autonomously and would eventually always steal away from its companions.

On summer days, the loud echo of woozy music heralded the arrival of the ice cream van, but my father forbade it from ever coming up our drive. It was torment to listen as it circled the lanes around our hill, without ever arriving. It wasn't us eating the sugary by-product of whale blubber on sale that Pa minded, but the quality of the soundtrack. We knew it was this because he would crank up the volume of Herb Alpert playing on the stereo to drown out the van, and because on Saturdays we were given a little pocket money to spend on sweets at Mrs Harris-the-Post-Office.

Over the gate above the house, across the switchback of the Thomases' cattle pasture, and then a difficult choice: left through the lych-gate and into the gloom of the ivy-choked churchyard, or right, past the neighbouring farm to the Thomases', with its three ferocious collies. Even though this church was the closest one to our house, it wasn't 'ours' and it emitted a gentle menace, unlike 'our' church across the valley below Gelli Ayr. The dog route was usually preferable to the graves, although they barked and snapped; each dog seemed to live in the belief that some imaginary glass boundary kept their teeth away from our flesh by a few inches.

In any case, this farm held voyeuristic attractions. Some years earlier, the farmer's teenage son had suffered terrible groin injuries in a shooting accident while hunting rabbits. He had crawled under a hedge and then pulled his loaded gun through afterwards, barrel first. A twig snagged the trigger and blasted him at point-blank range. The grown-ups' hushed mention of 'groin' seemed annoyingly vague. I longed for a glimpse of the boy looking wan and romantic, staring out from an upper window, but he was never there. It was my first realization that something profound and permanent can happen in an instant, and, worse, never be undone. It took a while longer to realize that life doesn't deliver a single such instance, but an endless series of them.

Mrs Harris and her post office had escaped off a page of Beatrix Potter. The post office itself was in the front room of her cottage. When we pushed open the front door, it knocked a little bell that alerted her to change from a grandmother crocheting doilies by her fire into a crisp postmistress doing her bit to keep the cogs of country business oiled. Her tight grey curls and knobbly hands were the only things visible behind a dark panelled counter with old-fashioned scales and weights and a brass-embossed till that went 'ca-ching!' On the far wall was a mass of pigeonholes filled with Parma violets, sherbet tubes that looked like little fireworks with liquorice fuses, and pink shrimps, which were the closest things to edible polystyrene. Above were glass jars containing a huge selection of gobstoppers, cough candy, bull's eyes and pear drops.

Clutching bulging paper bags, and not wanting to return home immediately, we would occasionally continue on to visit a family who lived at the bottom of the hill, a few fields away from a giant wreck of a house called Aberglasney. Bethan Jones was a little bit annoying and had hands with strangely crinkly palms, but she was our closest neighbour of the same age. She had a younger brother called Owen, who snivelled a lot and was even more annoying, and I didn't like sharing my sweets with him one bit. The Joneses were the closest things we had to friends, but at the time they didn't seem to be anything other than people who just happened to be the same age as us. The looming walls of Aberglasney were a bigger draw than the easy company Bethan and Owen offered. Pa said it was a shame about Aberglasney; that the owner was not able to look after it. I never knew what he meant by that – whether the man should repair it, or whether he should take a tip from Pa and hire a bulldozer.

There was a muddy, feather-strewn pond in the Joneses'

farmyard with bossy, swagger-bummed geese and red-wattled Muscovy ducks loitering around its edge, all wriggling and muttering to one another. To stop them mugging our sweet bags we would fill a small bucket with grain and throw it out in a great semi-circle.

Regardless of what time we visited them on a Saturday, their cat was always snoozing on the wall by their gate. Only its tail, giving a meaningful flick now and again, showed us that it was alive, well and perpetually tetchy. This was our only contact with cats because Pa was allergic to them. He loathed all cats, and cat owners too. They were fussy and suburban beside dog owners.

Once, as we were mooching about licking liquorice stains off our fingers, we spotted our father driving by. He often just waved, but this time he stopped and showed us a large chunk of bark on the passenger seat. Pa said it was a bit unusual and he was taking it home to check it in his field guide. It was all part of his fixation with trees. 'Hands up who knows what the name of this is?' he asked, pointing at a silvery green area speckled with minuscule turquoise and red spots. He was always testing. The answer was 'lichen'. We all put our hands up. Owen was leaping up and down as if he was about to blow his bladder, so my father chose him. 'OK, Owen, you tell us,' he said.

'TRRRREEESKIN!' Owen shrieked, with the same kind of certainty with which men roar 'Goal!' 'Where'dew buy it then?' he added, quite unaware of our stunned faces.

'I bought it in Woolworth's,' my father replied with cardinal-like solemnity, dropping the bark back into his car.

'Brrrrilliant! I'm gonna save up and buy one too!' cried Owen.

Pa gave him some small change from his pocket to kick-start the fund, and drove off. It surprised me that my father was so patient with him. If it had been one of us we would have got a poke in the ribs and our brains would have been compared to the size of an iron filing.

To get away from Owen we would go and find Bethan's Barbie, but it never lasted long. Three girls playing with one doll had its limitations, and eventually Emma and I would be rolling on the floor fighting. Bethan would heave us apart and we would head back outside.

Whenever we were with the Joneses for any length of time, we were inevitably drawn up the hill to the tunnel of yews that led up to Aberglasney. We would frighten ourselves witless creeping around the derelict rooms and rotten staircase, never once daring to go as far as the second floor. A sudden creak, the flutter of a startled pigeon, and we would flee the building screaming at the tops of our lungs.

But at the farmyard our greatest dread was to run headlong into Bethan's father, who used to shout at us. He was a mean-tempered drunk who had thrown his wife out and installed a wig-wearing 'fancy woman' with more 'compatible appetites to his own'. At least that's what we had overheard Mrs Harris saying one day. I felt sorry for Bethan and Owen having to live with this couple, but we never dared talk about it, and whenever we did encounter Mr Jones we would wish them a hurried goodbye and leave. My imagination never stretched to thinking what it must be like for them always to be abandoned to deal with his temper alone. Maybe once in a while we could have asked them over to our house; but we never once thought of it.

As for Aberglasney, it has now been restored and is heralded as having one of the great 'forgotten' gardens of Wales, but then it was the local Bates Motel.

He may have been our scariest neighbour, but at least Mr Jones had children. Pretty much everyone else we saw was a grown-up. Pretty much everyone else we saw worked for my father. Mr Teague helped my father run the estate, which seemed to mean that they met up, pored over charts, tapped pencils and said 'Yerrs, yerrs' in turn. Mr Teague lived in a wooden chalet-style house next to the Baptist chapel with its tidy borders of purple and yellow primulas. We never saw anyone going in or out of its peeling grey doors, and Old Mrs Thomas muttered that this was because they kept 'ungodly hours' – which made us think that the Baptist faith must be pretty odd and possibly even more dour than Presbyterianism, the church into which we were christened. I wasn't completely confident that I could tell the difference between Mr Teague and my grandfather Jack. They were both gruff and distant and looked old in the same sort of ruddy-jowled, white-moustached way. We saw my grandfather a lot less often, so when in doubt, it was probably Mr Teague.

Sometimes when he was driving us into the local town, Pa stopped off at the bottom of the hill to visit the estate workshop. Wylo, the head carpenter, and his assistant Zachariah would let us crawl under their workbench and gather up the ringlets of wood shavings. I wished that all men could be called Zachariah; it was such an exotic word, and what's more, he understood our love of putty and would hand out small lumps whenever we visited. The heavenly smell always compelled me to pop it into my mouth. Anyone who has tried it will know that chewing putty is a shocking anti-climax. It tastes of nothing, in quite an uncompromising way.

Then there was Stan, who cut the grass round our house with a tractor that pulled a gang-mower. He seemed very, very old, although he was probably only in his late thirties. His hands looked as if seedlings might be thriving in the creases of his knuckles. Stan hardly ever spoke and used a large yellow duster to blow his nose, but I liked him because he was kind and taught me how to ride a bike. He was the only person patient enough to keep pushing me until I learned to keep my balance. Whenever Stan, Wylo or Zachariah saw my father they pulled their forelocks and called him m'lord. And when they referred to him or Ma, it was as 'his lordship' and 'her ladyship', as if they were a small flotilla of privilege. Despite my parents only being in their twenties, everyone treated them with the utmost respect and cautious affection. Golden Grove felt like a wonderful nest surrounded by old people who had never been young, and would never die.

The person who became the most constant in our lives was Edith Griffiths, who turned out to be the world's most lachrymose cook and who stayed for ten years. Edith was in her fifties and lived across the valley with her father. When she came to work for us as a cook, she was leaving home for the first time. She was very short and had a pair of tragic brown eyes that swam with tears all day long like a heart-broken seal. Not a month went by without her appearing on her day off wearing her best hat and jet beads, ready for a funeral. If asked where she was going, the answer was always the same; only the protagonists' names ever changed: 'Alderman Williams/Barry-the-Taxi/Myfanwy's nan/Dillys-over-by-Gronga has passed on,' she would snif-fle. If asked the cause, 'Nerves,' she would intone, and then add with some emphasis, 'Shot to pieces,' before stumbling off clutching her handbag in one hand and her best lace handkerchief in the other. Whenever we came into the kitchen, Edith would, without fail, jump and clasp her neck, gasping, 'Holy Moses! You gave me such a turn!' as if she had quite forgotten we lived there. This was an 'OK' kind of turn, but if we found her slumped with her apron over her white-haired head, weeping like a tap, it was a 'bad' turn.

Edith was a desperately reserved woman and never explained what triggered the misery-go-round of 'turns' that ruled her life. It was incredible that her nervous disposition did not interfere with her cooking; she was very good indeed. I loved Edith, but she smelled funny, as if she had kept her sadness for so long some of it had gone stale.

To my six-year-old mind, life was bursting with early joy. Edith was an enigmatic anomaly.

Chapter 4

Beware! Beware!
His flashing eyes, his floating hair!
Weave a circle round him thrice,
And close your eyes with holy dread,
For he on honey-dew hath fed,
And drunk the milk of Paradise.

S. T. Coleridge, 'Kubla Khan'

THE CRUCIAL DIFFERENCE BETWEEN JACK AND HUGH WAS that while one was cautious and conservative, the other was a libertine. While Jack was taciturn, Hugh was outrageous, witty, attractive, sharp-witted and belatedly well read. These assets allowed him leverage to treat his sex life as if he were James Bond, in ermine.

Born after the Wall Street crash, Hugh had six years of World War Two as a backdrop to his early youth, followed by the post-war decade of rationed austerity. Slowly, the years of peace accumulated, the country's economy recovered, and liberal attitudes bloomed. Contemporary mores had long demanded as imperative male rectitude and female virginity. And then, ka-pow! The pill saw to it that everything changed. My father was up there being fabulous and going haywire with the frontrunners, while my mother had no appetite for free love whatsoever. As a young man in the early 1960s, my father typified easier times. He dressed like a Restoration buck, wearing scarlet velvet jackets with black frogging, floppy cuffs and outsize buckles on his belts and shoes, the heels of which were covered in red patent leather to match the jacket.

Not long after we had moved into Golden Grove, when my mother was pregnant with my brother Colin, Hugh took off to Africa where he embarked on his first extra-marital affair. On his return, he told Cath all about it, in great detail. He said he couldn't resist the temptation because the woman 'had a neck like a gerenuk'. It was hard to understand what he found attractive about an antelope with a neck the length of a camel's compared to my beautiful mother who had a lovely neck of her own, but it is naive to think that having a peach at home will stop some people from gorging themselves on raisins elsewhere. The gerenuk started a trend. Eventually my father's sex life had so many different strands and overlaps that it resembled an accomplished spirograph drawing.

Once, when my father arrived home from a trip to London in the post-gerenuk period, he scooped me up in his arms and kissed me. I loved the way he smelled; it was warm and woody with a whiff of lemons. Years later I realized it was the smell of nicotine and red wine with aftershave on top.

'I know where you've been,' I said.

'Where then?' he said with a laugh.

'You've been off kissing ladies.'

I have no idea how I accidentally managed an insight so alien to a small child, but my father put me down, climbed back in his car, and roared off back to London without coming into the house.

My mother turned as blind an eye as possible to his infidelities, and went on having babies, playing the piano and planting hundreds upon thousands of spring flower bulbs with a special tool like an outsize apple corer. When she was not busy arranging vases of flowers for our house or for 'our' church, she was fulfilling what she saw as the duties of her position: visiting the old people of the parish, bringing them Christmas boxes and keeping them company. She never ever let on to us that the goalposts of her marriage had been widened at one end only, but looking back, maybe her feelings did seep out. On the mornings she drove us to school we always sang:

> Early one morning, just as the sun was rising,
> I heard a maiden sing in the valley below –
> 'Oh don't deceive me, Oh never leave me,
> How could you use a poor maiden so?
> Remember the vows that we made at the altar,
> Remember the promise that you made to be true.
> Oh don't deceive me, Oh never leave me . . .'

Despite Hugh's peccadilloes, Cath never once caused a public scene for the duration of their marriage. As a direct result of her forbearance, my parents remained madly in love for a long time. When we arrived in the library to visit them after our evening baths, they were often dancing cheek to cheek and barely noticed us. He always touched her as she passed and she always stroked his thick hair as he read her passages from whatever book he was reading. I must have been six or seven before I realized my father's name was Hugh; he was only ever 'darling' to my mother, and she was Puddock (Gaelic for 'toad').

My mother was full of softness and love, but she so adored having babies that once we learned to talk she was soon distracted because another baby had just been born. Pa had no interest in babies and only woke up to us when we could make him laugh. He was always friendly, he just had a very abbreviated span of attention, and with my mother tied up with us babies, my father could enjoy a bachelor life in London. On sunny days when he was at home he wandered around in Speedos, and it was our special privilege to be allowed to rub sun lotion into his back as he lay sprawled on a sun lounger outside the library. We would sit crosslegged in the grass beside him and bombard him with questions. Pa knew everything. He knew the name of every tree, he knew about politics and history and art, he drew pictures and he wrote a little picture book in which we starred. He could make us laugh until Ma thought we would do ourselves a mischief.

My parents had a formal candlelit dinner every night, even when they were *à deux*. They always changed for dinner, often into matching outfits; he with a chiffon scarf tied over his black roll neck, she with hair extensions back-combed and sprayed into spun sugar. After our nursery supper of fish fingers and boiled eggs, we would chat to our mother as she had her bath, put on her make-up and chose jewellery from the lumpen collection of cardboard rings with op-art designs supplied by our cottage industry.

Dinner guests were often bizarre. My father had a series of E-type Jaguars and he would get into spontaneous races with other string-backed driving-glove wearers on the seven-hour journey from London to Wales. If they pulled in for petrol at the same filling station he would often impulsively invite them to come and stay, 'Any time!' And they did. In droves. 'Hey, man! We were the Jensen Interceptor that turned off at Gloucester! This is Boo, my wife. And Reinhardt. He's a dude from Basle. We picked him up hitching to Dover, 'cept he was on the wrong side of the motorway. We've got some friends following in a Winnebago. They'll be here soon.' And so on. While I helped Edith stiffen leftover egg whites for meringues, I could hear the hectic laughter of our guests through the baize-covered connecting door as my father regaled them with his witty asides just out of earshot.

Sometimes people would arrive asking for the 'rabbit guy', because Pa had once accidentally driven off with our pet rabbit Michele in his engine. On cold days my father would open up the bonnet of his car, check the oil and run the engine for ten minutes, so that it was capable of ramming speed by the time he got to the cattle-grid at the bottom of the drive. Michele lived in a cage in the garage.

On that day, Emma and I had failed to secure the latch of her cage properly, and she hopped into the temptingly warm metal cavern. When my father pulled into one of his pit stops, he asked the mechanic to check the oil level. The man ducked under the bonnet to reach for the dipstick, but instead lifted out Michele by her ears, like a magician. Her fur was singed and her paws were burned, but amazingly, she was alive. Pa brought her home, but Michele went into a decline and after a few days we decided we should liberate her by way of an apology. We took her hutch to where the lawn met the field and opened the door. After a few moments, Michele emerged and loped off up the grassy slope without so much as a backward glance, until her burned rump finally vanished from sight.

My father's racing habits had a downside: he wrote off six E-types in succession. The crashes got steadily worse. It was as if he was destined to die that way, but it was going to be by instalments. Pa's philosophy was that when in town, obeying a red light after midnight was a sinful waste of precious time, and in the country, when in doubt, take to the scenery. Typically he would crash at night, after dinner, while drunk. He modified hedges and then moved on to smacking into parked vans. For the next ten years, Cath extracted needle-thin splinters of glass as they slowly emerged out of his forehead after he had headbutted his windscreen.

Hugh's last Jag crash was almost fatal. After a heavy night, he set off to collect Cath from Swansea railway station. His car mysteriously spun off a straight, empty road, careened down a bank and did three somersaults, end over end, before coming to rest upside-down in a meadow. Pa got catapulted out through the sunroof and landed in a ditch with a fractured skull, five snapped ribs, a pierced lung, lacerations, a broken nose (for the seventh time) and two crushed vertebrae that left him a smaller man, with a pronounced hump. Cath waited and waited on the platform but he never came, and in the end she caught a taxi. On the way home, they pulled over to let an ambulance rush past. Only later did she realize it had been carrying her husband. For weeks, my mother ferried herself between the intensive care departments of two separate hospitals, one caring for her husband, the other her youngest child.

Instead of spotting any correlation between the drinking and the crashes, my father came to an altogether different conclusion: E-types were rubbish and their suspensions dangerous. The crumpled and horribly foreshortened wreck of his E-type became the heart of a growing car collection, and thereafter he drove Ferraris. Their suspensions were clearly vastly superior because he only managed to write off one.

If our parents were alone, we had a custom of going down to the library after dinner in our dressing gowns for a glass of Coca-Cola. Those were the days: no crash helmets, no safety belts, universal smoking and caffeine at bedtime. My father's nightly treat would be to let us eat the burned charcoal from the matches he had used to light his cigarettes, and on a lucky evening he would put down his drink and cigarettes to play hide and seek with us. It was during one of these games that I realized he had a genius for hoodwinking. I had counted to ten and was searching for him and Emma when I spotted the tips of his shoes peeping out from behind a curtain. I rushed up with a 'Ha!' to find only a plump moon soaring gracefully behind the windowpanes, and an empty pair of shoes.

Unlike my mother, Pa scared me sometimes. One evening I thought I was alone in the library, having failed to notice my father in the room as I took some sips from Emma's Coca-Cola. My mother would have scolded me with a few well-weighted words, but Pa gave a little cough, and when I turned round he sprayed me full in the face with the contents of a soda siphon. Totally shocked and soaked from head to foot, I burst into tears, not because my nightie was wringing wet, but because the punishment felt so out of proportion to the crime. Later on, when I looked back on this incident, it was a jagged rock in an otherwise calm sea of childhood, viewed from the forbidding continent where our family had washed up.

Our Welsh valley was a parochial backwater, but even here it was the height of the 1960s. The sounds of Donovan singing 'Season Of The Witch' were always floating from the speakers, and we ran around the house shouting 'groovy', 'psychedelic' and 'swanky'. I wasn't totally confident that I knew what psychedelia was. When they showed it on the television it seemed to be blobs and swirling circles that made your eyes go blurry, and then things went into a kind of spiral and a girl wearing white kinky boots and matching hat spun dizzily while waving her arms like reeds in a musical gale. My father said psychedelia was about colour, but our television was black and white.

Watching telly brought the world beyond Wales into our nursery: Neil Armstrong on the moon, *Animal Magic*, *Jackanory*, and the Beatles growing beards.

'I love John!'

'You can't have John, he's mine.'

'I love Paul then.'

'Nope, he's mine too. You can have Ringo.'

'OK, Emma.'

'But only for this week.'

There were anti-Vietnam war protests, *The Persuaders*, Jason King, *The Singing Tree* and Woodstock – 'It's just bad acid, man!' For me, though, the seminal experiences of the late 1960s were fruit-based. They peaked one Christmas when pomegranates came to our local town of Llandeilo. Although they are not instantly recognizable as totems of the Tune In, Turn On, Drop Out culture, they encapsulated thrilling modernism to me. When my father teased me, saying pomegranates were a new invention, I believed him. They were like turnips designed by a graphic artist. The outside gave no hint of the sweet-scented wonders within. When broken open they revealed a mass of translucent jelly-pips, like fuchsia tadpoles. They promised so much, but the energy you burned getting into them was greater than the goodness they bestowed – a bit like the 1960s. Nevertheless, no-one could deny that of all the fruits, pomegranates were the most psychedelic. Cherries, on the other hand, were groovy. I was always on the look-out for semi-detached pairs to wear as earrings. Avocados were swanky, especially if Edith placed a prawn on top of the Thousand Island dressing. Women were demanding equality, burning their bras and embracing political activism, but my 1960s revelations were confined to the seasonal stock in the local greengrocer's.

The only upheaval was when Emma got sent away to boarding school in Dorset at the age of eight. In the year she was gone I found relief from her temper, but I missed her desperately. Even though all our games were interspersed with her flying off the handle, she was terrific company and I adored her. I tried to play with Colin, but he was only four and a poor substitute. Whenever I tried to force him into a desperate dash around the back of the garage in search of our many make-believe children who had been cruelly abducted by pirates, he would stray off in express contradiction to my plot commands. His omnipresent tissue veil only added to my frustrations. 'You're meant to be a DOCTOR!' I would shout in despair as he forgot all about our thrilling crisis and shuffled aimlessly in a flowerbed.

Pa bought a gypsy caravan for us to play in; he had bought two at auction and gave the second to Boojum and Alexander. Theirs turned out to be haunted. Ours had a tiny bunk, no bigger than a horse's manger, and a couple of miniature wicker chairs. We spent hours fiddling around playing gypsies. I was the mother; Fred and Colin were my children, but they doubled as blacksmiths. Off-cuts of pastry doled out by Edith served as our lunch, but doubled as horseshoes. Father Cinelli came over on a special visit to see our caravan. He explained that in the States they had only had covered frontiersmen wagons, not gypsy ones. I knew that we would be dead meat crossing Pawnee country. Only a bunch of sissies would paint theirs in. primary colours with stencilled flowers on the shutters.

Father Cinelli looked in on us through the door, gave a low whistle, and then turned to Pa. 'You can understand why they had such a problem with incest,' he remarked. And they walked off into the house to have a pre-lunch gin and tonic.

'What insects?' asked Colin, taking the tissue away from his face and looking round.

'Not insects, silly,' I said haughtily. 'Incense. It's a holy thing.'

'Uh-hunh-huh,' said Fred, and fell down the short ladder, leaving a blue wellington boot behind at the top and the skin off his elbow at the bottom.

I joined Emma at Hanford boarding school a few weeks before my eighth birthday. I had never stayed anywhere without my parents, or rather, they had often stayed away from us but I had never stayed away from them. I went into shock when my mother drove away. Emma came to my rescue, and although she fell short of my desire for us to amalgamate, she did at least take me under her wing.

The school was a lovely place, run by teachers bustling with enthusiasm for their subjects. The headmistress, known to us as Mrs C, was a marvellous figure with purple tinted hair that would fade to a pale lilac over the course of a few weeks and then, with the help of her home-dyeing kit and a casual approach to any guidelines concerning the strength of the mixture, the shade got zapped back up again. She seemed as old as Mrs Noah, but whenever Pa dropped us off at the start of term she would get strangely kittenish and play with her amethyst curls.

Hanford was fanatically horsey. Our previous contact with livestock had been limited to the Thomases' herd of Friesians, and it became obvious that while neither of us had a problem with cattle, we were, like Pa, both violently allergic to horses. Emma developed hay fever and asthma in her first term, and as soon as I arrived I followed suit. My mother said it was another case of me copycatting, but however much I admired Emma, I did not enjoy sneezing until my nose bled, or the interminable nights spent propped upright by pillows, able only to think about the next breath I was going to snatch. I suspect it was more to do with a genetic predisposition, coupled with a dusty Jacobean schoolhouse in a damp Dorset valley where we all walked around covered in horsehair. Winter terms were bogged down by asthma, and as soon as the weather warmed up we were in the grip of hay fever. Whenever we went out on early-morning rides my eyes and nose would be streaming and itching within minutes of mounting. When I couldn't resist it any more I would claw at my face with a gloved hand, which only ever made matters worse. Snot would be strung between my nose and my hand, my hand and the reins, and the reins and my hat, like vile bunting. Pa suggested I stay away from horses, but at a school like Hanford that was a bit like telling a waiter not to touch the plates.

Mrs C ran the school with her two adult daughters. Rose, the elder of the two, was a wounded swan of a woman who had 'gone peculiar' at a previous juncture and now only spoke in an inaudible whisper. She wandered around with downcast eyes, one arm on permanent duty supporting her prize-winning marrow-sized breasts. Rose taught us art, and her beloved companion was Jack, a tame jackdaw that sat on her shoulder. He was a vicious, girl-hating bird. When he wasn't using Rose as his slow-moving chariot, he would lie in wait at the far end of the long, narrow kitchen passage and launch himself at us, tearing out hanks of our hair as we ran the gauntlet trying to fend off his scything beak and talons. If he missed, he would do the avian equivalent of a handbrake turn and dive-bomb us again from the rear, trying one more attack before we reached the sanctuary of a swing door. Somewhere in the school grounds there was the chicest nest in birdkind, lined with the human angora of little girls' hair. The strands of sauce-coated human hairs we regularly found in our food were known as Lotte's Trademarks in honour of the school's Polish cook – although the hairs were just as likely to be ours, as the ceiling beam above the kitchen table was one of the jackdaw's favourite perches.

The food was consistently bad. To distract us from the taste of the cooking, everything, especially the puddings, had exhilarating titles. We had the traditional Spotted Dick and Dead Man's Leg, but then things branched out into Thames Mud and Frogs' Spawn, and reached their imaginative zenith in a horrid confection of cornflour and jam, eagerly anticipated simply because it was called Tragedy in the Alps. When we complained, Hugh wrote back that we were naive suckers and that they could have served up custard-covered balls of putty if they had called it Humpty Dumpty's Post-mortem.

Behind the classrooms was a long yew hedge. Its hollow interior was divided into house sections that were occupied on a first-come-first-served basis at the start of term. Everyone else, when not riding real horses, was busy 'being' a horse and whipping themselves fiercely over home-made cavallettis. Some people's yew houses were stables where these human horses could come for imaginary hay and a bit of lungeing. I was going through a religious phase and had a chapel rather than a house. One holiday I was asking Pa what his favourite books were, and he said the Bible was a fantastic piece of literature. I took my copy out to my chapel and resolved to read it from cover to cover. I found it heavy sledding. After a while, as I leafed through I began inking out every reference to 'Satan' I could find. When the job was done I realized that rather than obliterate Satan's presence, the dozens of prominent blue scribbles had highlighted it, and now the blots scared me even more.

I could no longer go near my Bible, so I turned from my religious calling towards autopsy, which involved finding dead animals and poking at the maggots with revolted fascination. Until one day we found Miss Rose Canning's Jack. His head had been staved in. For school life this was as close as we had come to a murder mystery. I decided to bury him, then panicked, dug him up, and took the corpse to Mrs C. I knew that Rose was like Edith our cook and was likely to have the mother of all turns. An investigation began into the death, but seeing as Jack had attacked almost every girl there, Hanford was a school full of suspects. At half-term I told Pa the story and was taken aback when he laughed uncontrollably. After this, I knew that if I could only give all my stories a gothic tilt I had found a way of making him happy.

Boarding at Hanford prompted the inescapable realization that there were wrinkles and bulges in the space/time continuum. Clocks ticked slower, lessons stretched into the foreseeable future, and a week felt like a whole season, especially when the children who lived nearby got to go home and sleep in their own beds every weekend while our mother was far away and completely preoccupied with a sick baby. On Saturdays, we clambered into the branches of an old cedar tree from where we could watch a steady stream of cars come down the drive and pick all the other girls up. Our afternoons passed watching black and white movies of brave sailors searching for periscopes in the North Sea while impossibly brave heroines sensuously exhaled clouds of cigarette smoke.

In the evenings, one girl had the special privilege of mixing Mr Sharp the maths master's gin and tonic and delivering it to him as he performed his pastoral duties. The reward was a glass of Coke with a slice of lemon. Mr Sharp had thick, wavy hair, a roguish twinkle and a famously short fuse. I worshipped him; he reminded me of Pa, who was a gin drinker too.

Sundays were more formal, with chapel followed by letter-writing home – two pages minimum. I recently came across a badly spelled list that I had used as a prompt.

1. Send more pape and stamps
2. Nearly fell of the tree
3. Got your letter
4. Had a slipper fight
5. The incest in the chapel gave me the wheezes
6. Emma's better
7. Have a nice time in Ireland?
8. Made a hole and stired up earth and made a trap

Looking at it brought home just how young we were to be living away from home – and how wearisomely dull my letters were.

Ma was scrupulous in her duties and wrote to us a couple of times a week with details of the home life we had left behind. Pa's letters were far more sporadic and thus unfairly prized. They were half jokey and half lecture. Our messy handwriting was a running theme. One letter complained of my spelling being 'completely gerschmurgled' and accused me of writing lines that were so slanted that I must have been writing on the deck of the *Bismarck*. The same letter ended with a poignant PS – that he realized he'd forgotten my birthday: 'oh damn'. I think that a lot of the time we weren't particularly on Pa's mind, but when we were, he made spontaneous gestures that were often doomed to failure. Twice, Pa turned up out of the blue skies to visit us, piloting his own helicopter. It caused a tremendous stir, but on neither occasion were we there. By the second half of each term we had set about courting girls who lived near the school who might, just might, invite us out. To learn on our return that we had missed Pa's visit was much worse than not seeing him for months on end, and we were both stricken. Once was bad enough, but after the second time Emma and I were so traumatized we had synchronized asthma attacks. The worst thing was the certainty that after a double disaster he would never bother to try again. The second worst thing was that our recovery coincided with exams. The only cheering moment was a timely letter entitled 'Instructions from devoted, loving Papa for Exams'. It contained an eight-point plan for surviving exam time, exhorting us to brush our hair to lift the morale, to read the 'kwestions' and to try not to pick our noses. Finally he forbade us to pad out our 'ignorance with scronk', before signing off, affectionately, 'Good luck and I love you, vastly. Bless you.'

As consolation for our long absences from home – and because we were considered, if not more housetrained, then less feral – we were allowed to join our parents for supper in the dining room during the holidays. To stop us fidgeting in our chairs at the dining table my father offered a reward to whoever could keep still for five whole minutes. Emma struggled and gave up quickly. I stayed stock-still. I remember thinking, 'I can do this for ever! I *will* do it for ever if he wants me to.' Being motionless, that's what I was good at. I used to long for my father to place the statue bet because I was unbeatable. Once, when Emma had been sent out of the room for being insolent, I asked if I could freeze on my own for him. Pa agreed and said he'd be back after a pee, and not to cheat. The minutes ticked by. A shaft of light lit up the tips of my hair. A bluebottle clattering against the windowpane to my right would occasionally come dive-bombing across the room. I did not flinch; my father might be peeping through the keyhole to catch me out. My feet began to tingle a little. It got worse, and I gingerly wiggled my toes inside my shoes, but stared fixedly at the facing wall. I needed a distraction, and it came: my father's dog Wasp was outside and had started barking excitedly. Maybe it was a visitor. I wanted to look, but Wasp's barks came from the window directly behind me and I would have to break my pose. Finally the sound of the barks moved around the corner of the house to a window I only had to slide my eyes to look out of. My father was there, throwing a stick, taking Wasp for a walk. He never looked back. He'd forgotten all about the statue deal. I stood up to go to the window and shout angrily, but my ankles were so numb I took one step and keeled over.

One holiday we came back and were surprised to find that there was someone new living at Golden Grove. For once it wasn't a new baby; it was a grown-up. He was introduced to us as Tia Honsai, a martial arts expert. Pa had met him at a party thrown by a property tycoon called Felix Fenston. He said that Tia's eyes had 'bored' into the back of his head and he had spun round and said, 'I must know who you are.' And Tia had proceeded to mesmerize him. By the end of the evening, Pa was his latest devotee.

I was expecting to meet a wise old Japanese man with white, waist-length moustache strands, but Tia was middle-aged with a greasy quiff. He was not even Japanese, he was Welsh, and Tia was not his real name. It was Ronald Thatcher. Like many self-styled gurus, Tia was a bit of a showman. Later, as his powers waned, there was a small pinch of charlatan too.

The way Tia told it was that he had been born in the industrial sprawl of Cardiff, but as a teenager had stowed away on a merchant ship destined for the Far East. The ship was far out to sea by the time his hiding place was uncovered, so the sailors let him stay on board after punishing him – Tia maintained they had keel-hauled him – and he was put to work in the galley. When the ship eventually docked in Japan, he disembarked and wound up at a small city dojo, or gym, where he became apprenticed to a martial arts grandmaster who taught him aikido and how to speak Japanese. Like t'ai chi, aikido is a defensive fighting form that aims to convert the energy of an attack to the defender's advantage. Tia became a superlative fighter and was encouraged to develop his control of chi – the inner energy force – and harness it as a healing power. Years later he returned to England, found work as a body-guard, started up a small dojo in Hammersmith and began to get a name as a healer. His clientele gradually became grander and wealthier, and by the time Hugh met him he was quite well known.

My father was immediately and utterly in Tia's thrall. With Jack Cawdor as remote as Pluto, it was not so sur-prising that Hugh might crave an approachable father figure. The only framed picture Pa kept on his desk was a grainy photograph of Tia. The shot had been taken during an international randori tournament,, when individual contestants take on pairs of opponents. Tia is standing with his feet apart, his top is gaping open, but he has a passive look as he gazes downwards. The man to his left is sprawled face down on the floor. The man to his right has both legs in the air and is a second away from crashing onto the canvas. On the reverse of the photograph is a small typewritten note listing the two men's injuries, including several broken bones apiece.

Pa wanted to learn aikido, and in return Tia wanted total control over his life. Before you could say feng shui, Tia had moved in with us. He trained Pa very hard indeed. They would start with early-morning meditation that lasted an hour and was done squatting on their haunches. Then they ran a four-mile circuit of the valley, past the Thomases', past Wylo's house, through the meadow where the glider crashed, down the rhododendron-lined drive of Gelli Ayr and back past the church. When they got home, they stood on their heads for an hour before even starting on aikido. Tia dictated how much Hugh should drink, warned him off philandering, and even instructed him when he should abstain from conjugal sex.

In a moment of frankness, Pa told Tia that one of the reasons for undergoing this tough new regime was that he had a secret phobia of knives. This was something he had never even told Cath about. Now, at last, he had found someone who would teach him to develop the courage he suspected was lacking. Hugh wanted to become an unarmed killing machine so that he could walk the earth fearlessly. He could normally only ever achieve this state by drinking, but this method tended to tip him from confidence into aggression. What he never grasped was that courage lies exclusively in the hands of the fearful. Because of this fundamental misunderstanding, my father never achieved the poise he longed for, no matter how much he trained. He also never managed to grasp that the central tenet of aikido was to be humble and to walk away from trouble, not to instigate fights.

Adults must have seen something in Tia that children missed. To us, this guru had all the charisma of a traffic warden. When we eventually found out that his real name was Ronald Thatcher, we stopped calling him Tia and switched to Ron, but that was considered impudent, so it was Thatch thereafter. Emma and I would watch with vague disdain as Pa and Thatch, dressed in white judo kits, grappled with each other on the lawn. They spent hours looking fierce and chopping the air with their hands as they took slow steps in what looked like a strange version of Grandmother's Footsteps. We grew to resent Thatch's constant presence, and, later, that of his strangely silent, bewigged wife Val. Pa remained in awe. They moved in with us for three years.

As Tia Honsai, dressed in his judo clothes, he was powerful, charismatic, commanding. As Thatch, in his tight blazer, he was pretty unprepossessing. Pa didn't seem to mind, but he drove us mad with endlessly repeated anecdotes and – worst of all – his noodling on the

Hammond organ. Aunt Carey nicknamed him 'the Killer at the Keyboard'. As Tia, his followers were so deferential that they looked to him for guidance in every single aspect of their lives. As Thatch, the flattery of this attention would often lead him into pronouncing on business and financial matters – areas his gifts did not cover. Like many other spouses of his devotees, my mother was a sceptic. She could see that Thatch had a good influence on Hugh, but doubted his capacity to heal. She did not enjoy sharing her home with this guru when there was no departure date in sight, but was far too distracted by her desperately ill child to make a fuss.

Laura was still lying like a shrivelled leaf in a Cardiff hospital. When Pa brought Thatch in to visit her, Cath could see that he was at a total loss. Later, when massive doses of cortisone slowly began to restore Laura to health, Thatch announced that it was he who had saved her. Cath reserved her gratitude for the nursing staff. Val was an unforthcoming companion, and while the men had a shared goal, my mother struggled to find common ground with her. Val had no role unless Thatch was making notes on a course of action he wanted a patient or pupil to follow, and then he would dictate to Val in gabbled Japanese. She scribbled things down, but no-one was sure whether she understood a word he was saying.

Pa was under the impression that his improving aikido skills had given him curative powers. I viewed these embryonic abilities with the deepest suspicion, ever since he had tried to cure one of my asthma attacks using 'an aikido approach'. During one half-term I was confined to bed at a family friend's house when Pa came in. He stood me in front of him, told me to relax, and then punched me hard in the solar plexus. I fell to the floor shocked, insulted and gasping for air like a dying fish. My wheezes remained, and to them were added freshly bruised ribs.

Hugh's shortcomings as a healer aside, his climb through the belts was meteoric. By the time we moved to Scotland he was a black belt, three dan (like being a five star rather than just a plain 'general'). We sometimes suspected that, as his teacher-cum-examiner and beneficiary of free lodging, Thatch exaggerated his star pupil's skills, knowing that Pa responded to flattery. Pa's anxieties ran deep, and a lot of them had to do with knowing all his ancestors and wondering whether he measured up to his forebears who had been conspicuous for their gallantry. Six MCs, fifteen DSOs and three VCs had been won between twelve men of the family during the Boer and First World Wars.

Almost two hundred years earlier, the military excellence of John Campbell (the grandson of Joyless John) had earned the family an English barony, in addition to the Scottish thanedom. He was given the new title as reward for the pivotal role he took in repulsing the last foreign invasion of mainland Britain. But the phrase 'the last foreign invasion of mainland Britain' sounds rather more significant than the spool of events it describes. The affair barely registers, even as a' digression, in history books.

John's portrait hung in the front hall of Golden Grove

and every time a new guest enquired who he was, we would listen to Pa telling them the story of what had happened in 1796, when France was still in the grip of revolutionary zeal and an atmosphere of alarm was sweeping England. It was feared that the dastardly French republicans planned to launch an attack across the Channel and spread their anti-monarchist message through the land. Sure enough, in February that year a small fleet of French war-ships set off with an ambitious but sketchy plan to sail up the Severn estuary and destroy Bristol. As they slid over the horizon towards the English coast, the French fleet overhauled a merchant ship laden with madeira. Having captured the shipment but with little cargo space of their own, they were inspired to empty prodigious quantities of the booty into themselves. A sharp easterly wind blew them drunkenly off course, and on 22 February they ended up sore-headed at Fishguard, where John Campbell captained the local militia.

Thirteen hundred French soldiers, armed with ultra-modern flintlock muzzle-loading muskets, leapt ashore. With their intended target a hundred miles behind them, they boldly took Pencaer Peninsula. Until that day this bare Pembrokeshire headland had no strategic significance whatsoever, but it was at hand, and Bristol was not. There was not a great deal for the French to triumph over at Pencaer other than some sheep and a few trees. Wondering what to do next, they decided to fan out and foment some insurrection. This failed. News of the invasion had swept through the little seaside communities and the local militia mustered with all speed. After escaping a French ambush,

John Campbell, a handful of professional soldiers and his troop of six hundred yeomen engaged the enemy on a beach. The invaders outnumbered the Welsh force two to one, but their misfortunes were still on the wax. The local wives, daughters and mothers rushed to the surrounding cliff tops to watch over the fate of their loved ones as they formed up against the enemy on the beach below. In those days, Welsh women wore traditional outfits of red flannel dresses, cloaks and black stovepipe hats. The French mistook the tall-hatted silhouettes gathering on the heights above them for reinforcements, and promptly surrendered.

The death toll was six on land and sixteen on the French ships, plus John's horse, stolen and eaten by the prisoners as he attended a celebratory dinner with the local governor. Nineteen of the captured muskets were presented to John. They still hang in a fan-shaped display opposite the Tree Room on Cawdor's main staircase. And although Fishguard is long forgotten as a military encounter, it did have one significant repercussion. When word spread that the French were on English soil, a run on the banks for gold caused a dangerous shortage of cash. To bring the situation under control as rapidly as possible, the Bank of England issued paper money as a substitute for the first time.

While this all seemed interesting on a very small family scale, none of us felt particularly emotionally connected to John Campbell's actions beyond the thrill of the story. Hugh, on the other hand, identified far more closely not only with John but with all our other martial forebears.

Thatch's great importance to Hugh was to help him bear the weight of this burden of memories. Hugh wanted to be sure about his own mettle, and he gradually began to put his training into practice. Yet the uses to which he put his skills were all rather less orthodox than Thatch had in mind.

Chapter 5

Up the airy mountain,
Down the rushy glen
William Allingham, 'The Fairies'

OUR PARENTS TRAVELLED EXTENSIVELY WHILE WE LIVED
in Wales. I have a box of postcards that say 'Hello darling!
We are in Wengen!/Kashmir!/Madeira! We have seen an
ibex!/a rococo church!/Uncle George!' As children we
hardly went anywhere at all. Five small people getting lost
at airports was too much of a logistical headache. Apart
from Barafundle beach, our excursions were confined to a
couple of trips up to Scotland every year.

The drive north was a marathon, with suitcases, fishing
rods, children and a dog. My parents always chose to drive
through the night as it was just too awful to spend eleven
hours driving while we were awake. It was a shrewd plan,
but it never worked. We would set off in the early evening,

dressed in our nightclothes to advance the idea of impending slumber. It had, of course, the opposite effect. Home life was pretty quiet, so climbing into a car dressed for bed was enough to get us insanely hyped. We waved at every car we saw, and once we were at least twenty miles away from home we were allowed to stick our tongues out if they did not wave back. Sometimes we wrote notes and pressed them against the back window, hoping to electrify the occupants of the cars that came up behind us. Our favourite was Pleas Help! My Brother Has Turn In To A Dog!' And we would point dolefully at Hugh's dog, Wasp.

As soon as the sun had gone down, the back seats were folded flat to form a makeshift bed. Wasp slept across the end, crushing our feet. It was impossible to sleep as our bed became an instant lunar landscape of biscuit crumbs. We bickered our way north. I would whine about the discomfort until I was told to get up on all fours and give the bed a thorough sweep. 'You're behaving like the Princess and the Pea, missy,' my father would say, an impatient edge to his voice. He was right, but only up to a point: it wasn't like sleeping on a single pea, it was as if a catering pack had detonated. The journey was unbearably long and unbelievably boring. The one solace was passing through endless Midlands suburbs at night. I loved catching glimpses into homes whose occupants had been generous enough to forsake net curtains. The dark outlines of the houses, the warm glow of the lights within that revealed a captivating flash of strangers doing simple domestic acts, like ironing, laying a table, playing with a cat, or staring out of an upstairs window with their hair in a towel. It was like a living advent calendar.

We were limited to five 'are we nearly there?' questions each. If we exceeded our quota, my father whipped round and clashed our heads together – a formidable way of inflicting sudden pain that left no outward sign of injury. Another trick to keep us quiet was to allow us the normally strictly prohibited chewing gum, but on the few occasions we did nod off for a bit we would wake up with the gum matted in our hair. I would lie on my back, attempting the impossible task of extracting the sticky clod while listening to the drone of the midnight shipping news.

'Biscay . . . Finisterre . . . Sole . . . Fastnet . . . Lundy . . .'

'Where's Finisterre, Pa?'

'It's at the end of the world.'

'Is that near to Cawdor?'

'Careful now! That counts as another "are we nearly there", which makes it your third time. And we've still got hundreds of miles to go.'

Petrol stops were our only chance to stretch our legs. We would examine the hundreds of squashed moths on the car headlamps and chase after Wasp, who threatened to romp off into whatever northern county we happened to be travelling across at the time. Once we were north of the border, the road was a ribbon of moonlight, but it was also a busy abattoir for larger creatures as bedazzled hares, rabbits, pheasants and the occasional hedgehog went under our wheels. We passed the early hours playing roadkill-counting games in the matter-of-fact way of mortuary attendants.

'I think that was a mouse!'

'It could have been a baby rat.'

'Ooh gosh, don't start arguing, you two. Just add it to the hedgehog tally and call it "smaller mammals" instead.'

The only time a collision caused a proper stir was when my mother took out a hefty ram. Conscience-stricken, she turned the car round and drove back down the road to check if it was dead or, worse, injured. If it had a broken leg, we were duty bound to put it out of its misery there and then. I had no idea how we were going to manage it – bludgeon it with a suitcase? As we rounded the corner where we had hit it, the ram reared out of a ditch and my mother smote it a second time. It dodged off again and disappeared into a wood. And who could blame it? We seemed to be conducting an inadvertent vendetta against it. My mother turned the car round a second time and drove on, tight-lipped with horror.

As dawn thrust a sullen light into the car, we would cross the high passes that traversed the Grampians and finally reach the single-track road that wound its way over the last liver-coloured stretch of moorland before the land dipped down to the River Findhorn, and suddenly the landscape went from bleak to beautiful. Entering the Findhorn valley was like stepping into a Victorian watercolour. The river had carved its way through steep-sided hills of towering larches planted by Napoleonic prisoners-of-war. The place felt secluded, sheltered, secret. The Findhorn snaked sleepily over shallow rapids, a deep coffee-bean brown. The slow corners formed shady pools where salmon lay up on their journeys upstream to spawn, but in spate, the scene was transformed. The river could double in volume in a matter of hours, and the colour changed, as though seething milk had been added upstream. The force of water would chew up the banks, tear down the hazel trees that fringed the curves, and carry them away to the sea. Beyond the Findhorn, there was one last stretch of moor before we reached the Big Wood surrounding Cawdor. We would arrive in time for a breakfast of salted porridge and Arbroath smokies, with the closest thing to jetlag a car can provide.

While my grandfather Jack was still alive, this breakfast was the first and last meal we shared with the older generations. Thereafter we were despatched to the nursery wing at the furthest end of the house. The nursery was a gloomy room that had 'The Google Book', written by Wilma's father Vincent, in pride of place – the only evidence that she had once been resident. It was the single most petrifying children's book I have ever read, with pictures that even managed to make sunsets look creepy. It was too big to fit into the bookshelf so it would lie on a table, beckoning horribly. I longed to ignore it, but before long I had succumbed, starting slowly and nervously and then turning faster and faster, hoping to skip over the page with the awful Google creature on it and later, curled up in bed, trying desperately to keep its image at bay. I kept wondering what kind of a man my great-grandfather had been to write such a strange, nightmarish children's book. I asked Pa about him, but the only thing he could remember was being taken to London Zoo as a child and Vincent striding up to the llama cage, removing his bowler hat and flobbing a great gobbet of spittle at the animals, 'to get in there first'.

The nursery was in a 1940s time warp. The toys were ones Hugh and Carey had played with. All our late 1960s cultural references were to flowers, peace signs and cut-out fashion dolls, and it was hard to relate to the Tommy and Gerry lead soldiers, wooden Spitfires and laminated sheets showing the different types of battle aircraft in silhouette to help identify passing planes. They illustrated British and German planes from three angles: In Profile, Head On and From Below. There were twenty different sheets, each with six or more illustrations to dither over. Even if there had been whole enemy squadrons flying over, the nursery would have been strafed to rubble before Hugh or Carey had had time to furiously flick through all the options to recognize a Fokker (Head On). And despite Grandmother Wilma's worries, during the entire length of the war only one German plane ever flew over Cawdor. A fighter plane returning to its airbase on the continent after a raid on Glasgow strayed off course, ran out of fuel and plunged into the moor a little distance to the south. The crash left a deep crater in the peat that soon filled up with water. Twenty-five years later the dewpond was still there, and when Pa took us up onto that part of the moor we would tramp across the springy peat to study it. When we threw in a pebble, aviation oil rose up in rainbow-coloured hoops, and if we grubbed about among the heather roots we could still unearth scraps of coloured wiring.

'Visiting grandparents' has a cosy ring to it. It conjures up sitting on laps, looking through old family albums, hot milk and certainty. As with Pa's grandfather, Vincent, there was nothing cosy about our grandfather. He did not indulge us in any way. He never engaged us in any sort of conversation other than to bellow if he caught us picking moss off the drawbridge or scuffing the fine gravel in the driveway. A liquid diet of pink gins had turned his complexion to tones of magma. Jack was always dressed in a kilt, sporran, incongruously flamboyant socks and a hessian-strength tweed jacket. He only ever wore trousers on his infrequent forays south of the border. Among all the other unspoken rules, there was one that the wearing of a kilt outside Scotland was naff. The crepitus crunch of his hobnailed boots on the flagstones would echo across the courtyards, giving us time to skedaddle before he came marching out of the house, kilt swinging in stride. We would peep round the corner and wait for him to unlock the studded door that led to his offices and the downstairs loo. This was his private kingdom, despite it being the only loo on the ground floor. No-one, but no-one, aside from Jack Cawdor, was welcome. There was even a doorbell.

I finally got to see what was on the other side of the door after he died. The gents was tiny. It contained a Victorian thunderbox hidden by a large mahogany throne and had a porcelain-handled chain flush that needed several pulls followed by a long delay while pipes clanked and shuddered as if a train was leaving a station. Jack spent long contented hours in here with a newspaper, a surreptitious cigarette and a supply of arse-serrating Jeyes greaseproof toilet paper. As for many men of his age, his Spartan toilet habits were a hangover from the ascetic ways of the military, and the seed had rooted deep. The advent of soft toilet paper upset his cherished customs, and Bill, my grandfather's butler, would be sent forth to rummage through clearance sales to stock up on the dwindling supplies of Jeyes.

At least we could be thankful that we were not the grandchildren of his friend Jimmy Dunbar of nearby Spynie Palace, who had taken hygiene austerity one step beyond. Instead of Jeyes, Dunbar used bracken, and on the rare occasions he travelled to London he took along an extra suitcase packed with bracken fronds, since London hotels were unable to cater for this particular requirement. Jimmy Dunbar was my father's hero because he lived with his own coffin in the front hallway of his house and claimed to exercise his droit de seigneur over his tenants' wives. Hugh never prepared for death in the way Dunbar did, but we did go through almost thirty nannies, and it was not because we children were waking them up in the dead of night.

If the downstairs gents was out of bounds for children, then my grandfather's study made North Korea look like Heathrow. The study was where he dealt with all the correspondence brought to him on a silver tray each morning by Bill. Jack had one unwavering rule regarding brown envelopes: never, ever open them. Bills put him out of sorts. Yet they were never thrown away – that would have been grossly irresponsible. Companies had long ago learned that if they sent duplicates to the estate office, business quietly continued. Upon Jack's death, the study was cleared out and the slag-heap of accumulated mail was laboriously checked. Eventually a three-seater sofa, now buckled by the

111

sheer weight of paper, emerged. Many of the letters contained cheques rather than the dreaded bills, but they were all years out of date and could not be cashed, so everything was burned in a large bonfire, along with the sofa.

When my father took over the study he allowed us limited access but, in keeping with tradition, the gents remained out of bounds. It was now Pa's locked domain, where at the end of his life he hid out, just like his father, to puff at sly fags behind Angelika's back. He smoked four hundred cigarettes a week for thirty-five years and on the occasions he attempted to give up he described it as 'unfurling my will-power and brandishing it around like a flaccid brandy snap'.

There were only two occasions during our Cawdor visits when we would gather en masse as a generationally varied family. One was when we were put into the back of ancient Land Rovers along with all the dogs to go out shooting 'on the hill'. The moorland colours were constantly shifting. The keepers burned large swathes of heather to allow new growth, which provided food for the grouse chicks and left a patchwork of dark and light purple, of new and old heather, of silvery grey from older burns and blackened strips from fresh burns. It was usually cold and usually drizzling, and my main task on the day of a shoot was to keep out of sight. Hugh and his best friend, his stepmother Betty's son William Gordon Cumming, liked to stand side by side so they could try and 'wipe each other's eyes' by being quick enough on the draw to pot a bird flying over the other's position.

I would sit in the bottom of a butt, hands clamped over my ears, as Pa fired overhead. Shooting was deafening and dull, but I tried to keep my lack of hearty Highland enthusiasm quiet because it was such a treat to be with my father, even if it meant he only talked to Wasp and said 'Shh!' to me for the duration of an afternoon. There was not much to see from wellington boot level, other than a damp dog, and nothing to do except collect spent cartridges and sniff deeply on the warm cordite before popping them on my fingers as witch's gloves. When the headkeeper's whistle blew to signal the drive was over, I would scramble out and watch the dogs search the heather for fallen birds, their masters shouting, 'Hel-ooost, hel-oost! Good boy! Heel now, heeeeel!' Sometimes Wasp would retrieve a wounded bird and I was meant to wring its neck, but I just couldn't; and rather than by the neck or feet, I carried the dead ones in my arms as if they were still living. 'You weed,' Pa would grumble.

The highlight of the day would be getting back to Cawdor and clambering out of sodden clothes and into one of the gigantic Victorian baths surrounded by glass decanters etched with grapevines and full of purple bath crystals and soupy pine essence. There were long copper plungers instead of plugs, and the scalding water was a soft peaty brown. The baths were so long that if I lay down I had to hang on to the sides or float, and when I sat up the water lapped my shoulders. The bath towels were the size of spinnakers.

If it had been a good day out on the moor, with a big bag, it meant one thing: game on the menu for the rest of the week. I hated eating grouse. I hated eating pheasant. I hated eating teal and woodcock and snipe and jugged hare, especially when the meat was so rare that it might just as well have been left on a radiator for ten minutes. But my childhood took place in pre-fussy eating days and we ate what we were given. The only relief from the musky tang of game blood was when my teeth clattered against a pellet. This was very auspicious. On my privately calibrated scale of luck, it was one up from winning 'pull a wishbone' and two down from seeing a shooting star.

The only other occasion when we spent time together as a complete family was on Sunday mornings, when we would gather in formal dress and head off to kirk along with the house staff: Bill the butler, Mrs Wood the cook, Jessie and Annie Mary the housekeepers, and Mrs King the laundress, all in our Sunday best. Our tiny children's kilts had been handed down from Edwardian times. If you lifted the front flap, the tartan beneath had been reduced to lace by moths. It made for a draughty walk down the drive, across the narrow wooden footbridge that spanned the Cawdor burn and then along the village's only street.

Even though the kirk is a modest size with a short stump of a tower, its construction in 1629 had nearly bankrupted the 12th Thane. The interior complies with all the rigid stipulations for exemplary Presbyterian plainness. The only concession to decoration is a couple of wall plaques listing the dead of two world wars. There is no stained glass, no altar and no crucifix. Watching dust motes whirl softly in a light beam was the extent of visual stimulation.

The minister's sermon was as unedited as it was stern, typically commencing, 'This week I was inspired to put pen to paper on the subject of babbling fools . . .' followed by a pause as he glowered at us all over the top of his spectacles. A reading would follow that was most likely about Lot's wife, or Job and his malignant ulcers. The Presbyterian God was a dour one who must have thought up the rainbow while he had a temperature and was not feeling quite himself. The songs we sang were all wilfully obscure works from forgotten backwaters of the hymn book, and on the rare occasion that a hymn's words looked remotely familiar, any unholy confidence was expertly crushed by the opening chords of some Harrison Birtwhistle experiment on the organ. We were cajoled into trying to follow the cascade of random notes by the sterling efforts of a large-bosomed lady called Peggy Forsyth, who tapped her feet and gave it her all in a loud and warbling soprano. Pa used to hiss that her vibrato was due to her wearing a truss. Whatever the impact of her undergarments on her vocal cords, she kept the congregation singing. On the occasions when she was absent, voices were apt to falter and drop out one by one, as if poison gas was seeping from the vestry.

In keeping with Presbyterian tradition, communion was taken once a year only, at Easter, when we could look forward to a hunk of real bread and some port. The service would finish off with the congregation stumbling through that cheery foot-tapper 'By the Light of burrrning Martyrs, Christ thy bloody steps we trace', with my father singing it in a basso profundo that sounded like heavy furniture being dragged across the floor. In a pew at right angles to ours, Mrs King from the laundry at Cawdor would make no effort to sing. Ever. She would wave to us gaily while popping a succession of hard-boiled sweets into her mouth and spend the rest of her time flattening out and folding up the cellophane wrappers – as if she could never fully relax from her laundress's habits. Pa kept himself amused by glaring at his watch in full view of the vicar and making stage-whispered comments, usually about Peggy Forsyth's choice of hat, but if we tittered he produced a hammily pious 'Hush now!' This would only make matters worse, and with heaving shoulders I would wait for him to hand over his large spotted handkerchief to stuff into my mouth.

While I was away at school, my mother wrote to me about one of the more exciting services.

Pa and I went to kirk yesterday. The service was full of distractions. A small boy from Piperhill played tiddlywinks with his collection money through the prayers and shouted loudly all through the children's hymn. Not long before the sermon Jessie went a paler shade of grey and was escorted out by Bill, later joined by Peggy Forsyth who obviously felt she might be missing something, & one could but envy them all missing the sermon. I went to look for Jessie afterwards to see if I could drive them home, but she was recovered and giggling having been revived by a strong cuppa in Annie Mary's house.

*

When it was sunny, our holidays at Cawdor were spent grazing on currants in the vegetable garden, stroking the ginger noses of the Highland cows that were pastured beside the drive for ornamental purposes, and clambering across the acres of rooftop gables. From the top of the tower you could see the sea. On the southern battlement there was a medieval loo, a stone projection that jutted out from the vertical pitch of the tower walls with a little stone seat but no floor. If you peered between your knees you could see the courtyard far below. I never managed to pee down it; vertigo always gave me a stricture.

When it was miserable weather we went to the attics, or more often loitered in the windowless back passages behind the green baize door. If a bell rang we would run to where a long line of bells hung on coiled springs, like treble clefs. High up on the wall beside each bell the name of the corresponding room was painted in neat black letters. Even if the bell had stopped ringing, it was easy to spot which one in the line-up was still quivering. 'Gun room!' we would shout, and the relevant person would scurry off. Behind the green baize door we could chat to the house staff much less formally than if we met up on the other side of it, although there were some staff who weren't much cop whichever side you met up. Mrs King wasn't any fun outside church. She was amiable enough, but the omnipresence of a boiled sweet in her mouth made my contributions to our conversations an endless series of 'whats?' Jessie and Annie Mary were the housekeepers, and made a fearsome duo. They too were best avoided.

Bill, who looked as if he could be Grandpa's brother, was the one we wanted. He was friendly, but circumspect due to his catastrophic stammer. They said he had acquired it as a boy at school, when he was forced to write with his right

117

hand because it was considered improper to be left-handed. This information really bothered me since I was left-handed too; I could barely do anything with my right hand, other than pick my nose. I ate with my knife and fork back to front, which meant my elbows were always out of kilter with everyone else's on the long benches at school. But listening to Bill struggling to say 'More mince, m'lord?' made me determined to get mine the right way round and avert an unwanted remedial intervention.

The butler's pantry was orderly, meticulous — professional. In the middle, it had a big table covered with a thick damask tablecloth and padded by a green felt undercloth. Bill would show us how to fold napkins into origami lotuses or smear the clean cutlery with pink polish that turned grey when it was dry and ready to rub off. Emma and I were delegated the forks and spoons. We each wore one of Bill's cotton polishing gloves so that every curve got properly buffed. Only Bill was allowed to clean the knives because over the years the steel had been worn to razor sharpness on both edges. Guests had to be cautioned against pressing a forefinger along the length of the blade. People who didn't listen soon found out that it wasn't an idle warning and had the appetite-spoiling surprise of finding their flesh newly cloven. A lunch guest once inadvertently dropped his knife from his plate as he passed by my mother's chair. The knife fell silently, vertically, piercing my mother like a javelin and pinioning her foot to the sole of her shoe. Ma, for whom discretion was always the better part of valour, let out the smallest of gasps so as not to embarrass the guest, then seized the handle, pulled it out and left the room as her shoe brimmed up with blood.

If, after helping Bill with his chores, it was still too miserable to go outside we would be at another loose end – until Findlay Macintosh arrived, and then we would volunteer to help the bandy-legged gardener with his delivery of cut peat. Findlay was old and small but incredibly handsome with a shock of white hair and a face like a noble-hearted eagle. I thought that if I had been born in olden times I would have probably liked to marry him.

After helping Findlay empty his barrow we would mooch off to shout our names into the echoey old kitchen well, which was there in case of a siege. Anything was better than spending time in the nursery. Having Wasp to play with would have made a difference to our time, but all my grandfather's dogs were kept at the keeper's kennels and Wasp was banished there too. The only animal allowed in the house was an enormous grey cat with matted fur and a dewlapped stomach that scraped the floor. Its name was Catter and it belonged to no-one in particular. How it came to be at Cawdor was long forgotten. It never behaved like a pet. It had the attitude of a recalcitrant stranger and wandered the castle corridors sticking closely to the walls, lurking in the darkest passageway outside the pantry by the peat pile. Sometimes it would come towards us, but if we reached out to stroke it, it would lash out. On its infrequent forays into the drawing room my grandfather's eyes would light up and he would call it gently. 'Catter! Come here. Come, Catter.' Normally it paid no attention whatsoever and went about its business, rubbing against each of the piano legs before making a regal exit. But once in a long while Catter would be tempted by Jack's soft blandishments and move stiffly down the room towards his fireside armchair, using a curious sideways step as if it had quietly studied dressage but now had prosthetic limbs. As soon as it was within striking distance, my grandfather's boot, which he had been manoeuvring into position with glacial stealth, would shoot out and kick the cat back down the length of the carpet. This ritual was repeated until Catter died at some vast cat age and was buried in a flowerbed near the Tibetan irises, outside the kitchen. Common to the mystery of many human relationships, Jack conducted the interment with a sentiment unexpressed while Catter had breath.

Staying at Cawdor was not something I ever felt any enthusiasm about. If anyone had told me we were due to move there I would have thrown a shit fit.

Chapter 6

One Scot: the cleverest man on earth.

Two Scots: a quarrel.

Three Scots: four political parties.

Proverb

MY GRANDFATHER DIED SUDDENLY. HEART ATTACK. BANG. Gone. He was seventy. It was, without question, an impressive age for a man with a face the colour of a fire extinguisher.

Emma and I were at school when it happened. Mrs C called us into her study. I was nine and wasn't sure how to react, but saw that my immediate duty was to cry. I made myself think about Wasp getting run over by Stan's gang-mower until some tears came.

'Do you know what your father is now?' she asked. We were both blank. 'He's turned into something...' she prompted.

'He hasn't turned into Grandpa, has he?' I said, unable to conceal my alarm.

We left school and flew up to Cawdor for the funeral. Aunt Carey and Uncle Peebles were already there with Alexander and Boojum. Uncle James arrived on the train with his wife Bridget, their toddler Slaine and baby Cara – both tubby little girls. It was rare to have so many grand-children at Cawdor and there were only just enough kilts to go round. Jack would have been appalled to see children in such numbers.

The morning after we arrived, we came downstairs to find that breakfast had been laid out in a small anteroom with a barrel-vaulted ceiling known as the winter dining room. This was a completely new room to me, like eating in an upmarket grotto. There was no room at the table for all the grown-ups so they stood apart, sipping coffee and talking quietly. Aunt Carey was checking the cherry stones on Emma's plate using her own version of the counting rhyme. Instead of tinker, tailor, soldier, sailor, she said, 'Cowboy, playboy, sugardaddy, black.'

'Why are we here?' I asked.

'For Grandpa's funeral, you dope,' my father replied.

'No, why are we in this room?'

'Because he's in the dining room.'

'Who?' I asked, suddenly nervous.

'Why Grandpa, of course,' my father replied, and rang the bell-pull to order some more coffee. When we had finished our kedgeree, he said, 'Let's go and see him.'

I followed him out of the room. Bill the butler was in the hall looking pink and giving his nose a hard blow. I really,

really did not want to see my grandfather's corpse and prayed I wouldn't be sick or scream or do anything that would shame me. The dining room looked bigger and darker than normal, the table had been removed and the blinds were pulled halfway down; on the centre windowsill was the demijohn that my grandfather filled with cider and honey to trap wasps. It was packed with dead wasps. It seemed odd that it was still there, but he would no longer be inspecting the casualties with a satisfied grunt. To my relief, Jack's coffin was closed and lay on some sort of trestle with his walking crook and a tartan bonnet placed on the lid. I had no idea what to do. 'Is he a skeleton yet?' I asked. My mother gave me a cross look and told me to go outside and keep out of the grown-ups' way until it was time for the funeral.

I headed for the wild garden where I could hear voices coming from the thick stand of bamboo grown from shoots Grandpa had brought back from the Himalayas. Boojum and Alexander were having a disagreement about the direction of the earth's rotation that was growing a little heated, conducted in exasperated whispers. Then Fred and Colin arrived, having been sent out of the house too. Uncle James had brought his trumpet with him and the mournful notes started tumbling from an upstairs window as we busied ourselves detonating the tightly crammed seedcases of the touch-me-not balsam flowers, while Fred sat under the giant gunnera leaves and silently picked at the holes in his kilt.

A piper skirled laments as the pallbearers processed slowly to the kirk. Granny Betty and Pa led the mourners. She was wearing a trim black coat over a tartan skirt, her hair, as ever, in a miraculous white halo around her head without a single hair adrift, in the same periwigged style so beloved by our own dear Queen but more cumulo-nimbus and less like an Ionic capital. We walked behind Betty, friends followed behind us, and the estate workers brought up the rear. Silent villagers lined the road. Silent, that is, except for Mrs King the laundress, who was standing by the big beech tree noisily springcleaning her handbag as the coffin drew level.

The beech tree! A sudden chill swept over me as we filed slowly past its wide smooth trunk. The last time we had come to stay, we had spelled out on the bark 'Sex is Fun' using the free alphabet stickers inside our bubblegum wrappers. If anyone noticed it, surely they would instantly recognize it as Emma's and my handiwork and halt the funeral there and then to conduct a kangaroo court. I didn't dare check if the words were still there, in case the act of looking drew everyone's eyes to the spot; instead, I gave Colin a few hard pinches. It helped distract me, and besides, that boy just was not being sad enough. He had remained resolutely dry-eyed all day. By the time we reached the church I was feeling a little seasick from the sound of the pipes. Bagpipes are like a handsome man with halitosis: rather fabulous from far away, but taxing up close.

The kirk vault was up to the rafters with dead forebears – it was our Campbell version of my grandfather's wasp trap – so Jack was to be buried outside in the graveyard. The minister told us that life 'was an en-gyne and God was the en-gyne driver'. He made heaven sound like an

Inverness railway siding. As the coffin was lowered into the ground, Betty threw in a tea rose she had clipped that morning. On the way back to Cawdor, James's two-year-old daughter Slaine got lost in the thicket of mourners' legs. Being only knee height, she began to panic, tripped and measured her length on the gravel. My father gathered her up in his arms, dusting her fat little knee as she wailed. Everyone fussed around her, relieved to be distracted from their own sorrows by her much more transitory brand.

The whole congregation slowly gathered in the drawing room for drinks and I wandered around listening into conversations. Mrs King was talking to our great-aunt Helen. 'Did ye see that group of crows swooping overhead as his lordship's coffin was being lowered?'

'Really? No, I didn't notice,' said Great-aunt Helen.

'Well, I thought that was quite fitting in some way,' Mrs King continued, proffering some toffees.

'A sort of metaphor? Yes. But they'll have been rooks, not crows.'

'Rooks? Are ye sure?'

'There's an old saying that the keepers taught me. It goes: "If you see a bunch of bloody crows, it's a bunch of bloody rooks, but if you see a bloody rook on its own, it's a bloody crow." Crows are solitary.'

'Och, I'll nev'remember that.'

'Well, think of "rookery" then. Rooks like to live together. There's no such thing as a crowery.'

'Aye, that's good. Shall we be getting another wee nip of sherry?'

An elegant old lady wearing several dead foxes and lace

mittens was talking to Aunt Carey. I couldn't hear what they were saying, but Emma had and she pulled me aside and summarized it, imitating the woman's strong foreign accent. 'You know, in New York we knew heem as Mad Jacques Cord-ur. 'E was so crezee when 'e was yong.' We giggled with delighted amazement. We knew he'd been on expeditions to Tibet, but the teeming streets of New York seemed an impossibly unlikely place for our grandfather ever to have been. We had never once before thought of him as young. And crezee? So much intriguing inform-ation, and all of it coming a week too late for us to know him better.

My father was dealing with a steady line of people giving him their condolences. People were professing their con-fidence in his new role as Thane. Hugh was going to be the new hub, and his character was going to have an impact on the whole community. Years after, I remember wondering what the experience must have been like for Hugh suddenly to have all this wealth, this title, this *gain* that came with the death of a loved parent and the greatest sense of loss any of us can experience. What must it be like to have one's life predestined in this way? The convention of primogeniture recognizes but one child: the first-born male. All other siblings are superfluous. After Pa, Colin was destined for the role in our generation, a role Pa ultimately managed to betray. Like Emma, Fred and Laura, I have trudged life's path, following unmarked byways, jaywalking emotional motorways and thrashing around in the psychological undergrowth. The eldest sons in families like ours have a separate destiny: theirs is like a flyover, fetchingly lit, with fur-lined guardrails and clearly marked signs reading 'This Way, Buddy'. Does this make the chosen ones feel sure and steady, that their life's path is wide and clear and not going to be short on luxuries? Or do they bridle? Like most either/ors the normal reaction to a pre-destined future is a bit of both, circling in tandem like Phobos and Deimos, the twin satellites of Mars.

The mourners gradually took their leave, and when the wake thinned down to family and a few friends we noticed that Uncle Peebles had disappeared. My mother wondered out loud where he had gone, and his children replied in unison, 'Foraging.' On his way back from the kirk, Peebles had spotted some large ceps through the trees and had slipped away from the wake to pick them. The thrill of the mushroom hunt lay deep in his Teutonic bones, and once he had gathered the ceps he had spotted some shaggy inkcaps and so on until, as Alexander and Boojum said, he was on a full-blown forage. On his return, he delicately unwrapped a large white handkerchief and showed us his haul. He was particularly happy to have come across some unseasonably early boletus. 'Let's cook them immediately,' he said, heading for the kitchen. 'Mushrooms are the traditional remedy to cheer the heavy-hearted.' And I absolutely believed him.

The worst thing about our grandfather's death was that when we went back to school our parents packed up our life in Wales and moved us up to Scotland. Cawdor was our new home. The initial shock of knowing we were never going to return to Golden Grove started to wane little by little as we began to get a sense of place. Hugh began to tutor us on our Scottishness: how the name Campbell made us members of one of the most powerful clans in Scotland, but that over and above the Campbell name our pride dwelt in being from Cawdor. Our roots, he said, held us in an unbroken line of castle children from the times of snoods and heralds, when curses were cast and fairytales were true. Our family motto, 'Be Mindful', was etched in stone all around, and he told us it was a reminder and an instruction. Other family mottoes say pointless things like 'Only the Foolish Boy Pranceth at Dusk' and 'Specta Id Quod Feles Intraxit'.* 'Ours is concise and clear-cut,' he said. 'It means, "Think!" – and that means, of our history, and of Cawdor. There are laws of the land, but Be Mindful is the private law of our family and should *not* be confused with *other* Campbells.'

Our clan is vast. By far the largest branch is the Argyll Campbells from the west coast. The others, like Breadalbane Campbells and Cawdor Campbells, are spindly twigs on the sequoia-like trunk of the Argylls. Being born a Campbell comes with an inbuilt notoriety; on being introduced, a fellow Scot's reaction can range from jokily scandalized to sincerely cold.

For hundreds of years, since early medieval times, the ceaseless jostling for supremacy between the larger clans had made them all endlessly suspicious of each other. During medieval times, the Campbells had slowly emerged

*'Look What the Cat Dragged In'.

as the main source of the Crown's authority in Scotland. This closeness to the Crown had started with their fierce loyalty to Robert the Bruce, who won the throne in 1306 after murdering his rival John Comyn. Habitual proximity to power and their reluctance to relinquish the influence this gave them meant that when the centre of control shifted south of the border, so too did many Campbell allegiances. Their fellow countrymen deeply distrusted them as a result, but the reputation of the Campbell name only turned matt black at Glencoe.

In the seventeenth century, while most Scots of the time supported the Catholic Stuart line to the throne, the Campbells gave their loyalty to the usurping Protestant king, William of Orange. In a move designed to pre-empt Jacobite dissent in Scotland, King William issued a decree that all clan chiefs must sign an oath of allegiance to him by the deadline of nightfall on New Year's Day 1692. Those who defied the order would suffer the consequences. To oversee the job, William promoted John Dalrymple to be his Master of Scottish Affairs. It was a canny choice. Dalrymple was a former Jacobite and had the inside knowledge of poacher turned gamekeeper.

It is uncertain why, but Dalrymple had a particular grievance against the Macdonald clansmen who lived in Glencoe. Some say it stemmed from the Macdonalds' cattle-rustling lifestyle, but before the advent of pubs, football or television, rustling was a terrifically popular Scottish pastime. The Macdonalds were hardly going out on a limb in this indulgence. It is also rumoured that Dalrymple's enmity was inflamed by their Jacobite stance, but there were many others with identical inclinations. Whatever his reasons, Dalrymple set a trap. He ordered Alastair Macdonald, the Glencoe chieftain, to report to Inverlochy, a castle well to the north of Glencoe, where he was to sign the oath. Macdonald had been deliberately misinformed, and when he arrived at Inverlochy he was told, oops-a-daisy, there had been some sort of clerical error and he must sign at *Inverary* Castle, fifty miles to the south. It was the time of the mini ice age, a bitterly cold winter; the Highlands were snowbound and the only passable route was a winding road that hugged the deeply indented coast-line. Dalrymple's plan to force his enemy into missing the deadline worked. By the time Macdonald and his horse had struggled to Inverary, it was 3 January and he had committed treason by default. With the King's assent, Dalrymple instructed his ally Robert Campbell of Glen Lyon to exact royal retribution. He was to go to Glencoe and kill every male under the age of seventy.

There was little love lost between the Macdonalds and the Campbells; feuds had rumbled back and forth between the two for centuries. But there was no current feud, and Robert Campbell and Alastair Macdonald were related by marriage. Nevertheless, the Campbells rode up the glen with a detachment of 120 mercenaries on 2 February. It is a sign of the deception that the Macdonalds suspected nothing and did not rush to arms. Whatever the explanation given for the Campbells arriving thus, un-announced, it was evidently plausible and the party was welcomed in and billeted among the many homesteads.

The Campbells accepted every kindness proffered. They

gossiped, partied, danced, flirted and feasted for ten days. Ten long days. Then, at five a.m. on 13 February, the Campbells rose in the dark and slaughtered their hosts in their beds. The chieftain was one of the first to die, followed by two of his sons. As his wife screamed for help, she had her finger bitten off to get at her rings. She was so badly beaten that she died of her wounds the next day. Men were bound with rope and shot. Women and children ran from their homes as the thatched roofs were put to the torch. Their closest neighbours lived many miles away in a different glen. It was a wretchedly cold dawn and they fled into a blizzard wearing only nightclothes. The plan to eliminate every Macdonald male – they numbered nearly two hundred – was only botched because Dalrymple and his detachment, who were meant to have arrived in time to join the killing spree, got delayed by snowdrifts. Glencoe is a remote valley flanked by towering crags. It is a sinister, evocative place of imposing but oppressive beauty. Unlike many other historical sites, it is really not too hard to imagine the terror unleashed there three hundred years ago. Thirty-eight Macdonalds died from their wounds, but an unknown number perished from exposure as they hid out in the hills during the following weeks. By the time Dalrymple's men arrived they found the homesteads deserted, except for one old man, who they killed.

Murderous plots were not particularly rare between clans and the total killed at Glencoe was no more than at others. What thrust these particular events so deeply into the mass psyche was the violation of every tenet of Scottish hospitality in the days leading up to the atrocity. To ambush one's enemies and fall upon them without delay was an acceptable form of violence; to cosy up to them first was not. A ballad was written to chronicle the tragedy:

They came in a blizzard, we offered them heat.
A roof for their heads, dry shoes for their feet.
We wined them and dined them, they ate all our meat,
And they slept in the house of Macdonald.

They came from Fort William with murder in mind,
The Campbell had orders King William had signed.
'Put all to the sword' these words underlined,
'Leave no one alive called Macdonald.'

If there has been retribution for the betrayal at Glencoe, it is that the name Campbell carries the stigma to this day. There were occasions when I wondered what it would be like to have a less provocative surname, like Blennerhassett or Tibbs, rather than one that completed the phrase 'never trust a . . .'.

Alongside this screeching violin of a name there was another aspect of the Cawdor Campbells to consider: if you shake the family tree, bottles fall out. This is not to say that the family had somehow suddenly degenerated, for until the mid-twentieth century addiction was either ignored or wholly misunderstood – seen as wilful degener-ation, as if an alcoholic has the luxury of choice in the matter. Since alcoholism often runs in families, it could well have been doing so in ours for centuries; history wouldn't and probably couldn't relate. (Although one eighteenth-century unfortunate wounded himself fatally while trying to kill a seagull with his blunderbuss. A seagull. Surely a dead giveaway for a lush.)

Jack Cawdor had lived with a hand clamped around a tumbler of gin. Aunt Carey enjoyed a drink, and Pa seemed to have an insatiable thirst for anything except water. No-one noticed how many heavy drinkers there were in the family because only Great-uncle Andrew, my grandfather's younger brother, was seen as having any sort of problem. He was the family's designated drunk and was known as 'Drunkle Uncle', a name coined by Carey. He earned it after inadvertently driving off the end of the Kessock jetty and plunging into the Moray Firth, having misjudged the distance to a departing ferryboat by many yards. The spotlight never left him, and everyone else's drinking was studiously ignored. Although none of my immediate family dropped dead directly from alcoholic poisoning or from altercations with seagulls, most died as a result of their addictions in one way or another. 'Hold a woman by the waist and a bottle by the neck, and not the other way round!' Pa would cry if someone grasped the port decanter too low as it made its strictly clockwise orbit of the table. Strangely, of the men it was only Great-uncle Andrew, the boozy scapegoat, who ever truly got the gist of this comment: he remained in a calm and loving marriage to Great-aunt Helen, a woman my father once described as looking 'like her face had been set on fire and someone put it out with an axe'.

The degrees of contradiction in each human nature are what define our character differences. My father's dominant contradictions were that he was gregarious but painfully shy, and capable of generosity on a grand scale, not just materially but of the spirit, but also of a meanness that encompassed premeditated cruelty. One minute he could bounce with confidence, the next he seemed queasy in his own skin. He could do very little socially unless he had had a stiff drink first, but it was never just one, and as four went to five and to six, the alcohol in his system magnified rather than smoothed his moods. He became paranoid, belligerent, sexually incontinent and, on occasions, violent. He brushed off the ill-effects of his drinking with light-hearted explanations, on one occasion joking about loss of memory to the extent that, on waking, he was puzzled to find 'several bruises about my person'. 'They probably came out of a bottle' was his conclusion.

Drink does not explain all that happened to us as a family, but looking back, many things would never have taken place in the way they did if alcohol had been absent.

I felt bereft about leaving Golden Grove for a place I associated with a kilted curmudgeon and where we were only tolerated when sequestered in a distant wing. The three bits of continuity we had from Wales were the ubiquitous Thatch, all the portraits of our ancestors hanging in Golden Grove after the obliteration of Stackpole, and the cook, Edith. It was fifteen years before I could face returning to look at those river valley views again. The peaceful routine we had known in Wales was turned upside down; the course of our lives had changed for ever. But what changed the most was Pa.

Chapter 7

My heart's in the Highlands, my heart is not here;
My heart's in the Highlands a-chasing the deer.

Robert Burns, 'My Heart's in the Highlands'

LIKE ANYBODY ELSE, MY VIEW OF CASTLE LIFE WAS STEEPED in the books I had read and reread throughout my childhood. The only problem was that the girls in the stories were nearly always passive victims of the baddies. Bluebeard locked Fatima in a tower. All she could do was scan the horizon, hoping to spot the clouds of dust thrown up by horses' hooves, which would mean her brothers were coming to the rescue. They took their time. Rapunzel was imprisoned in another tower. Letting her hair grow and waiting for help was the extent of her escape plan. The Lady of Shalott would reap a deadly curse if she even so much as glanced out of her tower. Sure enough, her life was ruined when she used the reflection of a mirror to peek at

Sir Lancelot singing 'tirra lirra' by the river below. The poet Fiona Pitt-Kethley wrote a brilliant précis of that interminable poem:

> Saw Knight Pass
> In Glass,
> Left Room
> Full of Gloom,
> Stole Boat,
> Died Afloat.

As for Snow White, she ran away from her castle after her stepmother tried to kill her. And although she started a new life as a housekeeper in a commune of stunted miners, eventually she was rendered comatose by a poisoned apple. A sharp needle brought the same fate to Sleeping Beauty, who lay in her tower for decades, and both Sleeping and Snow attracted the attentions of princes with necrophiliac leanings. The only punchy heroine of a castle story was Macbeth's wife Gruoch, but she was heartless, on the make and an accomplice to murder. There was nothing on the nursery bookshelves that said the heroine was feisty, she had a good time, then left the castle and went out into the world and did something epic.

Our first school holiday with Cawdor as our new home was the cause of some trepidation, not least because Emma and I travelled north on the sleeper unaccompanied. No-one had told us that Inverness was at the end of the line, so we spent a sleepless night straining out of the carriage window to check the nameplates of every station we drew into, worried that we would miss our stop. Black-backed gulls wheeled over the platform and Bill the butler was at the barrier waiting to meet us. He put our cases into the back of the Land Rover. 'Dudududududududid you have a gugugugugugood jujujourney up, gugggugggu-girls?' he stammered, but we were barely able to respond 'Yes, thank you, Bill' before falling fast asleep across the back seat.

Bill woke us gently when we arrived and we staggered into the dining room for breakfast while he took our suit-cases to our bedroom. We were sharing a tiny attic in the eaves at the opposite end of the house and on a different floor from our parents. Edith slept quite near to us, but she seemed as traumatized by the move as we were. If we ever looked into her room, she seemed oblivious to our presence, vacuum-packed into her candlewick dressing gown, pink curlers in, teeth out and clutched in one hand, and mutter-ing in Welsh under her breath.

The exciting news was that we could now roam freely through the house. When we first arrived, I expected we would still be bound by our grandfather's rule of internal exile, and my heart sagged at the thought of that nursery with its subfusc wallpaper. It was not the only aspect of our Scottish life that felt a step behind the times. Every so often it felt as if Pa's constant harping on about our history was to the almost complete exclusion of any conversation about our future. What's more, the national newspapers always arrived a day late, and years after everyone else had got three we could still pick up only one television channel. And while our southern school friends went to discos, in the north we had huge, formal reeling parties.

After the insularity of Wales, Cawdor felt like and was a social hub, fishing and shooting parties regularly filling the house from August to February. Whatever the season, Aunt Carey and Uncle Peebles, Uncle James and Aunt Bridget and assorted children were frequent visitors, along with our more distant relations like Great-aunt Helen and Drunkle Uncle. Living nearby was William Gordon Cumming, who was married to Ma's sister Aunt E. Although Uncle William was Betty's son, he and Hugh had of course been friends long before they became related by Jack's marriage to her. The stepbrothers then married a pair of sisters, which made the Gordon Cumming children our double-cousins – or that is what I liked to think. They became our closest friends.

My parents suddenly had dozens of Highland friends, hardy, humorous people who thought nothing of driving forty miles to eat with one another. After dinner, the women would leave the dining room in advance of the men, who stayed behind to drink sloe gin and smoke cigars – an archaic custom that was meant to spare our blushes from strong talk. The women would go off to retouch their make-up and would then gather around the fire in the drawing room while Bill served tiny cups of coffee on a tray. Emma and I had the duty to offer around mint chocolate wafers and to push the end of a gnarled juniper branch into the hot embers until it smouldered, then to pace about, allowing the sweet-smelling smoke to fumigate the room. With that done, we would position ourselves on wooden toadstools in the inglenooks on either side of the fire, where we could listen and watch, and await the return of the men.

Flickering in the warm glow of the fire, portraits of long-dead family members jostled for space on the walls, like some unwieldy family album. In a full-length painting, John Campbell – hero of the Franco-Welsh encounter – looked windblown and dashing in a red velvet coat with deep fur cuffs, pointing to something unseen. Looking at him from my toadstool with half an ear on the conversation going on around me, I used to imagine he was saying, 'Sire, I assure you, my horse was tethered to the hitching rail yonder.' The painting was one of a pair: the other showed his beautiful wife, Caroline Howard, dressed in fashionable Grecian folds cinched under her bust with a pink sash, and trailing a straw sunbonnet. Pryse Campbell, the son of Joyless John and the father of John the French vanquisher, gazed out from his frame grey-wigged, hand on hip, in a kilt and tartan doublet, and swamped by what looked like a pair of tartan parlour curtains draped over one shoulder. His portrait was painted during the period after the Jacobites' final defeat, when the wearing of any tartan was banned. The English wanted to suppress the Scots' sense of a separate identity, but their plan proved unworkable. Pryse was not alone in flouting the law; it was a craze: young Scottish dandies saw it as a matter of pride to pose for portraits dressed in their forbidden clothing. Two hundred years later, my grandfather had still preferred to wear tartan, the sartorial rump of more dashing times.

Pryse's sister Elizabeth was there on the wall as well. Although she was far too beetle-browed to be thought a beauty, her facial characteristics can be traced down the generations. Her likeness to my father, born two hundred years later, was quite uncanny. It could have been him up there in a yellow silk dress standing in a flower-covered bower, even down to the faint five o'clock shadow. Every now and again I would try to persuade Pa to sit for a portrait, for his great-grandchildren's sake if nothing else, but he ignored me. Now, if ever I want to look upon the face of my dead father I need only go to the portrait of Elizabeth in the drawing room. I find it strangely reassuring, albeit an image of my father as a cross-dresser.

Hundreds of babies of both sexes were born at Cawdor in the centuries before us, but all the family stories were about the derring-do of hairy blokes – all, that is, except for one. There was one young thane who was utterly different from all the others. So different, he was even a she. She was my absolute favourite ancestor. I thought of her every day because her first name was carved into the ornate stone of the dining-room chimneybreast, behind my mother's chair. The story enfolded my heart and abducted my imagination. What's more, this story, unlike *Macbeth*, was a true one, about a real girl in our own castle. Her life seemed the very pith of romance and gave some indication of the rambunctiousness of the marriage market at that time. She was the reason we bore the name Campbell as well as Cawdor. Sadly, her name was Muriel, but you can't have everything.

In 1498, John the 8th Thane died young, leaving an only daughter as the heir to Cawdor. Such was the family's concern about kidnapping and Muriel's security that they branded her on the thigh with a red-hot key, for that same irrefutable recognition a farmer enjoys when checking the flank of a prized cow. They had good reason to be scared. With expansionism ever in mind, the powerful Campbells of Argyll gazed upon this peachy prize from their stronghold on the west coast, and in 1499 Archibald Argyll, the 2nd Earl, mustered a posse to kidnap the baby. They crossed the width of Scotland using the Loch Ness corridor, but when they reached Cawdor they found they were out of luck. Muriel was not there; she had been taken to stay over harvest time at Kilravock Castle, the home of her maternal grandparents, the Roses.

The Campbells might have been thwarted, but for an idiot who slipped the village limits and blurted out the baby's whereabouts. Kilravock was not far. The posse wheeled round, galloped through the stubble fields and splashed across the River Nairn to reach the castle on the far bank. Muriel was with her nursemaid in the grounds when they were attacked. In the frantic struggle the nanny bit off the last joint of the child's little finger, just to be absolutely certain, on top of the thigh brand, that she too would recognize her miserable charge in the future. Shocked and no doubt choking, the nursemaid staggered off to summon help as the Campbells escaped.

Some miles further on, they stripped off Muriel's cloak and wrapped it around a wheatsheaf. The majority of the posse kicked on with the tiny girl, while a small band stayed behind to hinder the Cawdors in their pursuit. They laid the decoy in the shadows of a hazel grove beside the track and then encircled it, swords drawn. When the Cawdor horsemen caught up there was a vicious skirmish. Seven Campbells were killed, but by the time the Cawdors realized they had been duped and the bundle was not Muriel it was too late. The kidnappers were well on their way to the Argyll lands in the west, and once they reached the west coast she would be beyond rescue. Muriel was held until 1510, when, aged twelve and legally 'of age', she was married off to Archibald's younger son Sir John Campbell and officially united with Scotland's answer to the Corleones.

Every time we sat at the dining-room table, my eyes would flick over her carved name in the same way they would over a grandparents' wedding photograph. I would look at my baby sister Laura and think, 'That's how big Muriel was when she was kidnapped.' Then at Emma and think, 'And that's how big she was when she got married.' And then across to my father and think, 'And there have been sixteen thanes between her and him.'

With Muriel's 'arranged' marriage, the tendrils of the Argyll Campbells' power extended into the north-east. The good news is that by all accounts her union was a happy one. She and John had grown up together, and given her experience of family love prior to the kidnapping and her scarred leg and slightly less than the full complement of fingertips, perhaps Muriel was thankful she was no longer in the Cawdors' care. Muriel and John settled in the clan heartland and did not return to Cawdor until 1523, after John murdered Lachlan Maclean of Duart, the husband of his sister Elizabeth. It was said that she could not give Maclean an heir, so, bored and estranged, he spurned a conventional separation in favour of dragging Elizabeth to the Firth of Lorne, where he chained her naked to a rock that got covered by every rising tide. Maclean then hurried to Archibald, his Argyll father-in-law, and sorrowfully but prematurely reported his young wife's death. Unfortunately for Maclean, a group of passing fishermen heard Elizabeth's cries as the seawater rose around her waist. They freed her and she fled to the sanctuary of her Campbell brothers. In a fit of fraternal indignation, John tracked Lachlan to Edinburgh and 'dirked him in his bed'. As the killing avenged a clear case of attempted murder, a judge gave John a pardon. Despite this official exoneration, neither Edinburgh nor the county of Argyll was safe for him any longer. He had to be forever on his guard against Maclean relatives exacting their revenge on his revenge. Suddenly, the very remoteness of Cawdor, on the far side of the Grampian Mountains, was attractive.

The Campbell party arrived at Cawdor to a hostile reception. Muriel's four Rose uncles had held sway there ever since she had been kidnapped and they had long stopped counting on her return. They did not welcome any shift in the status quo and saw the move as a greasy Campbell expropriation of Cawdor land. They dismissed Muriel as an impostor, but a quick flash of thigh and abridged finger proved otherwise. Muriel emphatically claimed her inheritance as 9th Thane and evicted them.

Her furious uncles called an emergency council. They resolved to resist her with maximum force and wrest back the castle for themselves.

In those days, the castle worked on a five-layered defence system; if one failed, the defenders fell back to the next. First was the curtain wall. Second was the drawbridge. Third was a hefty portcullis. For many years there was no conventional front door. The main access to the house was via portable wooden steps to the first floor of the keep, and this was the fourth defence. It can't have made bringing occasional tables into the house easy. As soon as the uncles' horde arrived, Muriel's party retreated inside the castle, hauled up the ladder behind them, and left the raiders milling in the courtyard below. If the invaders remained within the castle walls, the counter-attack would swing into action. Behind the battlements at the top of the tower was a cookhouse, the fifth defence. Here, come rain or shine, industrial quantities of waste could be heated up in cauldrons and the contents tipped down the 'murder hole' onto the enemy beneath. Knowing this, the invaders fell back and set about besieging the castle.

After some days, an intrepid Campbell broke cover, sallied forth and killed two of the uncles on the drawbridge. The deadlock was broken, and negotiations began. Muriel acknowledged her uncles' long trusteeship and granted the two survivors various tracts of her land in return for a yearly rent. The payment she levied was a single rose bloom from each of them, every summer, lest they forget who the rightful owner was. This elegant arrangement was sustained until their deaths, and thereafter the lands reverted to Muriel. Once matters were settled, John and Muriel started a family and their descendants have been defined as 'Cawdor' Campbells ever since.

Muriel lived to the age of seventy-five. Back then, a natural death at such an advanced age was as remarkable as her youthful trials – although her story was not such an unusual one for the Highlands. Quite aside from her two uncles killed at the siege of Cawdor and the stabbing of Lachlan Maclean, another brother-in-law of Muriel's fell to his death down the sheer cliffs below Edinburgh Castle while trying to escape from jail. Janet Douglas, Muriel's beautiful sister-in-law, was burned at the stake on trumped-up charges of witchcraft for daring to spurn a powerful suitor. And in 1571, in an incident that had echoes of Macduff's fate in *Macbeth*, Muriel's niece, Margaret Forbes, was burned to death along with her children and twenty-six of her household in an arson attack on Corgarff Castle. Corgarff was burned down a further three times over the next two hundred years. Muriel's eldest son predeceased her, so she handed the inheritance to her grandson, yet another John. He was murdered sixteen years later, shot at close range in a plot by 'Black' Duncan Campbell of Glenorchy, who was jealous of the influence Sir John had over the young Argyll laird Archibald 'the Grim'.

When I was trying to understand the strange things my father did, I wondered if he ever worried about how he would have acquitted himself in such situations from our family history. Would he have chased after the Campbell posse stealing the baby Muriel? Would he have stood up against the French soldiers like John? Would he have gone off to sea at sixteen to enlist in a war, like his father had? Would his grandchildren one day tell stories about his honourable deeds? After my father died, it slowly became clear that his idea of paternal tenderness would just about run to biting off the top joints of our little fingers.

Chapter 8

Today I saw a crow, and yesterday I had a distant view of a
rabbit.

The Revd Sydney Smith

FOR ANY CHILD WITH A THIRST FOR BLOOD, GROWING UP
at Cawdor was like a little corner of heaven. Pa's first ever
writing effort when he was a little boy was an essay lovingly
preserved by Wilma. It read: 'If you want to know how to
catch a rabbit, You'd better follow me. The End.'

His love of trees began when he first started creeping
around the Big Wood with his shotgun. When he took us
down the same paths, he would point out sessile oak, min
fir and northern hemlock, and show us where the trees
were scarred by lightning strikes and where squirrel drays
were hidden high up in the topmost branches. When Hugh
was a boy, the keepers would drag a ladder to the moat,
clamber up it and lure him out of bed by tapping on the

window with a Zippo lighter. Cap on head, flask in pocket, fingerless mittens, fag in mouth, he would join them to stump across frozen plough hunting hoodies (hooded crows) and pigeon. Pa was in his element when shooting, and one of the first things he did after Grandpa died was to order matching jackets and plus-fours for John Stewart and all the other keepers so that they were conspicuous as 'Cawdor men' in their tweed uniforms, with the new Thane as their general and birds as the enemy.

Pa encouraged the boys whole- and the girls half-heartedly to shoot. There were child-size shotguns to hunt vermin (not edible) and game (allegedly edible). With each new species potted, there came the crude rite of getting smeared in its blood. Sometimes, when John Stewart, the head keeper, took Colin flighting for duck I would go along to keep him company. We would take up our positions among the juniper bushes at the edge of a little pond as the sun sank and wait for the skeans to come in. 'Don't shoot until the bushes are black!' John would whisper before heading off to the far side of the pond with his spaniel. I liked going with Colin, because often he didn't fire and you could watch the whizzing silhouettes of the ducks as they dropped acrobatically out of the sky with an occasional quack, and hear the soft noise of the air wiffling from their wings.

Once they had all landed, John would reappear and ask, 'Why did yer no loose off a shot, Coln? Could you nay get a clear aim?'

'I just couldn't decide if the bushes had actually gone black.'

Jack Cawdor and the botanist Frank Kingdon-Ward on their 1924 expedition to Tibet

Cawdor Castle, east face

Hugh at eighteen

Cath and Hugh on
their engagement

Liza on her third birthday, perched on one of the remaining cannons at Stackpole

Stackpole after the Victorian renovations

The eight-arch bridge at Stackpole

With Pa at Golden Grove

Liza, Emma, Fred and Colin beneath the French guns

Fred and Pa
practising aikido
in front of Cawdor

Hugh at
Lochindorb

Cath posing with a garland for a *Tatler* photoshoot in the 1980s

Laura, Emma and Colin on the evening of Hugh's wake

Liza's two children, Storm and Atticus, outside Cawdor

Liza by the Tana River, Kenya

'Och, that again. You're a dreamer, wee manny.' And he would start chuckling.

John Stewart had been a young soldier on leave at the time of the German plane crash on the moor. A strapping young man who had already won an MC, he was content to volunteer for a solo six-mile yomp into the landscape to capture any survivors. We would beg him to tell us the story. Depending on his mood he would give us slightly different versions of it, but it always ended with him saying in his strong staccato brogue, 'Och, thut poor wee pilot laddie was jes' pollverrized, so I jes' concertinaed hum up into ma' rocksuck, hoisted it on ma back an' ran back doon the hull.'

'Oh, Johnny, please tell us again, tell us again – just once more.'

But he would shake his head and march off with a swinging stride.

Every summer he was in charge of making sure there was a steady supply of young heather for the juvenile grouse to eat. We would hear John's shouts and gaze up to see matchstick figures silhouetted in the distance, controlling the flames of huge fires. Some days, the optimum weather of a tiny breeze would turn at the drop of an isobar into a gale and the fires would gallop out of control. In one of his letters to school, my father described one such fire that 'took off like a scalded cheetah' on Holme Rose moor. When Hugh arrived on the scene, the flames had nearly reached a house at the edge of his beloved Big Wood. Two fire engines and the frantic efforts of thirty men brought the blaze under control, with the help of a helicopter 'that scooped water and rainbow trout' out of the neighbouring reservoir, before the rain came down.

Outdoor pursuits were so much a part of male life in Scotland that unless we girls joined in, there was not much for us to do. Alas, my shotgun calling was very brief. It was not because I disapproved in any way. I loved the taste of venison and wild boar and I was prepared, under duress, to eat winged game; but I could see that if you failed to kill an animal outright you were completely obligated to end its suffering. This meant either taking the animal by the legs and whacking its head against a stone, or pulling its head away from its body until the neck broke. I could not fulfil that part of the bargain, and it simply was not done to carry on firing at point-blank range to finish an animal off. I never graduated to shooting driven grouse from a butt, I was far too excitable and dangerous. I remained a crouching witness, breathing in the cordite and erroneously shouting 'Over!' at the sight of a bumblebee.

Shooting with a rifle turned out to be much more fun because a rifle didn't have a kick that left your shoulder bruised black and yellow when you got the positioning of the stock wrong, but I only went out stalking once. I loved creeping silently over the moor with Pa and John Stewart, keeping out of sight and upwind of the deer until there was a chance of a good free aim on one that had moved clear of the herd. But when I looked through the cross-hairs of the telescopic sight at this shy, elegant animal, the very last thing in my mind was to squeeze the trigger. I only really enjoyed plugging oranges and bottles – nothing with lungs.

Being inexperienced and in charge of a deadly weapon is nerve-racking if the intention is 'to be safe'. If we inadvertently pointed our gun at anyone, Pa would give us a clout and a tongue-lashing. Like learning to drive, there were actions that had to become second nature. Unlike driving, you couldn't fire a gun slowly, and if you messed up you ended up like the farmer's son in Wales who shot himself in the groin. Accidents did happen, and when they did there was a strict protocol about who you could hurt. If someone peppered a fellow guest, it was a regrettable but standard risk run by any group of people carrying arms. If, however, you hit an unarmed beater or a keeper, it was a scandal. There was a strict etiquette to follow:

- The guilty party must put down his gun *immediately*.
- The guilty party must ensure the injured party is taken care of and seen off to hospital with all speed. It is inconsiderate for the guilty party to travel with the injured party. If the man is in pain, he should not have to feel obliged to exchange pleasantries with the trigger-happy schmuck who nearly killed him.
- The guilty party must then leave the moor without delay, return to his lodgings and reflect on his shame in solitude.

Leaving the hill was an act of contrition, so someone who 'didn't even put his gun down' and continued shooting would get a name as a bit of a shit. The grown-ups generally closed ranks and refused to let us in on these scandals, but once we wore our mother down until she gave us a name. It turned out that Pa's cousin David was one. We asked what had happened to him, but she explained that he had already been in the doghouse for years, ever since he had been caught spitting in a great-aunt's bath when he was a child. The doghouse? I could see it for his gun crime, but for spitting? This seemed strangely harsh. Aunt Carey described it as the family scandelabra.

Every couple of weeks from August to February there was a houseparty at Cawdor with a dozen guns accompanied by their wives, plus Thatch, who never carried a gun. I assumed he had never learned to shoot because in aikido you needed only two fingers to bring death. In the intervening weeks, invitations to other estates took my parents to every corner of Scotland, all over England, and across to the Irish bogs, if there was snipe shooting on offer. Hugh followed the principles of Ready! Aim! Fire! to remarkable effect on the moor and in the woods. At home, it was different. If he was in a temper, it was Ready! Fire! Aim! And with women, he was Fire! Fire! Fire! Because of this, keeping Pa company on these excursions was not always a barrel of laughs.

When I was twelve, Pa also insisted that I learn at least the rudiments of casting. 'You never know,' he said, 'you might spend your honeymoon fishing, like Uncle William and Aunt E.' This made me marvel that their marriage had survived at all, let alone produced four children. We drove to the river and Pa chose me one of the hand-tied flies he had made as a boy, using a snippet of his sister's bright red hair. Ten minutes into my first proper lesson I hooked an incredibly unlucky salmon quite by chance, and under a tirade of enthusiastic threats and instructions I tried to reel it in. When the fish came into the shallows, Pa waded in with a net, scooped it out onto the bank and bludgeoned it with a little cosh that ghillies dryly call a 'priest'. He was thrilled that I had succeeded on my very first attempt. I tried to hide it from him, but the fact was he was a deal more excited than me. I was pleased, but my first thought was, 'Well, at least I've got that out of the way. I won't have to do it again.' The second thought was, 'We're going to have to eat this thing.' At the time, I could never have imagined that one day I would be fishing almost every day for years, including on my honeymoon.

My brother Colin wrote a short letter to our parents from his new prep school. It read: 'My heart's in the Highlands. At Cawdor Castle to be precise.' If I was to be precise, the bank of the River Findhorn was the place that captured my heart. It became my favourite place in the world after Wales.

In the summer, while Pa was casting in a distant pool, we would don goggles, jump into the freezing water and swim down to the lines of salmon. They took no notice of us. Sometimes we would find six or seven resting in a vertical stack, motionless but for the gentle twirl of their fins and an occasional punkah-like swish of their tails. Close up, their heads were streaked with scars, and the great jut of the males' underslung jaws made the experience a little eerie. As we kicked down into the murky water, Jacques

Cousteau's television commentary would play on a loop in my head – the time when his son was filmed swimming into a tunnel only to vanish for ever. 'And zat eez ze last . . . we saw . . . of Philippe.' I would kick back up to the surface, heart thumping. We would clamber out of the water blue-lipped with cold.

After pulling on clothes over dripping limbs, we would go and find Pa and hope the sight of our juddering jaws would persuade him to pack up for lunch. Luckily he was far less fanatical with a rod than he was with a gun, and he would join us on the shingle and give us nips from his hip flask. We would then scramble into his Land Rover and drive upstream to Drynachan, where Ma was already feeding the Smalls on a large picnic rug. Thatch would be sitting to one side wearing an over-tight blazer, awaiting his pupil.

Drynachan was our shooting lodge on the banks of the Findhorn. The house had started off as a bothy where hunters slept after a day on the moor. In the days before cars, the game was brought off the hill in large wicker panniers slung over packhorses and it was too tiring for the shooting party to try to reach Cawdor after a long day's shooting. Drynachan was enlarged in a gradual and completely haphazard way: some kennels were added here, an extra bedroom or two there, and it finished up an un-photogenic mess from the outside, but heavenly within.

When we came to live at Cawdor, our holidays were made even more hectically social by the presence of a colourful Parisian called Sheila de Rochambeau, who began renting Drynachan for the summer months. Sheila

154

was a Francophile American with Scottish roots. She embraced every Highland tradition with gusto and filled the lodge with a steady stream of French and Italian friends. Her three teenage sons were tricked out in extravagant tartan outfits that owed much to Pryse's portrait in the drawing room. To complete the look she equipped them with sporrans made from beaver heads, and skean-dhus – short, sheathed stabbing knives carried in the sock for easy access, though theirs were more like canteens of cutlery than switchblades. The boys' girlfriends were a source of fascination to me. Drynachan acted as a tester on their relationships, and each succeeding summer new ones replaced the old. The boys always seemed to be attracted to women who made you wonder how on earth the word 'charming' and 'French' ever got uttered in the same breath. They were invariably pretty, spoilt, humourless and appalled to find themselves stuck out in the middle of nowhere and at the mercy of their boyfriends' rather over-powering mother, who ordered them out on rugged hikes when they were the types liable to give themselves a bad gash while crossing a lawn.

Going out to shoot rabbits in the dark was their idea of hell, but our idea of a treat. We would be in quiet raptures as we sat on the metal floor of the Land Rover having rabbit corpses thrown in at us in the dark. Myxomatosis had been ravaging the British rabbit population for years, and as we drove through the fields with a searchlight sweeping from side to side you could see exactly which ones had contracted the disease. The healthy rabbits scarpered; the myxi ones stayed where they were, eyes swollen shut.

Blam! Fish in a barrel, but nothing you could eat or feed the dogs with. They would be left for the scavengers.

Sheila's eldest boys were twins. They joked that unlike Colin and Fred they would have no problem over just one of them inheriting their father's title of Vicomte de Rochambeau, because Eric would have it in France while Marc would have it in England. This was because when it came to twins, the French took a perverse view of the 'first born'. In England we believe the first baby out into the fresh air is the eldest, but in France they believe that the first baby conceived is then 'blocked in' by its 'younger' twin, so the last one out is considered the eldest.

Eric and Marc were identical but fairly easy to tell apart – until they had a minor shooting accident. For their birthday, Sheila bought them each a high-powered rifle for a chamois hunting trip in the Alps. The guns were enormous. The twins were unaccustomed to shooting anything, let alone chamois, with a weapon the size of a rocket launcher, so Pa agreed to give them both a lesson. He set up targets on the far bank of the river and zeroed in the sights before getting them to lie down in the grass and get used to the weight of the guns.

'Marc, you go first,' my father said, and crouched down beside him. 'There's quite a wind from the west, so aim very slightly to the right of the bull. Settle your breathing and then squeeze the trigger, gently. Don't wrench it; and whatever you do, don't press your eye against the rim of the sight. This thing's got a kick like an angry kangaroo, so—'

KERBLAMM! The rifle report drowned out the rest of the advice. Marc was thrust back across the ground by

Newton's second law of physics. He stood up looking dazed. Blood began to course down the side of his face from a perfect crescent shape cut above his eyebrow. Sheila took one look at her son and led him off to her car to go and get stitched up in Nairn. Eric wanted his turn regardless. My father crouched down again.

'OK. Well, you can see that Marc was a bit hasty. So, take your time, breathe and – don't press the—'

KERBLAMM! Backward thrust, suppressed groan, identical crescent-shaped cut, same position. Sheila stopped her car halfway up the drive, collected her second son, and returned from the doctor with them looking more identical than they ever had before.

At the end of the summer, the Rochambeaux returned to Paris with fresh scar tissue and battered relationships, and Drynachan returned to being a working lodge where people came to shoot partridge, grouse and pheasant. My father wrote describing a party there one late November, which included a bad-tempered duchess and Valéry Giscard d'Estaing, whose name John Stewart found so hard to pronounce he just referred to him as 'yon other Frenchman'.

Cawdor brimmed with guests every Christmas holiday. The foresters brought in wagonloads of holly branches with which Ma garlanded all the portraits. Decorating the Christmas tree was a group effort, but my mother's beady eye would be watching out for symmetry. We had a free hand, just as long as the tree was topped off with a battered gold star; the biggest glass baubles went on the lowest branches, the smaller baubles went on the higher branches

– all evenly spaced – and tinsel was laid along the lengths of branches until everything was just so. The whole tree was then studded with real candles. The presents were heaped in an artful cascade of intriguing shapes around the bottom of the tree, ready for Christmas Day. Locked in her dressing room, my mother took days to individually wrap the myriad presents needed to fill five children's stockings and Pa's. She used colour-coded tissue paper to keep the gifts distinct from one another, before stuffing them all into Jack's old shooting socks. Carol-singers came to the court-yard on Christmas Eve. They were shepherded into the drawing room for mulled wine and we would strive to look serene as Peggy Forsyth trilled,

> en the bleak mud-wuntaah
> frrowstee weeand mead mowahn.
> Erruth stoood harrd as eye-Ron . . .

Pa thought turkey a very overrated meat, so we ate goose. When we were so full we could barely fit our chairs under the table, Edith would stagger in with the brandy-doused cake, which she had prepared several months before and left to ferment in a larder somewhere in the furthest reaches of the house. By late December it was so alcoholic that when she put a match to it, it ignited with a great eyebrow-singeing 'whoomph'.

Present opening on Christmas Day was a strictly ordered affair. We were allowed one small present on Christmas Eve, followed by stockings before breakfast on Christmas Day, and then one present at lunch. The main event came in the early evening, after we had changed for dinner. We weren't allowed to open any present unless it was handed to us and we weren't allowed to open any subsequent present until we had finished thanking the giver or noted down to which aunt or godparent we must write our thank-you letter. We were not allowed to rip into our presents; paper must be preserved for recycling. By the end of the opening session, Ma would have assembled a huge pile of discarded wrappings to fold away for future use. Her presents would remain unopened as she trimmed off bits of sellotape and salvaged lengths of scattered ribbon, and we would murmur 'war baby' to each other in a solemn, knowing way.

Our last Christmas treat would be a trip to see a performance of *La Fille Mal Gardée* at Covent Garden towards the end of the holidays. The ballet tells the story of a beautiful young girl whose ambitious mother wants her to become the wife of a rich landowner, but her suitor is a clod and she wants to marry a handsome farmhand. Love triumphs over status. Later on, the story seemed an odd choice. Pa's plans for us were identical to the mother's and quite the reverse of the ballet's outcome.

At Easter, we now went to the Alps. A local family called Hilleary would organize the booking of a sleeper train and fill it with their cousins, their cousins' cousins, all their neighbours and their neighbours' cousins, including us. The journey out was rarely completed without someone, dressed only in a kilt and a pair of socks and nursing a whisky hangover, wandering out onto a station platform in eastern France to buy breakfast and then being seen shouting and trying to flag us down with a half-eaten croissant as the train gave a sudden lurch and pulled away.

Our ski party would fill a whole hotel, and evenings were spent reeling to Dhileas Hilleary's accordion and her mother Sheena's yodelling. Ma had good skiers to keep her company: Mrs Hilleary, her sister Vora and their two brothers had all been Olympic skiers. Pa was the one who normally shone in sports – blood sports at any rate – but on skis he was overshadowed by Ma's abilities. Pa was competitive, so the disparity in their skills annoyed him to the point that he declared that he hated skiing and insisted they go to the beach instead. But he couldn't win: Cath was equally good on water skis.

Over and above this rivalry was a loathing for 'groups'. A party of people venturing out onto a moor was fine, but doing something as a group in a foreign country was repellent to Pa. In his opinion, it was that dread thing: middle class. Whenever he found himself in a group, he felt obliged to catch a taxi and take it in the opposite direction. Rejecting his peers made him feel superior. It was a habit that reached its zenith towards the end of his life when he and his second wife became notorious for snubbing their companions and flouncing off.

After a couple of trips to the Alps with us as a family, my father refused to join in any more. Instead, he started initiating an alternative holiday. This pulling apart was the very first tear in our family façade. The first separate holiday, when I was twelve, was to Jamaica, and I went with him, along with my cousin Mosh Gordon Cumming.

It is clear from one letter I wrote to my mother that spending time with him on my own was not something I was used to:

I'm so excited about Jamaica. Wot on earth will I wear? I think Pa is so lovely, I really won't know wot to say to him. He's so incredibly generous and sweet, how are we going to pass the time on the journey? I wish I was seeing you more, you sound so miserable about your holiday to Courchevel with the smalls.

My anxiety proved unwarranted: we had a wonderful time. Pa was good at holidays and being a host. He loved being in the Big Wood or the dojo or his London club or a mistress's arms; what he was not good at was the rest of his life, the bit that involved decisions, management and accountability. As children at far-away boarding schools for much of the year, we remained blissfully unaware for a little bit longer of the effect this was having.

Chapter 9

Ghost: The outward and visible sign of an inward fear.

Ambrose Bierce, 'The Devil's Dictionary'

WE HAD NOT BEEN AT CAWDOR FOR VERY LONG WHEN MY parents hit their first big problem. It was the vexed question of the widow. The death of a patriarch always heralds a period of musical chairs, but to turf Betty out in the immediate aftermath of Jack's death would have been grossly insensitive, so my parents moved in alongside her. The house was fuller than it had been for years with a family of seven, Thatch, his wife Val, a stammering butler, a weepy Welsh cook and our step-grandmother. As the months moved towards a full year and Betty showed no intention of leaving, Hugh began to find our new domestic situation untenable. Questions hovered. Who sat at the head of the table? Who invited guests to stay? Who slept in the master bedroom? Who would turn off the logs in the grate?

Hugh had always had a civil relationship with his step-mother, and it continued while he tried to work out how to gently broach the subject of her departure. Betty had been thinking hard too, and things suddenly reached a head when Hugh discovered that she had been in talks with the Scottish National Trust behind his back. She had been quietly trying to negotiate a deal to hand over Cawdor to them – on condition she was allowed to stay on as tenant. This was way beyond her remit, and Betty was no match for my father. Although she had sufficient steel for Machiavellian scheming, Jack's will had left Hugh with all the power. Within weeks of Hugh uncovering her plans, a dower house was bought and furnished, and Betty was forcibly relocated. When the move came, Hugh virtually had to prise each one of Betty's fingers off the house.

Her new home was five miles from Cawdor, in Nairn, a gracious town renowned for the wholesome roughage of the eponymous oatcakes. In 1886 an excitable Victorian entrepreneur had styled Nairn 'the Brighton of the North' in an advertising campaign that overlooked the town's lack of pier, pavilion, Regency architecture and indeed anything else remotely resembling Brighton. Sure, both are seaside towns, but in size, temperature and action, Brighton makes Nairn look like a defunct crypt. The townsfolk note its pin-drop quietness by referring to their local newspaper, the *Nairnshire Telegraph*, as 'The Three Minute Silence'. Betty found it galling to relinquish her role as chatelaine of Cawdor for the mundanities of small-town life. For months after she could be found sneaking into the house like Hunka Munka, to remove knick-knacks without which she fancied life in Nairn would be less satisfactory. Time after time we would arrive back home from a walk or a shopping trip and bump into our step-grandmother in the courtyard weighed down with ornaments, vases and lampshades. Ma would greet her politely, walk her to her car, help her load it up and wish her goodbye, in the belief that kindness and good manners would make it the last raid. Eventually Betty's house was tricked out to her satisfaction and the raids stopped.

As they acclimatized themselves to being in charge of Cawdor, my parents began slowly to modernize it. First, the fake log fires were put onto a real fire, and then they moved the kitchen from the far end of the house into the room next door to the dining room. The former kitchen was then converted into a dojo where my father and Thatch practised aikido. Pa's aikido training had moved on to weapon work to counter his fear of knives. We had to take care when we went down to the wild garden on the west side of the house because Thatch and Hugh would often be crouching in the bamboo using the huge soft trunk of a redwood as a target. Thatch chose a pair of antique samurai swords for my father to buy and hang on the wall behind his desk in Jack's old office – symbols of his new mastery. Pa held a great reverence for the swords and told us that the final forging had taken place at the point of dawn to symbolize the nobility of the Land of the Rising Sun. That they had to be sharp enough to cut a hair dropped on their upturned blades. That their sharpness had been tested on executed criminals. That the corpses had been strung up and cut diagonally, from right shoulder to left hip, in one smooth bone-slicing swipe. Sometimes Pa would take down one of the swords and let us have a closer look – occasionally to hold, but never to unsheathe. These were sacred objects, not to be used lightly.

But something had gone wrong. Despite all Thatch's teaching promoting physical dexterity, inner strength and peace of mind, Pa was growing increasingly disturbed. If a doctor had sat us down and asked us, 'When exactly did your father's thinking segue into shades of Macbeth?', in retrospect it would have been around about this time. Unbeknown to anyone, Hugh had found the forcible eviction of Betty far more traumatic than his blasé attitude suggested. Her plot to wrest Cawdor from him had left him angry and shaken. Despite Betty's living arrangements having been resolved, and the fact that she had now stopped trespassing, he still could not relax. How come she had always been in the house when we were out? He became increasingly convinced that staff members had been acting as informants. This may have been true, but only by default. The staff were in an awkward position: he had not told them that if Betty phoned and he and my mother were out they should deny the fact. He became properly haunted and thought that his stepmother was a witch. This was not a euphemism for his dislike of her, but a real belief that she had supernatural powers.

My mother noticed his behaviour getting stranger, and tried to find out what the trouble was. Late one night he finally unburdened himself and confided that he feared his stepmother's intention was to possess him, like a succubus. Ma put it down to a drunken rant, but later realized he was genuinely disturbed when he began to lay scissors, with the blades open, in what he thought were 'strategic' places around the house. He said they would act as hexes to keep Betty's presence at bay. With small children running around Ma kept picking up the scissors, but Pa became furious and laid them all back down. Cath turned to Thatch for help. It was the first time we had really needed him to use his authority over Hugh and point out to him what was really happening – that in the turmoil of inheriting Cawdor our father was throwing his marbles out of the window in handfuls. Instead, Thatch merely bolstered Pa's conviction that he was indeed a super-receptive psychic.

In the central courtyard opposite the drawbridge there were three old horseshoes propped up against the tower wall. No-one took any more notice of them than they did the water butt or the ferns growing in a damp corner beside them. No-one, that is, until Pa was in the full grip of his hex obsession over Betty. The superstitious say that horseshoes must sit upright in a 'U' shape to bring good luck; if they are turned upside down, it invites bad luck. One day, as my father was crossing the courtyard, he noticed that someone had upended one of the horseshoes. The 'someone' was most likely one of us children who had accidentally kicked it over and shoved it back the wrong way round. We were not only clumsy but untutored in white magic etiquette. When Pa saw it, he was horrified; terrified. His 'stepmother-as-evil-witch' fantasy busted out into the open. He brooded on it overnight and the next day accosted our old woodman, Findlay Macintosh, accusing him of being

Betty's 'familiar' and of knowingly tampering with the horseshoe. Mad words falling into a sane world finally brought my father to his senses. Seeing Findlay's expression of utter bewilderment, he apologized for his outburst. The old man reassured his boss that no offence had been taken, but it had, and soon after Findlay took his retirement and tended his garden in the village.

It is impossible to know why my father suddenly decided that a delicate family situation had paranormal elements, but maybe becoming solely responsible for such an old house played on his imagination. Absolutely every last thing at Cawdor is infused with our family's bumpy history. Every painting, bed and tapestry has a story. But Hugh's *crise de nerfs* notwithstanding, there were two things from which Cawdor was joyfully free: it was haunted by neither curses nor ghosts. Our neighbours were not so lucky. In the Highlands, it is not uncommon for families to be contending with curses passed down from the Dark Ages.

A couple of miles west of us, Kilravock Castle, from where Muriel was snatched, had a curse: if a gooseberry bush that grew at the top of their main tower died, so too would the male line. Why there was a bush on their roof in the first place is not clear. Maybe it was wind-seeded; maybe a gardener was going for a Babylonian look. In the late 1980s, the bush started to wither. The owner, Elizabeth Rose, a descendant of Muriel's grandparents, made numerous frantic attempts to get a cutting from the original to take root, but it failed each time. Replacement with a brand-new gooseberry bush was apparently not valid in the small print of the curse. The bush died, the male line died out soon after, and Kilravock became a Christian youth hostel.

Fyvie Castle, the home of my father's great friend Sir Andrew Forbes-Leith, had a much harsher curse on it: that no eldest son would survive to inherit. It had been working like gothic clockwork ever since. Andrew's older brother had died in the Second World War, as had his father's older brother in the Boer War, and so on. Their curse was particularly taunting because it dangled the possibility of a solution: the curse on the men would lift when three 'weeping' stones could be found within the castle walls. The clues were described in a poem by Thomas the Rhymer, in what my father liked to refer to as 'olde kakke shoppe' spelling:

> Ane in the oldest tower,
> Ane in the ladie's bower,
> And ane below the water-yett [gate].
> The third one, ye shall never get.

After a forensic search, two of the strange, perennially damp stones were found where the poem said they would be, but the third remains elusive. Andrew Forbes-Leith vowed to break the curse. He moved to another house to bring up his children and allowed them to stay at Fyvie only for holidays. When he died, his eldest son was the first in generations to have lived to see his own father's funeral.

As a rule, curses were on families and buildings, but some natural features had enchantments on them too. The 'Fairy Hill', overlooking a gorge on the Findhorn eight miles or so from Cawdor, was such a place. It is a pretty spot, thanks to the great landscape gardener in the sky, and is enhanced by artistically grouped bracken clumps and elegant stands of silver birch. It was safe for walkers except on midsummer's day, when anyone foolish enough to climb the hill would be abducted by 'the wee folk' and kept for ever. This might seem a bit of whimsy nowadays, but everyone stuck to a rule handed down from a distant time when there was a law against 'Kyllynge, wowndynge, or mamynge' a fairy. Superstitions were part of everyone's beliefs, not just the preserve of backwoods simpletons.

The arrival of Aunt Carey at Cawdor soon after Hugh's confrontation with Findlay was a godsend. She teased him mercilessly. Pa enjoyed being a tease but was normally incandescent if he was teased, unless it was by Carey or William Gordon Cumming. Her teasing was so warm and wicked that he could not help but laugh off the episode.

As things settled down at Cawdor, Hugh would often list job descriptions that set off a shudder at the mere mention of their name – dentists, estate agents, proctologists, traffic wardens, tax inspectors, executioners and arms dealers – but the list was always topped off with stepmothers. He would explain his thinking thus: 'No dentist has ever been sufficiently bad to form the backbone of our fairytales. I never want to go through anything like that ever, ever again. No-one should have to go through it. Father should have sorted Betty out beforehand.' Of course, Jack had not meant to leave the mess; death had pounced on him before he had got his affairs in order. And who knows, maybe they were in order, but buried somewhere deep within the Himalayan letter pile in his office.

In fact, Hugh had it easy compared to some neighbours. My grandfather's bracken-loving friend Jimmy Dunbar had stipulated in his will that his heir would not be entitled to any of his property or money until he had been witnessed crawling naked for several miles across rough country, for no reason other than Dunbar's desire to humiliate. Hugh was always fascinated by this strange, cruel man, but what is incomprehensible in the light of his reactions to the whole Betty debacle is that seventeen years later he went to the trouble of orchestrating similar circumstances for his own son – only nastier by far.

My grandfather had overseen Cawdor in a calm and timeless way. Everything ran smoothly, people stayed in their jobs for life, change was avoided, surprises were unwelcome. Within a year of Jack's death, the managerial side of Cawdor was a mass of rapidly widening hairline cracks. Word got out about Findlay and the horseshoe, and after decades of service, Bill left. He had been the butler since Hugh was a boy, and his loss was like the hour hand of Big Ben falling off. By contrast, Peter, the new butler my father employed, was a total neurotic. It was an uphill task getting to know the mechanics of such a big house, and whereas Bill was practised in dealing with guests, Peter was forever gasping and throwing his arms in the air. His Lippizaner-like walk did not work well with small rugs on highly polished floors and he regularly went arse over tit while bringing in the tray of after-lunch coffee. 'That man is a one-man Greek wedding,' my father would sigh before going over to help him clear up the shards of Spode. Soon the housekeepers, Jessie and Annie Mary, were handing in their notices in protest over Peter's temper tantrums. Only Edith stayed on, jumpy, damp-eyed and forever bent over a bucket of feathers and entrails as she prepared endless grouse lunches.

At this point, Granny Wilma was added to the mix. It was the first time she had returned to Cawdor in nearly twenty years. Hugh had kept his relationship with her on a distant, arctic horizon, but when she broke her hip he resolved to be the good son and invited her home to convalesce. Betty was married to our grandfather by the time we were born, and I had never knowingly met Wilma before. Pa put her into the furthest-away room in the house and left the bedside visits to Ma.

I was intrigued by this heavy-lidded creature, wreathed in smoke and propped up in snowy sheets like a wrinkled djinn, who managed to pull off a remote and regal air despite a boy's haircut and a stained satin bed jacket. The ceiling above her bed time-lapsed through an impressive array of unpainted colour changes, starting white and progressing to rich umber via old ivory, sand and manila. The wainscoting around the bottom of her bedroom door underwent a similar transformation as the smoke found an escape through the small gap under the door. Wilma spent her days in bed making learned, private poetry critiques in a swirl of fumes like dry ice. Years later, despite several redecorations, the smell of tobacco lingered.

Wanting to find a way to talk to her, I took my pocket money, bought her a pot, and left my offering on the bedside table as she slept. The next day I went with Ma on her daily visit. Granny Wilma was very upset. She thumped her newspaper down on the bed. I hung back. 'Cath, darling, I am beside myself. Last night I read a long article on the terrible plight of those poor dear slum children in São Paulo. Really, it breaks my heart. And then, this morning, there are even worse things to read about orphans in Mozambique. I've been unable to sleep a wink for fretting about them. Not one wink.' She sighed and gazed soulfully out of the window while she tamped down her unlit cigarette in the way that Mr Sharp's black and white movie heroines did when receiving ghastly news about a loved one. 'By the way, thingy, oh, whatishername? Your blonde daughter has given me a present.' She flicked the pot with the back of her hand. 'I can't think what possessed her. It's quite hideous. Take it and put it somewhere, will you?' My mother whipped round to check if I had heard and made a grimace when she saw I had. She grabbed the pot and said, 'I'll leave you to your concerns about children on the other side of the world.' And shut the door rather hard before taking my hand and saying, 'Well, I love the pot. May I keep it?'

When her hip was better, Pa built Wilma a cottage in the village. It was a conciliatory gesture in their long estrangement, but it was not a success. As she grew older, Wilma's grandiosity had warped into a form of paranoia. Her voracious appetite for reading, once a salvation, became a curse. She believed that 'she knew too much'; that the CIA,

MI6, and probably Mossad as well were all keeping her under surveillance. Clouds over Cawdor concealed spies. Planes flying overhead had been 'diverted to snoop' on her. Agents skulked in many guises. She accosted the postman and ordered him off her property. As far as she was concerned, he could only be opening her letterbox for one thing: intelligence gathering. No-one could convince Wilma that if she really did know 'too much' her elimination could be carried out with the greatest ease, yet 'they' didn't seem to be crouching in the bushes waiting for a clear shot.

My father was already exasperated by her without any of these eccentricities. After the postal confrontation, he strongly suggested Wilma go elsewhere. She left Cawdor for a second and last time, this time moving to Herefordshire where she could be close to her youngest son, James.

Chapter 10

All those moments, like tears in the rain.

Philip K. Dick

MY PARENTS SENT THEIR FIVE CHILDREN TO FOUR DIFFERENT boarding schools in four different counties; only my brothers shared a school career. We all stayed in touch, haphazardly, by letter.

I was sent off aged eleven to Cobham Hall, an all-girls school at the other end of the country, in Kent. Emma had gone off to school with our Gordon Cumming cousins, so I was on my own at Cobham and did not enjoy it at all. I still cherish a grudge against the entire county. My letters home were full of complaints and wistful hopes.

Darling Ma,
I am writing to cheer you up a bit. Thank you so much for my lovely holidays. I saw you getting into the car after you

had said goodbye, so I banged on the coach window but you didn't see me. I still hate Cobham and I always will. I am dreading this term; I suppose you won't be able to take me out as exeat is on January 30th. Our dorm is so cold (the heater is working for the second time this term) you have to take a deep breath before you come in . . . I pulled my tooth out last night but no fairies came.

I love you so dearly,

Your second, unmarried daughter, Liza

xxxxxxxxxxxxxxxxxxxxxxxxxxxxxxxxxxxxxxxxx

P.S. Please send special love to old Findlay.

A volatile parent creates children who want a quiet life, and none of us was badly behaved at school. But, having excelled in the vibrant atmosphere of Hanford, I slumped at Cobham, and felt very far away from home. My mother came down to the school once or twice while I was there, but my father not at all. Unbeknown to me down in Kent, he had got into the habit of taking Emma out, accompanied by various women he always introduced as 'Olga Nethersole'. Emma didn't care that the face of Olga was ever changing, or what they were doing with him; she was just overjoyed to see Hugh. But it meant she was drawn into a partisan subterfuge of keeping secrets from Cath. Years later, when Emma was reading a James Thurber short story, she came across the joke my father had been making. A character called Elliot Vereker introduces a young woman as 'my niece, Olga Nethersole, despite being neither his niece, nor called Olga Nethersole'.

To assist with all our different half-term and holiday schedules, and to cope with stopovers on our way up to Cawdor, Pa bought a flat in London. It was in Embassy Court, a 1970s high-rise on a busy main road that connected Baker Street with Finchley Road. Down the road was a graveyard, and opposite it was Lord's cricket ground. Pa was not a cricket fan and my mother shopped in Chelsea – a three-mile drive across the city. The only reason we were in St John's Wood was that my father's current Olga Nethersole lived around the corner.

Our roadside bunkroom was unbearably noisy and we had to wear wax earplugs to get any sleep at all. In the mornings, the whole chewing-gum-in-the-hair scene from our car trips to Scotland was reprised with pink wax grafted firmly onto our eyebrows. There was little to do in the flat and no television, so we would press our noses against the filthy windows and watch a life-size mannequin dressed in overalls with an electronic arm beckoning cars into the garage opposite. The decor in the flat was self-consciously trendy. The hall walls were covered in brown wrapping paper, the lamps were made of smashed-up bottle ends. The pictures were abstract: top half blue, bottom half yellow – and if we were in any doubt about the desert theme, sand had been mixed into the yellow paint. The armchairs were inflatable, which was unfortunate because Pa's chain-smoking meant that very soon they were sad puddles of transparent plastic on the floor. This Olga was an interior decorator whom Pa had given a free hand to do the place up. Someone should have handcuffed her.

I could not put my finger on it, but Cawdor in the holidays was no longer the home I had grown to love. The idea of taking friends there was awful. We were on constant shimmering alert, desperately eager to please, trying to keep Hugh's mood sweet. It was tricky work, like trying to juggle soufflés in front of a hostile audience.

Days were fine; it was the evenings that were worrying. We were expected to change for dinner every night. Emma and I would hurry up to our rooms to climb into stripy Biba dresses before the gong rang for dinner. My mother would appear wearing floor-length creations trimmed with pink marabou feathers and numberless minuscule buttons that ran from a high neck all the way down to the floor. Colin and Fred's way of approaching Pa was to immerse themselves in his cinematic obsessions: *Bad Day at Black Rock*, *Harold and Maude*, *The Italian Job* and any of the Marx Brother movies that didn't feature Zeppo too prominently. Fred watched *Butch Cassidy and the Sundance Kid* at least once a week, and Pa enjoyed quizzing him on the film's more abstruse details. Sometimes it seemed to have become the main point of reference with his son. They communicated in quotes. Fred's favourite line was, 'Boy, I've got vision and the rest of the world wears bi-focals'; Pa's was, 'Never hit your mother with a shovel; it leaves a dull impression on her mind.' Their favourite song was 'Sweet Betsy from Pike', sung by the old mine boss for whom Butch and Sundance work when they are on the run. Pa scoured old American songbooks until he unearthed the whole thing and then sent us all copies of it so we could learn it by heart. It became his hospital-bed swansong.

Emma and I found we could jolly Pa along playing a homegrown version of *Call My Bluff*. Unearthing a truly peculiar word from the dictionary was capable of making him happy for the rest of the night. The game reached its apotheosis when we happened across the word 'carphology', defined as 'the delirious fumbling of the bedclothes'. We also tried to keep abreast of his ever-changing reading crazes. Sometimes it would be Dylan Thomas, then Logan Pearsall Smith, then Robert Graves. When he was in the grip of a Raymond Chandler obsession we leafed through the oeuvre like a pair of research librarians trying to memorize quotes that might amuse him: 'She looked as if she'd been poured into the dress and someone forgot to say when', and 'It was blonde. A blonde to make a bishop kick a hole in a stained-glass window.' My father was especially thrilled when he came across a rare Chandler poem, and it became his favourite for a while.

> He left her lying in the nude
> That sultry night in May.
> The neighbors thought it rather rude;
> He liked her best that way.
>
> He left a rose beside her head,
> A meat axe in her brain.
> A note upon the bureau read:
> 'I won't be back again.'

At Pa's instigation we also had nightly Scrabble and backgammon tournaments, and then, having researched the rules of cribbage in the encyclopedia, he taught us how to play it purely because he liked the idea of a game that had conventions, which involved us shouting 'muggins' and 'his nibs'. At other times he would get us to dowse for coins hidden under the rug while my mother swayed along to Neil Diamond songs and we relaxed and laughed and tried to avoid glancing at him surreptitiously to anticipate if his mood was about to blacken. Once when he was having a disagreement with Ma, we thought it would blow over when he stalked off. Instead he reappeared with a bucket of water and threw it over his wife's head, drenching her. I never knew what sparked off such excessive reactions. Sometimes he would just get up and go to the loo, and on his return he'd be freighted with paranoia, as if he had just overheard that there had been a mix-up and he was not the Thane of Cawdor after all but the son of a Slovenian sanitation worker. Moreover, they wanted him back home right now.

I was also beginning to realize that our family's values were a cosmic league away from anything the school's career officer talked about. By all outward appearances we looked contemporary, but scratch the surface and archaic traditions were not only still going strong, they went unquestioned. I appreciated this for the first time when, aged about twelve, I was sitting with Ma in the Land Rover waiting for a sudden downpour to cease before we made a dash for the drawbridge. She had parked under some lime trees that were dripping fat raindrops onto the roof of the car and I was looking at my mother's pretty, tanned profile and asking her what I had been like as a baby. It was one of those conversations that reassured and fascinated me, to hear about my tiny self. She laughed about how oddly I had crawled – straight legs, bum in the air – and then, as an afterthought, added that she had despaired at having given birth to a second girl. She laughed at the memory, but the hairs on the back of my neck stood up. My mother was an intelligent woman brought up in a family less tied to its past, but she saw no contradiction in championing the opposite sex over her own to fit the customs of her husband's family. I had no idea how to digest this information smilingly: not only was the deliverer someone of the same gender, she was my mother. Until that moment I had had no proper inkling that girls were a disappointment. It was as if Emma's birth had been the equivalent of a toothless couple entering a draw hoping for the first prize of false teeth, but winning only dental floss. On entering it again, they had won a toothbrush.

At Golden Grove, I had felt we were a family of equal parts. Some of us were big and some of us were permanently small, but there was no difference in importance between the sexes. I had, however, overlooked some clear hints. My father, for instance, always arranged to fly separately from Colin, but not from us. I vaguely understood that Colin was the 'heir', but it was a wholly abstract concept. To me, he was just my tissue-sniffling little brother and Emma was clearly the alpha-female queen-bee boss-lady. I regarded Pa as a progressive on the flimsy evidence that he had long sideburns, wore flares and listened to Lee

Hazelwood and Nancy Sinatra. I understood that any system that kept Cawdor intact would necessarily be unfair, but within that system, age discrimination seemed to have the edge of fairness over sex.

But it was pretty naive to think that Pa was going to depart from opinions so assiduously reinforced since biblical times. Girls were presumed to acquiesce innately to such bigotry, but it was like being invited to smile while swallowing gravel. There was absolutely no-one with whom I could discuss these tangled feelings. I looked at our family with new eyes and saw that everything had a male tilt. We were so steeped in the surrounding history I had overlooked that it all applied to us too. If Colin and Fred had not been born, or if they had died before they were able to produce sons of their own, the next nearest Cawdor male, however distantly related, would be favoured over Emma. In our case, given the preponderance of girls in the immediate extended family, it would be a far-flung cousin many times removed. The only male first cousin with Campbell blood was Alexander Friesen, but he was out of the running since Aunt Carey's female blood did not count. Pa's only brother James had produced five daughters across three different relationships. There were no candidates at one remove because Drunkle Uncle, Jack's only brother, was childless. The Cawdor heir would be a remote, unknown cousin – a melancholic harbourmaster living in Nova Scotia perhaps, or a reclusive tap dancer from Adelaide. Even if these hypothetical men had no interest in Cawdor whatsoever, as long as they had exterior genitalia, it was all theirs. It seemed to me completely absurd that male blood differed from female. I was told that it was because the title could not be passed down the female line – no medals for guessing who had made all these rules up. All privileges were reserved for men because that was just how it was. The women supported that, and didn't rate their own kind. The most successful form of repression is when it is invisible, and when the repressed assist in its reinforcement. Ma was not some sort of freak. The vast majority of her generation in the same position had never thought twice about what they were supporting.

In case this misogyny needed any further underlining, before the seat belt laws became mandatory Pa was forever telling me to strap up, saying, 'Your face is your fortune, so you'd better not smash it up.' Eventually the mantra began to drive me crazy. The subtext was that we must not expect a share of the family wealth, although there was never any discussion of careers, only of remaining physically un-damaged and nubile. A small nest egg had been set aside for the three girls, which went towards our education and a future roof over our heads, but otherwise we were excluded from his will. This draconian tradition was peculiar to our family. It was not the seat belt advice that irritated, but the tedious harping on about our faces. 'Success' would be the auspiciousness of any future marriage; any failure in that regard would be down to our looks. Hugh's vision for us was to be another nob's wife, an elegant flower who must never express any anger. That would be terribly vulgar and awfully unfeminine. It smacked of hairy ankles. I didn't know what I wanted to do with my life, but I knew I didn't aspire to being the consort of some red-faced landowner merely because he had status. We had sat through *La Fille Mal Gardée* enough times to know that.

Nothing gleaned from the outside world really applied at home. It was very confusing. All around, the sexual revolution seemed to have moved the world on. Even Hugh was a fan of Germaine Greer, though it turned out his admiration extended only as far as her bralessness. I tried, once, to talk with Hugh about primogeniture. Big mistake. As sole beneficiary of an antiquated hierarchy, Pa was the least likely person to enter into a reasoned debate.

'What do you think would happen if we three girls took you to the equal opportunities commission?' I said.

'What's it like being a half-wit?' he retorted, and then attacked this impertinence with such anger I was scared he was going to hit me.

The zeitgeist of enlightened egalitarianism was something 'other people' embraced. By the 1960s, the aristocracy was no longer the ruling class, but it still stuck to medieval rules established during a time when, among other things, women got burned as witches and rapists were treated more leniently if their victim was attractive. I gave up ever trying to discuss with my father what I wanted to do with my life after an argument on a damp autumn day when we had driven over to Rait Castle to look for puffballs.

Rait was a tiny wreck. No floors or roof remained, but there was an elegant stone fireplace halfway up the interior wall – evidence that the main living area was on the first storey with livestock stabled beneath to provide a natural form of underfloor heating. It was more pied-à-terre than castle, and it was ours, as much as it was anyone's. It came as part of a medieval compensation package for the 1405 murder of Andrew Cawdor, heir to the 4th Thane, by Sir Gervaise de Rait. Although his name was better suited to a choreographer than an assassin, he had not only put the Cawdor bloodline at risk, but his audaciousness had threatened the family's local reputation. As deaths go, it was infra dig. If it were a farmyard bust-up it would have been like a stud rooster getting savaged to death by a blue tit, in front of all the hens.

The Raits already had a reputation for punching above their weight. Some time before, the Rait Castle thane felt he had a bone to pick with another of his neighbours and invited the family over to dine with him, with the express intention of murdering them all between courses. Unbeknown to him, one of his daughters was having an illicit affair with the son of one of his intended victims. The prevailing culture of endless hostilities made enemies so thick on the ground that it was frankly hard for a girl not to get romantically involved with one of the enemy's sons every now and again. When she overheard her father detailing the plot with his stewards, she rushed off to their trysting spot and warned her lover. The boy alerted his family, but instead of cancelling the dinner date, they kept it. At a prearranged signal, the Raits drew their skean-dhus. Instead of being taken unawares, their guests followed suit. In the midst of the snickersnee, it dawned on the girl's father exactly who had betrayed his plans. He raced to his daughter's room and burst in upon her just as she was escaping. She was hanging from the windowsill, about to drop down onto her lover's horse tethered below. Rait ran straight over and hacked off both her hands.

Sir Gervaise fled into exile after killing Andrew Cawdor. The confiscation of the castle in his absence was intended to discourage any further challenges to the Cawdor authority. Rait Castle was too small and too close to Cawdor to be of any use so it was left to fall into disrepair.

As we gathered our mushrooms among the thistly tussocks, my father and I discussed the hand-severing story.

'What do you think the moral is?' he asked.

I thought a bit. 'That family loyalty trumps romantic loyalty?'

'Go on.'

'Well, what the father does is seen as a betrayal by the daughter, but what the daughter does to stop it is seen as a worse betrayal by the father.'

'Very succinct,' he said sarcastically, 'but wrong. The moral of the tale is that meddling children get their just deserts.'

'Ha di ha, very funny. You mean to say that you would have done that to me if it had been us back then?' I asked.

'What d'you mean?'

'Would you kill me for loving the wrong man?'

'God no!' My father laughed. 'Unless it was a left-footer. Believe me, I'll be grateful to any man prepared to take you on, especially after your last school report. All indications are that you will be unemployable. If you're not careful, you'll be shacked up with a diddicoy and a brood of dribbling cretins.'

185

I stomped off to sulk in the car.

My mother did at least broach the subject of careers with me once. She saw me as an air hostess, and the conversation came to a shuddering halt.

Of course nobody had told us anything at all about Betty and the hexes, but the atmosphere at Cawdor during the holidays grew steadily more peculiar. After much persuasion, a writer friend, Roger Longrigg, came to stay, but the moment he and his wife arrived, Hugh turned on them. A ghastly weekend ensued as he scorned Roger at every opportunity. On the Longriggs' last morning, Cath joined them for breakfast before they caught their flight south. Hugh was still in bed, but as they signed the visitors' book she asked them to wait. 'Hugh will be down in a minute,' she said. 'I know he would want to say goodbye.'

To which they replied in unison, 'Must we?'

Emma's and my escape was to go and stay with our Gordon Cumming cousins who lived at Altyre, near where the real King Duncan died. We would plead with Cath to drop us off after doing the shopping chores in Nairn. It was no distance for Scotland, only about seven miles further east along the main road to Forres and the tiny hamlet of Dallas beyond (once upon a time someone had emigrated to Texas from there). Compared to Cawdor, Altyre seemed utterly carefree – and this despite the presence of Mrs Mac, their nanny, who ruled with an iron oven-glove behind the green baize door. Mrs Mac had ferociously short hair shaved at the nape that lent her more than a whiff of the military. She ran a household rating system of gold and black stars for good and bad behaviour. Alastair and Sarah, the two eldest, were beyond her jurisdiction, so her efforts were concentrated on the two youngest. Emma's contemporary, Cha, was Mrs Mac's pet; gold stars were strewn across every day of the week after her name. Mosh, my friend, was the opposite: by Thursday, Mrs Mac had usually run out of black stars and was having to continue charting her crimes in black marker pen. As a nanny she was firm but fair, but life wasn't. Cha thrived because she had natural cunning, while Mosh was always in the doghouse because she was incapable of lying.

Our cousins were all incredibly horsey and talked in a special patois to their animals, and among themselves. They would burble impenetrably all day long and were just as happy communing with one of their dogs as chatting to a parent. We would trot about all day long, being cowboys on their home farm – a startling architectural oddity for the Highlands, built in the style of a Tuscan monastery with arched cloisters and a campanile. It was our very own spaghetti western backdrop. We would shamble about practising with homemade lassoes, talking about 'dogies' and lying in wait for our enemy, in the shape of a hapless tractor driver. These games ended for me when yet again I came home unable to breathe from an asthma attack and Pa drunkenly bet me a thousand pounds not to ride again until my twenty-first birthday. It was an unimaginably huge sum and I agreed immediately.

Neither Uncle William nor Aunt E ever said anything to us, or asked us any questions, so I never knew if they were aware of what was going on at Cawdor. It was just heaven to be away, even if Mrs Mac insisted that we join in her star system. Pa was a different person when he turned up at Altyre. Betty's expulsion from Cawdor had not ruffled his friendship with Uncle William in any way. They adored each other and sat around drinking gin and tonics and telling each other racy stories that would end up with them lying on the floor crying with laughter. The Gordon Cumming daughters spent their evenings practising song and dance routines and Uncle William, Aunt E and Pa would sit there politely as we jumped around doing clankingly pedestrian moves to words from 'Ode To Billy Joe' by Bobbie Gentry. What our cousins lacked in tunefulness they more than made up for in self-belief. They were always bellowing to anyone who cared, or dared, to listen.

The bad thing about Pa being one third of the audience was that it inevitably meant the end of our stay, that he had come to take us back. If he arrived at night, our faces and any subsequent fortunes just had to hope for the best as we crammed into the passenger seat of his Ferrari and he drove home flat out. He had a habit of switching off his headlights as we careened towards a sharp corner or a hump in the road. He did it, he said, to check for the lights of an approaching car, which would mean he should move back onto the right side of the road; but after a few drinks he often forgot to turn the lights back on, until I started whimpering. I would pray that we would soon reach the Wee Manny's Grave, because it was the only place where he was guaranteed to slow down. It was a small cairn of stones, now mossy with age, that marked the spot where a wounded Highland soldier had finally collapsed and died after escaping the disaster of Culloden. The man had staggered fifteen miles before succumbing on this lonely brae, anonymous but never forgotten. There was always a jam jar with flowers in it perched on the topmost stone. We took a momentary pause in any journey to inspect the current offering. They were just wild posies – harebells, buttercups and a couple of foxglove stems – but they were always fresh, even through the winter months, when there would be a sprig of heather and some holly berries. Who tended it so diligently was a mystery.

Memorials like the Wee Manny's were all over the Highlands. In the wake of the Battle of Culloden, the English were so remorseless in their suppression of the Scots that all tributes were low-key and allegorical. In the county of Angus, the locals planted a beech hedge by the roadside to mark the failed uprising. They swore to keep it growing until the English no longer governed them. It grew and grew, and today it is a vast wall of a hedge as high as any tree. Fire engine ladders are required in order to clip it. We knew all this as if it had happened just a few months before, yet we knew sweet zero about contemporary Scottish politics.

The Betty incident had flipped a switch in Pa that never flipped back. His temper, which had always been fierce, was now frequently out of control, and he seemed to revel in it. Outbursts multiplied, and the excuse could be minuscule. Thatch had successfully helped Hugh over his knife phobia, but the outcome was that he now regularly used knives to threaten people. He once threw a small dagger at a guest who was irritating him, the blade digging into the carpet between his feet. The man's 'crime' had been to drag a chair from the far end of the drawing room in order to join in a conversation going on around the fire.

Hugh gloried in these sudden cessations of hospitality. When he found out that a visiting acquaintance called Sonny Marlborough had moved Aunt E's car away from the drawbridge without her permission, he tried to wrestle Marlborough off the drawbridge. Another man, by the name of Murlees, came to Cawdor to discuss the restoration of his castle in Aberdeen, but during the course of dinner Hugh fancied he heard his guest say something offensive, although Cath, who was talking to Murlees at the time, remembered only desultory chatter. Hugh stormed up the table, grabbed his wife by the wrist and said, 'Come on, we're going.' He dragged her to his car, locking the portcullis behind them, and after he had driven aimlessly around the county she eventually persuaded Hugh to return home. They found Murlees talking to his driver through the iron bars of the gate, imprisoned in a house where he had been made to feel totally unwelcome.

Our mother had always been a level-headed woman and she did her best to calm her husband. Until now, the main cause of strife had been Hugh's hectic extra-marital adventures. Hugh was a dashing figure to us, but a wife and five children in wellies did not fit with the personal vision he had for himself as a samurai playboy. His new best friend was the photographer Patrick Lichfield, who had a conveyor belt of model girlfriends. Hugh hoovered up Patrick's cast-offs. They shared everything: tailors, cars, hairdressers, girls. The only difference was that Patrick was single and Pa was married. The phrase 'scoring birds' fitted him perfectly; he was a twitcher. It was as if, on a fundamental level – a level on which his very survival depended – Pa felt fully validated as a human being only when he was seducing someone. A succession of his lovers came to stay at Cawdor as guests, with my mother as their hostess. Years later, when I reread the letters my mother sent me at school, I suddenly saw them in an entirely different light.

Dadda went south the day I came north. He is off to a hidden destination where he is breathing deeply and trying to write a 'book'. He wanted total peace so none of us knows where he is!

The book, needless to say, never materialized.

The only reassurance Cath had was that however sexually tactless her husband was, after each sortie he returned to her declaring his love. To keep sane she concentrated on the idea that this was a sign of his under-lying devotion, but beyond all the giddy pleasures of his macho bullshit there lurked something darker: a total in-ability to articulate his frustrations. If he had been able to talk about them, he might not have kicked his cars, smashed his fist into doors and thrown books across the room. It was not clear if Hugh was concerned about such lapses of self-control. It was clear, however, that his drink-ing had increased – or his resistance had diminished. If Cath were a stick of rock, she would have the words 'For Better Or Worse' printed down the length of her core. She had taken a vow, and come what may she would stand by her man. When Hugh went plain mad rather than just sex mad, she stood by her maniac.

The next person to succumb to the tensions was Peter the butler. It all started to go wrong during a course of driving lessons he was taking. He said the stress of crashing gears was causing him to suffer from dandruff. It seemed like a minor neurosis, but the next thing we knew Peter had gone straight from his three-point turns to Raigmore hospital in Inverness, where he requested immediate admission to the mental health ward. Initially the doctors refused, but Peter was adamant, and they relented. A consultant psychiatrist contacted my mother to inform her that he would be unable to return to any form of work due to a tentative diagnosis of manic depression. My mother was amazed at the trajectory of his illness, from a light dusting of scurf to total collapse, but volunteered to deliver a suitcase to the hospital.

My parents went to his room to pack his belongings, and what they found there made them realize that the things going on in Peter's head were a little stranger than public appearances suggested. Behind closed doors, his room was crammed with plundered memorabilia. There were a dozen framed photographs surrounding his bed, but none of them was of Peter's family. They were all Campbells: Hugh as a child, Carey in a ball dress, and great-great-aunts wearing straw boaters, sitting stiffly on Welsh ponies in front of Stackpole. His cupboard was crammed with my grandfather's clothes. It was a bizarre magpie shrine. Cath thought it was quaint, but harmless; Hugh said it gave him the creeps. 'I don't understand. What kind of phoney would want to graft someone else's family life onto his own?' he kept asking no-one in particular. For a while it almost looked as though Hugh was going to reprise his there's-a-witch-in-my-house meltdown.

Then, just as rapidly as he'd first fallen for him, Hugh suddenly tired of Thatch. In the end, it all came down to money. After Hugh had his freak-out about domestic arrangements with Betty, he became a little more sympathetic to Ma's aversion to sharing her home with Thatch and Val. Hugh moved them out of Cawdor and into a house at the end of the drive. Even so, Thatch drifted in most lunchtimes. Pa had happily bankrolled his svengali, but it had never been clear whether Thatch was a guest or an employee. My father was often an extraordinarily generous man, to the point where he could be seen as a bit of a pushover to the wily. His patience finally snapped after Thatch touched him for extra money, naming some lofty cause, and then, a couple of days later, he popped into his house unannounced and found him excitedly unwrapping what Hugh interpreted to be the lofty cause: a frosted-glass, electronically operated indoor fountain, complete with Mantovani soundtrack. The flowering of their relationship had been unusual, but the disintegration followed the normal pattern: tracer fire, burning bridges and the total annihilation of any friendship. Perhaps this typifies the actions of someone who surrenders his autonomy as totally as Hugh had to Thatch. The only way they can work out how to reclaim it is with maximum force.

To appease his sense of guilt over his sudden rejection,

Hugh took the same course of action he'd followed with Betty and Wilma: he bought them out of our lives and broke off all contact.

While Thatch was still in Pa's life, he insisted that Pa pass on his self-defence skills to girls only. It was meant to be a homoeopathic remedy for his womanizing, but it was a bit like my attempt to ink Satan out of my Bible. As soon as Thatch left, the self-defence classes collapsed, but to keep up his aikido practice my father decided to teach us. We would go to the dojo one at a time and be shown how to throw ourselves around the room in a martially artful way. In one letter home from Cobham it seemed that it was all top secret: 'I have told no one about the Aikido, but when someone is going to hit me, I automatically put my arm up.'

My aikido career came to a halt the day I arrived in the dojo and Pa showed me an enormous hunting knife – the type used for eviscerating deer. He told me that he would shortly leave the room and conceal the knife on his body; when he returned, I was to frisk him. If I didn't find it and disarm him, he was going to come at me with it. I·did as he said. I patted him all over – all over, that is, except for high up in his inner thigh, and that, of course, is where it was. I knew after patting him down that it couldn't be any-where else, but I certainly wasn't going to touch him there. He pulled out the knife and I ran from the room slamming the door behind me. Later I bundled up my judo kit and threw it in an attic cupboard.

Hugh persevered, but put his own private spin on what aikido was all about. The self-discipline that was meant to give aikido practitioners an inner calm and serve as a spiritual path went out of the window. He decided to form an elite squad of fighters: four male friends and Cath. He handed out leather belts made to his own specifications that were going to serve as the group insignia. The brass belt buckles were formed out of each of the six's initials and were to be worn so they 'could recognize each other' during some future crisis, when they would annihilate 'unacceptable people'. What sort of characteristics or behaviour would be judged 'unacceptable' was hazy, as was why the squad needed belts to recognize each other. Perhaps they were all going to be in a different dimension. If he had thought of a slogan for his gang, it could have been: 'Bespoke Murder! In the Name of Good Taste!' My mother didn't even do aikido. Perhaps Hugh expected her to stand around like a magician's assistant. It was all quite bonkers, and not in an entirely harmless way, but mercifully, the crisis that would force Pa to spring into deadly hand-chopping action never happened and mankind was spared.

Chapter 11

In the real dark night of the soul it is always three o'clock
in the morning.

F. Scott Fitzgerald

THE SCOTTISH ESTATE WAS PREDOMINANTLY FOREST, SHEEP
pasture and moor: wild and beautiful, but poor-quality
land. The Welsh estate was beautiful too, but it was bursting with arable land that sustained fields of tulips and
daffodils, and its profits took care of Cawdor. We found
this out when in 1972 my father suddenly sold Golden
Grove and the entire Welsh estate. The land that had come
into the family in the seventeenth century had lasted
seventeen years in his hands. His decision to sell was
many things, but most of all it was short-sighted. He
had halved his land ownership, and the loss of Wales
turned the financial equilibrium on its head. Running
a pile like Cawdor was a whirling drain; the heating

alone cost tens of thousands of pounds every year.

Although Hugh was cash-rich in the short term, most of the money needed immediate reinvestment to bankroll Cawdor. Somehow, the study of budgets and accounts quietly turned itself into a shopping list. Hugh went on a spending spree. Another Ferrari arrived. And then another. Then a pair of Range Rovers, their insignias doctored so that they read 'Hang Over'. There were a couple of souped-up, *Italian Job*-style Minis in bright blue and bright yellow. There was a paint-it-any-colour-as-long-as-it's-black Model T Ford, a Hafflinger, a wartime Chrysler with gangster window blinds, a couple of canvas-roofed troop trucks and a cheesy, over-restored *Chitty Chitty Bang Bang*-style Bentley. The older cars just sat under dustsheets in the garages. I never got the car thing.

When the garages were full up, next on the shopping list was the ruined castle of Lochindorb (Loch of Trouble). It comprised fragments of a curtain wall with crumbling corner towers and stood on a small island in the middle of a remote loch, fifteen miles from Cawdor. Hugh bought it at amazing expense, given that buildings without doors are hardly private property, and in Scotland there is no law of trespass. He could have gone there at any time, for free.

Lochindorb had originally belonged to Robert II, grandson of Robert the Bruce. He gifted the fortress to his third and most wayward son, 'Big' Alexander Stuart, better known to his subjects as the Wolf of Badenoch. My father admired the Wolf in the same way he admired Jimmy Dunbar, my grandfather's friend with the fern toiletries. When asked why he liked men like these two, he was wont to reply, 'I suppose the love of one monster by another is strong.' Even in those casually barbarous times a hundred years before Muriel was born, the Wolf was notorious for his cruelty, and used his position as the king's deputy to terrorize a wide region bordering the Moray Firth. He imposed his will by burning people out of their homes, and it became quite a habit. He graduated from individual crofts to razing villages, then whole towns. In 1390, his delinquency reached its zenith when he torched the gothic glory that was Elgin Cathedral. This arson was committed to vent his fury at the Bishop of Moray, who had been supportive of Mrs Wolf's complaints of abandonment. (A woman who clearly didn't recognize a stroke of luck when it poked her in the eye.) Once the cathedral was gutted, the fire swept on through the chapter houses, and went on to destroy Elgin's college and, finally, the hospital. The Wolf was excommunicated for this outrage – a punishment as meaningful as giving a football hooligan a lifelong ban from visiting art galleries.

King Robert eventually despaired of his son's recidivism. He ordered the Cawdors, who were the local sheriffs in their brand-new shiny castle, to 'neutralize' Lochindorb, and paid them twenty-four pounds for their trouble. The Cawdors approached with caution and waited until the Wolf had set off on a pillage before rowing across to the island with a raiding party. They wrenched the yett, or wrought-iron front gate, off its hinges, rendering the stronghold ... less strong. They hauled the yett back to Cawdor as proof of their work, and it still hangs outside the Tree Room as a piece of gigantic wall bling.

The Wolf's reputation was such that it was said he finally lost his life at Ruthven barracks playing chess with the devil. As the devil growled 'checkmate', a cataclysmic storm erupted overhead. When the clouds finally cleared, the bodies of charred sentries littered the barrack walls. They found the Wolf's body inside. The nails on his boots had been torn out, but otherwise he was unmarked.

For Pa to buy the wreck of Lochindorb in the late twentieth century was a piece of romantic whimsy that perfectly encapsulated his typical response when faced with a serious problem. It was a phenomenon one of his subsequent girlfriends defined as his 'morbid fixation with Never Never Land'. For a while Aunt Carey poked fun at her brother by ringing up and saying that it was 'Red Riding Hood hoping to have a word with His Big, Bad Wolfship'. Lochindorb was really nothing more than a staggeringly costly picnic spot. As it offered no shelter, picnics there happened only in the summer months, but in Scotland, a small island surrounded by still, fresh water makes a perfect breeding ground for midges. Being supper for a million biting insects makes an otherwise beautiful day unbearable, and before long we were visiting Lochindorb only a couple of times a year. The thrill of ownership dwindled to Pa impressing guests by majestically pointing at it from the car window as he raced across the moor.

After Lochindorb, more money was frittered on a variety of vanity projects, none of which flourished. Unlike a lot of wealthy people (John-Paul Getty was widely rumoured to have a pay phone in the front hall for his guests' use), Hugh was incredibly generous and enjoyed splashing money about, but his extravagance was in inverse proportion to his business acumen. He learned to fly a helicopter, he had a fleet of sports and vintage cars; he constantly bought jewellery, mostly for Cath but often for himself, in the shape of chunky cufflinks the size of golf balls. Whenever Pa put his money where his mouth was, it was only to kiss it goodbye. He bought flats in London and Paris for himself, his mistresses and a few lucky hangers-on. He invested in crackpot schemes from Canada to Australia. In due course, he owned a jewellery shop, a helicopter company and then went into film production. All these businesses failed. To fund his lifestyle he sold off a bit here and a bit there in a steady trickle.

My father's mismanagement and profligacy need not have been overwhelming to us as a family. Fortunes rise and ebb – that is, after all, why they are called 'fortunes' – and there were trustees in place to put the brakes on irresponsible behaviour. But as my father's inheritance shrank, so too did his heart. He grew older but he did not mature, and his conflicts deepened rather than abated. There were endless little ironies afoot: as a trustee, he managed other people's estates quite brilliantly but left his own in a God-awful mess; as a host, he was usually convivial and generous, but as a father, he was intolerant and often unkind. Towards the end of his life, his family relationships shrank into the background as material things increasingly obsessed him. The more he pushed us away, the more we tried to connect; and as he grew more acquisitive, the more reckless he became with long-cared-for possessions.

On a practical level, the sad evidence is that the inheritance of Cawdor overwhelmed Hugh utterly from the start. When it became his, at the age of thirty, he was far less ready or capable than his father had been at fourteen. In order to conceal his panic, he became autocratic. He despised anyone disagreeing with him, and therefore was hard to help. The only reliable course of action he found that helped him cope with these shortcomings was to drink. When he was drunk, he could take all the pain he held inside and inject it into those close to him.

The sale of Wales had been a huge error of judgement and the answers to the questions raised were not 'more cars' or 'a brand-new landlocked island' or 'topaz mines in Tasmania'. Hugh struggled to work out what to do next. We still had house parties and dinners at which my father was genial and witty and the commander-in-chief of anec-dotes, but as soon as we were alone as a family he often dispensed with his considerable charms, and his *joie de vivre* was seamlessly replaced by a perplexing darkness. It was always a bad blow when someone cancelled a visit because it meant that there would be no wadding. And taking his moods out on Ma was becoming habitual. On a quiet day, my father stomped around the house slamming doors and sighing like an angry buffalo whenever my mother spoke, even when it was not to him. The most innocuous tele-phone call could trigger him.

'Is that Rose Brothers?'

'Urrrrgh.'

'I ordered a side of ham last week and I . . .'

''Struth!'

'. . . wondered if it had come in yet? It's Lady Caw . . .'

'Jeeezu.'

'. . . dor.'

And he would storm out, slam!, shaking the pictures on the walls.

Pa hogged a wide range of settings on our emotional dials. If a guest arrived, the static would die away, as if his transmission mast was set to retract as they walked in. After they left, his bulbous moods were instantaneously readable. Edith, who ventured out of her kitchen only occasionally anyway, would be sent scurrying back if she caught sight of him. The moment I walked into a room where he was, or where he had just cut a vindictive swathe, I would feel clotted with anxiety. Emma used to call him 'the amateur barbarian', although privately I thought he was turning pro. I concluded that only poor people got sectioned on psychiatric wings. Rich lunatics raved free with everyone looking the other way.

And then, without warning, the sun would come out from behind its cloud and everything looked as if it might improve. He would take me into the Big Wood with him so that he could inspect some rare tree or other. As we passed each stand of trees, he would test me to see if I could name them. If I dithered, 'I'll have to hurry you! Chop! Chop! Two seconds to answer, or here comes the chopper to chop off your head!'

'Um . . . sycamore?'

'No! Velly velly bad, cloth-ears. Minus one thousand points.'

But his chiding was warm. He had a habit – a relic from when I was very small – of clasping my hand; we would take it in turns to squeeze each other's fingers. In moments like these I could imagine that one day, even one day fairly soon, we might all feel happy and loved and secure. I gave him the benefit of the doubt every time. To do otherwise was just too scary.

I didn't know what was really wrong with Pa, couldn't even guess. Alcoholics were stinking tramps in doorways, drinking from cans of Special Brew. Alcoholics did not wear moleskin boots and hamster-lined coats; they did not drive Ferraris. One evening, after another fraught dinner of unilateral insults, I sat down beside Pa by the fireplace in the drawing room. I wanted to speak to him, to appeal to his better nature, to beg him not to be so aggressive. I didn't know how to put it, how to order my thoughts. So I just opened my mouth and out it came: 'Please, Pa, stop drinking.' I think I was more surprised than he was. I had no idea I was going to say anything like that. He looked at me, his eyes filled with tears, and then he looked into his glass and said, 'Yes. I'm going to stop drinking. I'll stop tomorrow.' And a tear plopped into his gin.

Pa's drinking followed a standard trajectory and the effects on him were archetypal, but none of us could see that. We circled around a black hole. I didn't realize in the morning, when we were all feeling fragile after the venomous things he had come out with the night before yet he was behaving as if nothing had happened, that he did so because he simply had no memory of what he had said, and never would have. It was almost impossible to articulate what was happening. Family life had gradually become nightmarish. Yet I loved him. We all did. We really adored him. Within the almost permanent state of exasperation he lived in, he needed only to make a tiny gesture for us to feel that one day all might be well again. As soon as we were away, he wrote us funny letters filled with affection. But the thing that really messed with my mind was that the soft world he conjured lived only on the page. My mother's letters showed another side.

> My darling Liza,
> The boys left yesterday on the aeroplane. It all seemed horribly short, but I think they were both very happy here. Colin went shooting after lunch yesterday and only arrived back just in time! Fredbox was very upset about going. It was Steve's birthday and he had been asked to a small party. There was only really time for him to give his present, seize a piece of cake & into the car. He was a bit slow coming out of the Websters' house and Pa strode out & pushed him so roughly. It was awful – desperate tears & unhappiness & I felt frantic too. I wept like a baby when they finally walked to the plane, and came back to Cawdor looking like a rag.

*

Without Wales as the cash cow to take care of Cawdor, my father eventually realized that he was going to have to open the house to the public. Once he had made the decision, it took a year to prepare. Signposts, ropes and cameras were installed. A pitch and putt course was created, our old gypsy caravan appropriated as a ticket office and golf club store. A cafeteria replaced the laundry rooms where Mrs King had steamed the linen. A gift shop, stocked with fudge, mugs, Loch Ness monster oven gloves and make-your-own-Cawdor-in-cardboard packs, was created in a cellar beyond the old, old kitchen with the siege well in one corner. After years of there being just one, jealously guarded, loo on the ground floor, there were now rooms lined with them in Bill's old pantries. There was no need to install many wheelchair ramps as most steps already had them in place for the wheelbarrows that carried firewood and peat into the house. Pa ordered a flag of our coat of arms that was hoisted at the top of the tower when we were open for business. Later, after he remarried, the flag came to mean that the Thane was 'at home', like the Queen.

We were still at school when the first visitors started to arrive but Pa sent us letters that gave us an idea of what to expect when we got home. He described giving a large group of travel correspondents a guided tour. After he had delivered a detailed lecture on medieval life to explain the reason for the well in the old kitchen, he reported that an American in the party had piped up, pointing at the well and asking, 'So this is where they junked the trash, right?' He gleefully recalled that the same man had taken the stuffed goat's head for a deer. Another visitor had given him one of the 'stupid-looking badges' on his hat that said 'Stand up for Ohio.' My father had pinned it to his sporran.

In another letter he asked that I come up with a more

suitable family motto for the new circumstances at Cawdor. His own suggestion was 'the stranger who tries locked doors within the house should be watched with zeal from behind the hedge'.

When we arrived back home at the end of term, he presented us with name badges of our own. Mine read 'Lady Elizabeth Campbell'. It ran almost the entire width of my chest, and if I turned sharply the laminated corner stabbed me in the shoulder. No-one ever called me Elizabeth; Elizabeth was a bothersome name. It started well enough, and the zed was deadly chic, but just as things were looking good it got ambushed by an enforced lisp and everything fell apart. It is small wonder that it has more shortenings than any other name: E, Eliza, Liza Bette, Betty, Bess, Bessie, Beth, Lily, Libby, Lezzer, Liz, Lizzie, Lilibet, etc. The badge made me feel that we were no longer at home on our holidays, but being paraded as these little exhibits my father had fashioned earlier, *Blue Peter* style.

For the first few days, Emma and I obediently wore ours and, as instructed by Pa, our kilts too. We felt self-conscious and ridiculous. It made us look like part of the management, and visitors bore down on us. We fielded their questions as best we could.

'Where is the Blasted Heath?'

'About seven miles east of here, near Brodie Castle.'

'Can we walk to Dunsinane from here?'

'Not unless you are hiking. It's fifty miles back down the A9, near Dunkeld.'

'What were the names of the three witches?'

'Oh. I don't know.'

'What d'you mean you don't know! You live in this castle. What d'you do all day, young miss?'

Emma gave me a nudge. 'Just make it up,' she mouthed, but I couldn't think of any convincingly witchy names, and anyway, the questions kept on coming.

'Who would have been King of Scotland if the Jacobites had won?'

'Um, well, Idi Amin is King of Scotland at the moment.'

'What utter codswallop! Now you're just being plain cheeky!'

But it was true. At least, according to Idi Amin it was true. He had proclaimed himself 'His Excellency President for Life, Field Marshal Al Haji, Dr Idi Amin VC, DSO, MC, Lord of All Beasts of the Earth and Fishes of the Sea and Conqueror of the British Empire in Africa in General and Uganda in Particular & King of Scotland'. Why Amin included the throne of a distant country in this splendid list is a puzzle in which logic has no function. Amin's rise to power by toppling his mentor did have echoes of Macbeth, although his murderous temperament did not need any encouragement from a wife – of which he had a few.

That night I lay in bed trying to come up with three names I could trot out if someone asked me the witch question again, and fell asleep trying out Rhiannon, Gudrun and Beathag ... Agatha, Hannah and Dot ... Lilibet, Lizzie and Bess ...

By the end of the week we were back in our jeans and had quietly dropped the badges into one of the many new litterbins. As soon as I was anonymous again the anthropological roles were reversed and I could roam about and indulge my furtive twin fixation. If I spotted twins, all I wanted to do was grab someone and whisper, 'Look! Twins!' like a twitcher spotting a pair of chanting goshawk.

My favourite perch was by a small window on the stairs leading from the Tower Room down to the Tree Room. On one of the little lead-latticed panes was a piece of two-hundred-year-old tagging. Pryse Campbell, the saucy one painted as a tartan-themed dog's dinner, had scratched his twirly signature into the glass with a diamond. From this position I could peer down on people coming across the courtyard to the front door. To my right was the Lochindorb yett, and to my left I could hear people scuffing down the stone spiral before I saw them.

I liked to look at people's faces and envisage the youthful face in an old one and the aged one in a child; to detect family similarities, and eavesdrop on exchanges like, 'Ooh, it's steep! You go ahead, Dermot, and tell me what's next.'

'Looks like a dead tree, Gran.'

'Well, I don't think I need to see one of *them*! I'm still trying to get Gramps to cut down those laurels.'

As I watched the world go by from my corner, I liked to imagine what kind of holiday the visitors were on. Was it the morbidly obese man in the leather catsuit and dog collar who was touring the Highlands on that Easy Rider Trike parked in the drive? Had those peevish-looking children with Art Garfunkel halo-hair absconded from the vile county of Kent? Did their fathers kick the furniture and cannon into passage walls at night too?

*

Every summer, the arrival of parachutes from out of the sky marked the launch of the Highland Games in Nairn. Canisters attached to the parachutists' heels belched coloured smoke as they spiralled down to a canvas landing apron in the main arena while a regimental pipe band marched around the perimeter playing Scottish standards. The bagpipes made the tunes blurry and sub-aquatic, but when the snare drum rolls came in, they sharpened up the sound just as a pair of goggles clears your vision underwater. Throughout the afternoon there were displays of the Highland fling to polite, rather than wild, applause. These dances were nothing like the reeling we did. Overdressed children in waistcoats, lace jabots and leather pumps pranced like nimble but enraged pixies in a complex hopscotch around two swords lying crossed on the floor. Maybe this is where Pa subconsciously picked up his anti-hex ideas. It was all taken very seriously, and there were endless heats. Finally, as the audience was drifting towards a collective nap, a cup would be awarded to some grandchild of Rumpelstiltskin. Far more exciting were the sweating, topless men, mostly itinerant New Zealanders, having shearing races. Huge, docile sheep were held deftly between the men's legs as they peeled away the fleeces to reveal skimpier, balder models that pronked skittishly away on release.

There were high jump and pole-vaulting events too, then the sudden appearance on the running track of scrawny men who, unbeknown to us, had been racing towards us in a bobbing filament from some anonymous field on the other side of the county. Burly men in kilts hefted cabers into their cupped hands and balanced them vertically with the help of a bulging shoulder. A few steps and then, if they could produce sufficient momentum, the pole was flipped onto its opposite end and into a lumbering somersault. The novices were easy to spot: they staggered about like a drunk making off with a keepsake from a sawmill. When they lost their balance, the caber would topple sideways with a thud and a sympathetic groan from the crowd. If you caught a glimpse of underwear, you knew you were watching a Sassenach. It was anathema to a Scot to wear anything beneath his kilt. A proper kilt had enough material so that however far the pleats swung out, you never saw their bits.

In a second arena there were flower displays and raspberry jam contests, pet races and sparklingly clean combine harvesters for sale. Farmhands in manila-coloured coats led outsize bulls wearing outsize nose rings to compete for the title of most fabulous beast. Some were creamy and sedate, others were piebald and mad-eyed, but neither type looked anything like the average joe bull seen in any pasture.

Best of all was the fair set up on the parade ground by the sea. We would have go after go on the waltzers, screaming for the sleazy-handsome boys to straddle the back of our chair and spin us faster, faster, faster until the g-force pinned us to the dirty velvet backrests.

The Nairn Games had been going for a hundred years, but similar Highland events had been held for almost a thousand, organized by Highland chiefs to give their clansmen a festival with a useful sideline: messengers were recruited from the fastest runners, bodyguards from the strongest, battle drummers from the musicians and castle entertainment from the dancers. Seeing the size of the crowds the modern Nairn Games drew, Pa inaugurated the Cawdor Games, in the hope of attracting more visitors to the castle. It started as a tiny affair, with a few races, a tug o' war and piano bashing, where teams would race to demolish two upright pianos into pieces small enough to pass through a small square frame. To the wild amusement of all the children watching, the pianos produced loud, discordant tunes as mallets thwacked the ivories. The star of the Cawdor Games was an Obelixian mink farmer called Hamish Davidson. He smashed pianos, threw curling stones, tossed cabers through the air, and soon found regular work on the hugely popular television programme *Britain's Strongest*. The show's champ was an ex-policeman called Geoff Capes, who had won the nation's heart with his ability to haul tractors and lug piles of paving stones. The two men became friends, and when Hamish invited Geoff up to the Cawdor Games there was a meteoric rise in audience numbers and Cawdor benefited accordingly. At the end of the season, when the figures were collated, Pa wrote excitedly that visitor numbers at the castle had gone up by 10 per cent, going against all other economic indicators 'except for the price of crude oil and the birth rate in Nigeria'.

My father adored Hamish. They drank in the same way, and when Hamish bought a Ferrari with his television earnings they jockeyed with each other whenever they met in the local lanes. Hamish's drinking kept getting him into trouble, and eventually he was caught out after ringing the local police station as he was leaving a bar in Nairn and daring them to catch him. The police could not outpace his car, but they easily outpaced his thinking. They made no attempt to chase him, but followed him at a leisurely speed, confident that there would still be plenty of alcohol in his bloodstream when they arrived at his house. On another occasion, he opened up all his cages just for the sheer bloody hell of it. Hundreds of mink ran amok in an undulating mass across his neighbours' farms, like a luxuriant plague, leaving countless dead chickens. Just as he quietly admired the Wolf of Badenoch, so Hugh thought Hamish's mink laying waste to neighbouring farms was all rather stylish. 'What chutzpah,' he kept murmuring.

For a couple of years we attempted to live at Cawdor while it was open. At night, the ropes were taken down and the room notes set aside so that the kitchen and dining room could be recolonized for dinner. As soon as the food was cooked, poor Edith had to clear up the kitchen to operating-theatre cleanliness in preparation for the visitors the next day. Moreover, at the time my father was going through an experimental food phase.

'Right,' he would say, 'I think we should see what all the fuss is about swans.'

'Oh please!' we would beg. 'A swan? Can't we just eat something normal?'

'Like what?'

We would all then chime in with food suggestions that we thought were exotic enough to grab his interest.

'Smoked eel.'

'Devilled kidneys.'

'Silverside?'

'Chops!'

'Dish dingers?'

When we won him round, it was, 'Good thinking! We'll have silverside, with gulls' eggs to start with.' When we lost the battle, he would get Edith to cook red squirrels (without announcing what they were – to keep our palates free from prejudice). Another time it was hedgehogs that were packed in clay so that their spines snapped off when it baked hard. Edith mumbled in horror at the smears of clay all over her kitchen and the horrible little cooked corpses that she had to serve up. When squirrel and hedgehog were on the menu, it became pretty obvious why they weren't in great demand, but they were more unpopular with us on compassionate grounds for Edith had artfully masked the taste with garlic and herbs. It seemed especially churlish for us to eat red squirrels when their numbers were already so depleted. North of the Grampians was one of the few places grey squirrels hadn't driven them out, so the last thing they needed was a mad earl with an avant-garde palate.

Supper was a meal the whole family came to dread, not because of the menu, but because it guaranteed our parents were confined to the same room. I longed for Aunt Carey to come and stay. I knew none of this would be happening if she were with us. Now when my father drank, he lashed out viciously as a matter of course. We were all in the firing line, but Cath took the most direct hits. She was stalwart and refused to react. Sometimes I thought her commitment to him was actually the very thing that was goading him and if only she would tell him to shut the fuck up he might actually comply . . . inshallah.

Ma's refusal to engage led to a change in tactics, and Pa's spotlight swung round and settled on Laura. She became the butt of his most vicious persecutions. The totality of her deafness in one ear was still undetected, so when anyone spoke to her on her hearing side she was animated and engaged, but if they were on her deaf side she was oblivious, and appeared to ignore them. For Laura, all conversations at the dining-room table were like watching a tennis match with a view of only one end of the court. She was an undemanding child, never loud or brattish, happy for hours on various important decorating jobs in her dolls' house or patiently colouring a picture. She had a placid self-containment – her logical response to a half-silent world. Hugh, however, would call his youngest daughter 'odious' and 'stupid' and would spitefully mock her, saying, 'Go on, make me laugh.' If Laura arrived for lunch in fancy dress – hardly unusual for a child of five – he would react with the same sort of distaste as if she'd vomited under the table. And when her little face crumpled in fear-filled confusion he would sneer, 'Got your period?'

At this point Cath could no longer ignore Hugh. She would leap to Laura's defence. This was her baby, whom she had spent long months watching over in hospital, who had so nearly died and who held a very precious place in our mother's heart. My father had spotted the chink in her armour and Ma was in the game now. Whenever she waded in to protect Laura, it only excited Pa to further extremes. One lunchtime it became too much for Emma to bear. She grabbed her fork and tried to stab Pa in the hand. She missed, but only just. He snatched his hand away just in time and the fork whacked into the tablecloth, drilling four neat holes. This was a truly daring affront. There was a stunned silence. Which way was Pa going to go? He already had a knife in his hand and we all knew exactly how sharp they were. Feeling that I must support her, I jumped up and yelped, 'You've got cancer of the soul!' It was the only time I ever stood up to him. And then we both legged it and hid in Lovat's Hole for the rest of the afternoon.

Lovat's Hole was a secret room under the eaves above our bedrooms. You could not reach it from inside the house, but had to pass through a low door onto the roofs and up a ladder, where a stepped gable hid its tiny entrance. It was named after Lovat, the chief of the Fraser clan who had sought refuge while being hunted for high treason after the Battle of Culloden in 1746. It had a little window that overlooked the front door so he could spot the English soldiers coming. It had been an effective hiding place during the brutal mopping-up operation after the disaster of Culloden, and it still was now.

If there was a handbook for Scots with advice on how to conduct a battle, Culloden would merit few entries. Sometimes, Pa would pull up the car on our way back from Inverness and walk us through the forestry plantation to find the burial mounds of the different clans and explain the messy disaster on the notorious battlefield so close to our home.

During the final showdown between the Scots and the English, the Cawdor Campbells found themselves in an invidious position. There were Campbell clansmen on both sides, and by the early spring of 1745 our family found themselves sandwiched between the two enemy armies. If they sided with Bonnie Prince Charlie, they would earn the enmity of the much more powerful Argyll Campbells who marched under the English flag; but if they sided with the royalists, and then Charlie's Highlanders won, Cawdor and its land would be slap bang in the middle of a victorious enemy army. The thane at the time was Joyless John, and he decided the only answer was to get the hell away. He hustled Pryse and his brothers off to Italy and retreated to Stackpole to catch up with some tutting and moody wall staring. While the decisive turning point in Scottish history was taking place on their doorstep, the young Cawdor Campbells were on a cultural Grand Tour, buying Venetian glass and comparing the prices of Neapolitan watercolourists.

The charismatic young Prince Charlie had achieved the near impossible: he had united the clans in their loyalty to him. The English responded to the uprising by sailing an army of eight thousand men up the east coast of Scotland to Aberdeen, ninety miles to the east of Inverness. The general in charge of the enemy troops was Bonnie Prince Charlie's own cousin, Prince William Augustus, Duke of Cumberland. Poor intelligence led Bonnie Prince Charlie to believe that Cumberland's army was half its actual strength, and a false sense of security pervaded his men when the royalists showed no signs of marching on Inverness. As the weather softened, many of the Highlanders took 'seedtime' leave. This thinning of Jacobite ranks was just the beginning of a sequence of events that led to the catastrophe at Culloden on 16 April 1746.

On 12 April Cumberland's army broke camp. Bonnie Prince Charlie assumed that the fast-flowing River Spey would act as a natural obstacle to the enemy's approach, but the water was unseasonably low, the English found fords in three different places, and they easily saw off a small Highland troop that had been sent out to harry them. The English set up camp outside Nairn. Bonnie Prince Charlie responded by marching his men out of their winter quarters in Inverness to await the enemy on Culloden Moor. Although he had chosen this site in advance, the long, gently rising slope was perfectly suited to cavalry and cannon – and these were the chief military strengths of the English, not the Scots. One of Bonnie Prince Charlie's Highland generals implored him to move their men across the River Nairn, to the opposite side of the valley. It was only a mile away, but the land there was far more rugged and rose sharply to a height of a thousand feet above the river. To engage Cumberland's men from this position would not only make a cavalry charge impossible and favour the Highland fighting tactics of close combat, it would allow their soldiers to melt away into the desolate expanse of hills behind if needs must. The young prince ignored the plea and listened instead to his French advisers who recommended a surprise nocturnal attack. The Duke of Cumberland's twenty-fifth birthday was on 15 April and they guessed that the royalist soldiers would have a drunken celebration.

This strategy might have worked, but a massive catering oversight meant that no rations had arrived from Inverness for the Jacobite troops since bivouacking at Culloden. After three days with nothing to eat, the Highlanders were starving and far from battle-ready. The situation was so dire that when all the stores had been scoured and emptied there was only enough food to hand out a single rough biscuit to each man – and this was meant to sustain them on the eight-mile night march to Nairn and then into battle. They were already outnumbered and outgunned by the well-fed English, who had been accompanied in their advance by relays of supply ships. Now a third of the soldiers deserted to scavenge for food.

Despite the food situation and the vanishing troops, Bonnie Prince Charlie persisted with the night march and marshalled the remaining Highlanders into two rather long, rather spindly columns. A dozen short, broad columns would have been capable of covering the ground much faster; in narrow columns, the front had to travel a considerable distance before the men at the rear could advance a single pace. In order to retain the element of surprise the columns zigzagged back and forth across country, slowing them even further. The night was pitch-black and unmooned, and there were soon hundreds of stragglers. By the time the head of the column reached the beech woods around Kilravock, men were quietly slipping away to sleep under the trees. The plan had been to cross the river here, using the same ford the Campbells had used when they kidnapped Muriel 250 years earlier. They would then march past Cawdor, re-cross the river parallel to Nairn and attack the English flank and rear. But it had taken most of the night to reach Kilravock and by two o'clock in the morning it was obvious that the Highlanders were in quiet pandemonium, and that they would never cover the ground ahead before daybreak. Instead of thrusting at his enemy with his men grouped like a pair of deadly javelins, Charles Stuart had a plate of mercury in human form. In fury and frustration, the attack was aborted. The troops trudged back to Culloden, hungrier, more exhausted, and now having lost any psychological advantage they might have gained by seizing the initiative. They arrived back at their starting point as dawn cracked across their failure. Despite the bitter cold, many just lay down in the open and slept. Yet more deserted in search of food.

By noon, word came that the English were approaching. There were more debates about making for the high ground to the south, but Bonnie Prince Charlie again refused. As the royalists neared the bottom of the long slope, the two armies fanned out in front of each other and Cumberland's men opened fire with cannon and artillery. The Highland ranks were thinned instantly, without even engaging their enemy in return. And the fusillade continued. The Scotsmen struggled to maintain their positions while waiting for orders to charge. They needed to be in close combat to wield their claymores; until they could do that, they were just standing targets. While his men took a terrible pounding, Bonnie Prince Charlie vacillated. Finally he sent an envoy with a briefing to charge, but the man was killed by a cannon shot and the message never arrived. In desperation, the Highland soldiers took it upon themselves to charge, but it was without any sort of co-ordination. They ran forward waving their swords and yelling their hearts out, and were cut to ticker tape. Bodies piled on bodies until they lay three and four deep. The whole calamitous encounter lasted just forty minutes. Superior technology won the day. As usual. Over one thousand Highlanders died. Among the dead were scores of unarmed day-trippers who had ventured out from Inverness to witness the unfolding drama. A piece written at the time described the aftermath:

> Immediately after the conclusion of the battle, the [English] men, under the command of their officers, traversed the field, stabbing with their bayonets, or cutting down with their swords, such of the wounded of the defeated party as came under their notice. This was done as much in sport as in rage; and, as the work went on, the men at length began to amuse themselves by splashing and dabbling each other with blood.*

Cumberland's intention was to put the Scots down so hard they would never rise up again. Bloody reprisals

*From *Chambers*, 6th edn, p. 258; *Scots Magazine*, vol. viii, p.192.

continued for five months under the order 'It will be no great mischief if all should fall.' Women and children were not exempt, and in Scotland the royalist general has been known as Butcher Cumberland ever since. For those left at Cawdor, the only thing to do was open up the house to the English troops as they came and went. While being expedient rather than rampantly principled, Joyless John probably saved Cawdor for the family.

After months on the run, Bonnie Prince Charlie was able to escape back to France, where he sank into alcoholism. His drunken excesses eventually alienated even the staunchest Jacobites. The English built the colossal and stunningly beautiful Fort George on a peninsula outside Inverness and for years after any murmur of dissent was met with extreme prejudice from the government troops garrisoned there. The only way Highlanders could express their affiliations was silently. When they drank to the king, they passed a finger over the top of their wine to indicate it was the king across the water they were saluting. And scores of young blades, like Pryse, saw it as their subversive duty to be recorded for posterity looking as if a tartan haberdasher had attacked them and won.

Chapter 12

Now I am cabined, cribbed, confined, bound in
To saucy doubts and fears.

Shakespeare, *Macbeth*, Act 4, sc.1

SCOTTISH SUMMERS WERE DOMINATED BY KILLING AND dancing. The only aspect that was markedly different from the previous centuries was that the killing was now confined to animals. When the young men came off the moor, they changed into their kilts and sporrans to dance with their hands in the air in imitation of the antlers on the stags they'd just been stalking.

If you gazed around any ballroom, you could see the distinctive livery of each clan and make the connections between brothers and sons and cousins and uncles and fathers by matching up the tartans of their flying kilts, and the women by the sashes tied across their bodies. Ma and Pa were both beautiful dancers, but being a sophisticate from the Welsh valleys, I initially loathed reeling. I considered it little more than esoteric prancing and stubbornly boycotted the reels, but eventually the boredom of not joining in wore me down. As I gradually came to understand the pattern repeats as we wove down the line of dancers, I started to love it. It was like being a crochet thread with a brain. Sometimes I even fantasized that it would be possible to modernize our parties if only we could try doing these same dances to contemporary music, but no-one was ever interested in trying out the Dashing White Sergeant to T. Rex. The bigger parties were amazingly old-fashioned and there was an unspoken etiquette to follow: no dresses above the ankle; men might remove their jackets only if they happened to slip off from a surfeit of sweat; men could clap and leap and holler, but a girl doing the same was viewed as off colour – she must move smoothly and avoid hearty skipping; newcomers who couldn't do the dances were quietly frowned upon for cocking up the flow. People drank copiously and then sweltered it all out again.

When we were old enough, we were allowed to go to the Northern Meeting in Inverness and do the round of formal balls in Skye, Perth and Oban. They were held in rooms lit by chandeliers and with specially 'sprung' floors so that the whole room bounced gently with the thud of six hundred feet stepping in time. The most old-fashioned of all the old-fashioned aspects was that you had to pick up a numbered dance card. It came with a printed running order of reels and an attached tasselled pencil. You filled it in if and when a boy came up and asked for a dance. He then noted you down in his and you sought each other out when the programme reached your booking. All the girls lived in terror of having an unmarked card. If Pa was my only entry, I would scribble anything – Godalming Flats, Red Corpuscle, Arc Welder – in light pencil so at least it didn't look as if I was a wallflower.

Writing such nonsense had an advantage when it came to the opposite end of the problem: you couldn't easily rebuff people you didn't like unless your card clearly looked full. I began to grade the reels on how much you touched your partner. The Reel of the 51st was the most flirtatious – best kept for someone who made your heart beat faster. Hamilton House gave you the least physical contact with your partner – good for dealing with mossy-handed boys. Speed the Plough was so impenetrably complex that it was seldom on the dance lists, but it would be included from time to time so that it did not slip entirely from our cultural canon. When it featured it was not just a clinically efficient passion douser, it could cause a novice not only to lose the will to flirt, but the will to live.

It all seemed so unutterably, endlessly innocent, but what did I know? Peep under the social lino of any county life and beneath you will find swarming sexual intrigue. The twin counties of Nairn and Morayshire were no different. As we moved away from childhood, it slowly dawned on us that gracious lifelong couplings were far fewer than we had presumed. Everyone gossiped about the landowner and the wife of his neighbour who went off together on extended diving trips every summer. This was a passion that ran along seasonal lines with rather admirable self-discipline. Another woman who tangled with almost every married man north of the Grampians, including Hugh, had Emma and me echoing 'Uncle' George's familiar refrain, mouthing 'From Genesis to Deuteronomy!' at each other whenever her name was mentioned. When she embarked on yet another affair, her new lover went to Asprey's and ordered a brooch that spelled out the splendid announcement 'I love fucking you' in diamonds. This became known only when the stricken lover came to my father in hysterics because the enormously expensive gift had got lost in the post. The man swore Hugh to secrecy, but he told us about it (without mentioning names) over lunch, laughing so hard that his claret came gushing out of his nose. I loved the idea of the dignified shop assistant charged with taking his order. 'Would sir like the phrase in a straight line, or in a circle? I could ask Mr Ledbetter if we could add an exclamation mark at a reduced price. You may like to look at an example we have made for another gentleman, which was inspired, I believe, by some art on a tree. Here it is, sir: "Sex is Fun", in emeralds.' I liked to imagine that the brooch had slipped silently from the postman's sack and lay unnoticed in the penumbra of a sub-post office until Mrs Harris started shutting up shop. I could hear her saying, 'Crikey Moses, what's that glinting down by 'yur? Dew! Must have come out of one of them foreign caramel creams.'

Tales like this were hilarious to me as a teenager, mostly because it was happening to 'other people'. When it came to my own father it was a different matter. I hated the arguments between my parents, which I could hear through the floorboards of my bedroom. I would lie in bed in a conflicted tangle of trying to ignore and straining to hear the names of the women mentioned. Our own burgeoning sexuality was, in turn, a source of quiet horror to my mother. When Emma lost her virginity, Ma took her aside and said sadly and solemnly, 'You've played your ace card.' From her viewpoint, chastity was a priceless coin to be sewn into a velvet pouch and locked inside an ironwood chest set on a high shelf, in a distant belfry, on a remote island, with no anchorage. Of course, she had reasons we knew nothing about. She had no control over her husband's sexual behaviour; maybe she felt a need to keep ours in check.

Thanks to Highland reeling, the job wasn't hard. For years, it was all one big chaste blank. I envied all my school friends, whose parties offered contemporary music, drinking cider and groping in the dark. Such debauchery was out of the question in Scotland when, far from being exclusively teenage, our parties were nearly all 'for the nine-to-nineties!' Rather than sloping off into the bushes between dances, everyone just sat about trying to catch their breath before the start of the next reel. While all my school friends appeared to have snogged several boys, I was having an agonizingly vestal time spinning to the sound of an up-tempo accordion. I fretted that not only would I die a virgin, I would never even experience what it was to be kissed. How the hell did you kiss? I had no idea. Did you move your tongue around like a gear stick? Did you just rest it there like a salmon in a pool? How did you breathe? Were there any rules? No-one would say.

Growing up was full of mortifications. I finally got kissed at the age of fourteen. The son of one of my mother's cousins came to stay and we exchanged smouldering looks

for a couple of days before he found me alone in the drawing room and invited me 'to go for a walk'. I knew what
that meant. I was more nervous than excited, not least
because moments before I had rammed a fistful of peanuts
into my mouth. I could only nod and follow him out across
the drawbridge, chewing as fast as I could. We crossed over
the burn and into the woods. As soon as we were out of
sight of the house, a damp hand clamped onto mine. He
went into a droning monologue about how he wanted to
follow his father's example and sell 'top of the range' sports
cars when he grew up. It never crossed my mind that he
might be nervous too; all I noticed was that he was being
astonishingly boring. The hand, the peanuts and the car
talk had annihilated any lust, and in a wan attempt to abort
the mission I took him on a path that cut back in a short
circuit through the rhododendron bushes. If I could get
him back within sight of the house, nothing would happen.
But then suddenly he said 'Hey!' loudly and urgently, as if
stung by a hornet. I turned in surprise and his mouth fixed
on mine. How come I could see his teeth? Lips, teeth,
tongue, saliva, teeth, nut particles, tongue, more teeth. It
was not a success. I ignored him for the rest of his stay.

A week later, we were all sitting around the breakfast
table watching a pair of red squirrels dancing across the
larches on the far side of the burn. We could always
tell if the squirrels were there, even if we couldn't
see them, because of the sudden shudders as they bounced
across the branches. My mother, who read through her
mail at breakfast, finished her grapefruit and
began reading out loud a thank-you letter. It was from

her cousin, and it went something very like this:

> Burble, burble . . . you must tell me how you grow those
> marvellous miniature yellow tomatoes . . . burble . . . can't
> believe how much stronger Laura looks now . . . burble,
> burble . . . & I'm so very sorry about the incident between
> Rupert and Liza in the woods. He is still very puzzled and
> upset because he feels she encouraged him, but he has
> given me his word that it will never happen again.

He told his *mother*? He'd treated my face like an ice cream
and then he'd snitched? And now she who must be kept in
the dark about these things was reading it out to the whole
family? I silently thanked God that Pa was still upstairs
nursing a hangover. Meanwhile my mother seemed
oblivious to my embarrassment; she even seemed to be
rather enjoying herself, as if this exposure might work as a
powerful tool against my trying anything so beastly again,
until well after my silver wedding anniversary. Not only
was this going to mean years of therapy, she had neatly
handed my head on a marmalade-smeared plate to Emma.
To her great credit, instead of mocking me Emma rolled
her eyes in a conspiratorial way, as if to say, 'Parents, eh?'
The only lasting fallout was that the name Rupert still gives
me the chills.

As a teenager, I longed for my mother to ease up a little
and for my father to do the opposite, but instead a new
secretary arrived. This Olga Nethersole had soon helped Pa
out of his trousers. My mother guessed what was happening when she noticed the girl wearing an identical necklace

to one Hugh had recently given her. Emma had seen them grappling with each other in a Range Rover, and I had overheard private laughter coming from behind the locked office door. None of us said anything, each of us thinking we were alone in carrying the secret.

When Cawdor opened to the public, my father installed huge floodlights. Before they were installed I could see Cassiopeia and the Pleiades in the night sky from my attic window, but no longer. Now when I went to bed my room was bathed in a sickly shade of municipal orange, against which my curtains were no match. It was strange: we were deep in the country, but it was like sleeping on a motorway slip road.

My bedroom was above my parents' suite of rooms and I would lie awake in the eerie tangerine twilight listening to my father shouting and slamming doors and praying that he would not hurt Ma. Like a terrified flyer, I stayed awake to check that the wings of their marriage were still on. But if they fell off, what was I going to do? I could never think of a plan. The racket would continue into the small hours, and then I would hear the glass rattle in its frame as the front door slammed shut behind Pa, the scrape of his footfall and the faintest chink of his shoe buckle as he crossed the courtyard below, then the clump of heavy feet on the timbers of the drawbridge as he made his way out to his vile lime-green Ferrari parked in the drive. When he screeched off, a new worry would start: what if he had another crash? The compressed carcass of his last E-type lay rusting in the garages, a neglected talisman. Once Pa had gone and I could no longer hear the engine dip as he shifted gears on the corners, the fretting faded into the bliss of silence and sleep would finally come. Peace.

There were nights when Pa had reached the falling-down stage and lacked the co-ordination to drive. When this happened, he would just sit at the wheel and rev the engine until it screamed. Other times he could not even make it out to the car and appeared at breakfast covered in grazes. He would explain that 'the drive came up and hit me'. He would look over at Ma and say sarcastically, 'What's eating you today? You look like a whited bloody sepulchre. Why are you looking at me like that? Did I *do* something?' In truth, he really had no idea. One morning he came down in his Tibetan dressing gown, bleary-eyed and unshaven, saying he had had the worst nightmare of his life, so terrible it still terrified him, even when he had woken up and realized it was a dream. He said a huge werepig with a russet pelt had chased him all over the house until he was cornered. In the end, he said, he knew he had to get out of bed and go down to his study to draw it. It was hard to imagine an animal more frightening than the ones in 'The Google Book', but I took his word for it. He said he couldn't show the drawing to anyone because it was so monstrous we would be haunted too. As he talked, Emma and I glanced at each other. In a tiny exchange we knew we were both thinking the same thing: the werepig had been with us for some time and had no plans to leave; it was the nocturnal part of him.

Soon after this, my father developed a virulent strain of eczema. He had deep, tickly fissures between his fingers

230

and on his throat that got inflamed every time he shaved, and the itching drove him mad. Or the madness made him itch. Either way, his flesh was in torment. For a while, the subject of his affliction took over in his letters as he searched for a cure. His skin doctor, a tiny, twinkling hunchback, tried to guide him through the maze of irritants. Comments like 'Your observation about deterioration of the skin condition when you gave up cigarettes may be quite valid' endeared him greatly to my father. The 'cure' turned out to be only a short respite and the eczema soon returned – on his testicles as well as a stigmata rash across the palms of his hands.

Now when Pa turned on Ma it was physical. One afternoon he thumped her so hard she got whiplash. Acting without any provocation, he hid behind her bathroom door and waited there until she had finished freshening all the flower vases around the house and had gone in to wash her hands. As she leaned over the basin, he clouted her on the side of the head.

Another day he hid again and then cornered her with one of his samurai swords drawn. 'I'm going to chop you in half,' he hissed. Thatch had helped him learn how to handle knives, but an unarmed wife was clearly not quite the target the aikido master had intended. Cath fled the room and searched the house until she found another adult. Her saviour came in the unlikely shape of Martin Newell, an artist friend who had come to Cawdor to paint a mural on Emma's bedroom walls. Pa had commissioned Martin as much for his painting style as for the fact that he was almost permanently pissed. As things grew increasingly confused during the course of any given day, Martin would woozily dip his paintbrushes in his whisky glass rather than the glass of turpentine. The entire mural reeked. Martin rose unsteadily to the occasion, calmed Cath and, when he strolled in ten minutes later, rounded on Hugh. 'What the hell d'you think you're playing at, man?' Pa looked at him in surprise and then stared blankly at my mother. He asked her why she was crying. Such amnesia was commonplace. When people talked about blackouts, I thought it meant someone falling unconscious, not someone so drunk that they went on functioning while the cognitive, mindful part of their brain had shut down.

The craziness started to seep out of Cawdor. The first sign of a leak was when Cath went off to a local drinks party on her own one evening after Pa had refused to go with her, predicting it would be tedious. Half an hour later, however, he strode into the party as Cath was chatting to a group of friends in the middle of the room. He got straight down on his knees and started yanking at the rug she was standing on, trying literally to pull the rug out from under her feet. After a moment of simple maths – the great expanse of rug, the large number of people anchoring it – it became obvious that his plan had fundamental flaws, and he stormed off. He did not utter a single word throughout. When he came home, he found his three oldest children watching television in the Blue Room. Still nursing a frustrated desire to intimidate, he gave the television such a kick that he broke his toe. The Blue Room fireplace had a carved stone cipher that read 'Feare the Lord'. As he landed the screen a pointless thwack, the message suddenly seemed less biblical incitement than a warning to Hugh's nearest and dearest.

I prayed that my mother would find the strength to leave him and these increasingly demented attacks, but she did not. Nor did she see it that way. To her, leaving would be a defeat, though it took all her courage to stay. I tried to tell her how frightened I was for her, but Ma always tried to rationalize the situation with a cock-eyed perspective born out of extended exposure to Pa's irrational excesses. She drew comfort from the fact that she didn't draw his fire exclusively. 'He often lashes out at other people; it isn't always at me,' she would say. She didn't know how nutty she had begun to sound when she said she really did not think things were that bad and Pa's behaviour was only a little blip. Her optimism came from the sudden, unexpected lulls in the storm when he would sit close to tease her as she sat in front of the fire, knitting us long winter scarves. As her needles clicked, he would playfully wrap the finished end around his face until only his eyes showed. This was a glimpse of the old Hugh. There would be no edge to his humour. He would walk around humming, hold my mother's bird-like hand, call her Puddock and dance with her. My friends were appalled when their parents danced, but I adored it when mine did. And by the time they reached their eighteenth wedding anniversary they were happy enough to have a party in celebration.

Chapter 13

When the lamb they is lost on the mountain, they is cry.
Sometime come the mother. Sometime the wolf.

Cormac McCarthy

TOWARDS THE END OF THE 1970S A SERIES OF UPHEAVALS
changed the family landscape for ever. Four key figures
went and four new ones were thrust into our midst, all of
them women. I cannot now remember in what order they
happened; I can only recall them in terms of rising impact.

The first to leave was Edith. Even though she was a
quiet, introspective loner, Edith was the only person who
had made the transition from Golden Grove to Cawdor
with us. She connected us back to happy times in Wales.
While all the other staff had upped and left, she had been
our one constant. Edith had never really assimilated into
local life, however, and had pined for her home on the
banks of the Towy all the years she was in Scotland. For

someone whose nervous disposition was so profoundly ill suited to the goings-on at Cawdor, Edith had shown remarkable tenacity. She had survived by tucking herself away and carving a separate existence within the house, her presence hardly ever being anything more tangible than a disembodied voice behind the green baize door of the dining-room hatch. There was no goodbye party – her nerves weren't up to it – so my parents had a quiet sherry in the sitting room with her while she sat slumped in a chair clutching her handbag, on the brink of a turn. The last I saw of her was a sodden handkerchief waving out of the train window as the sleeper pulled out of Inverness station, taking her away from us for ever. As the train climbed the hill towards Culloden Moor and vanished into the trees, I wondered how many of her salty tears had flavoured our food over the years.

Next was Granny Wilma. She got ill and died quickly. My father did not go off to be with her. A stroke killed her, brought on by an incident a few days earlier when the poor woman had lashed out at one of her nurses in an exasperated fury. She had cracked under the unendurable strain of having to listen to pleasantries peppered with persistent grammatical blunders. We were in the Tower Room when Pa took the telephone call.

'Is she dead?' I asked as he replaced the receiver.

'As a ruddy doornail,' he replied. As if she was a parrot in a comedy sketch.

I didn't know what to feel. I looked to my father to give me an emotional lead, but there was nothing. She was my grandmother, but I had never had a normal grandchild relationship with her, had not seen her for a couple of years, and in that time my father had never made reference to her; she was a closely related stranger. Nevertheless, she represented a large chunk of the family tree closest to us.

We are all equal in front of the Lord, but not in his graveyards. As an ex-wife, Wilma was not allowed to be buried at the Cawdor kirk. She had requested to be buried at Daviot, a tiny church near Inverness. Uncle James brought her home on the overnight sleeper. I said to my father that I was worried about what an ordeal it would be for James, on his own, knowing his mother's body was lying in a coffin in the guard's van as the train rattled its way north. Pa gave me a look like I was an idiot and replied briskly, 'Oh no, it's only a small casket – they grilled her first.' We buried her ashes in Daviot graveyard with Pa glancing impatiently at the minister, as if the man was a trainee bank clerk being frustratingly slow in completing a very basic transaction. There were six of us at her funeral. On the way home I said, 'Are you very sad?' He did not reply. 'Didn't you love her?' He gave a tight little smile. It was hardly encouraging; it followed that if he failed to feel love for the woman from whom he had come, what was to stop him doing the same to us, who came from him?

Of all the losses, the next one was the most unexpected. One sultry day in summer, we were drinking coffee in the Tower Room after lunch when the telephone rang. As soon as my father picked up the receiver, an instinctive hush came over the room. It was obvious from the way Pa was listening that this was not a routine call. It was Uncle Peebles ringing from Spain; something had happened to

Aunt Carey. We could hear only one end of the conversation, but Uncle Peebles was plainly worried. He and Pa talked for a long time and we slowly picked up the details of an accident. They were on the way back from seeing his parents in Majorca . . . they had stopped off with friends in Cadaques . . . Carey had tripped and fallen over a garden terrace . . . she was in a hospital . . . her ankles were broken . . . she might have chipped her coccyx . . . there was something wrong with her blood . . . her kidneys . . . the cottage hospital was run by nuns . . . it was ill-equipped . . . he needed help getting her back . . . she needed English doctors . . . it was an emergency.

Pa placed the receiver back on its cradle with a heavy sigh and stood looking at it for a few moments. At first, he thought Peebles was panicking unduly – broken ankles did not sound too bad – but several calls later it was clear that the situation was grave and getting worse. For the next couple of days my father tried to organize a flight to bring his sister home, while France was paralysed by an air traffic controllers' strike. An air ambulance was chartered, but getting permission to cross the disputed airspace was an unbearably slow process. An increasingly desperate Uncle Peebles kept Pa informed as Carey's condition deteriorated. At last the plane got the go-ahead. Peebles took their daughter Boojum and set off ahead by car. Alexander, who had just turned fourteen, stayed behind to accompany his mother. Carey died as the plane arrived at the Spanish airport. She was forty-two. The plane crew flew her back to Scotland, but instead of taking her to a hospital they brought her to Cawdor to be buried.

Throughout her life Carey had been Hugh's intellectual sparring partner; his older sister and boss lady; his strongest stabilizing influence. He turned his mourning inward. I knew that he had no love for Wilma and that he had adored Carey, yet there was no discernible difference in his reactions to the two deaths. I never saw him cry. I never heard him reminisce. With both his parents dead, Thatch gone and now Carey dead, fate had left Hugh answerable to absolutely no-one. Carey's death was not only incredibly sad for all of us, it triggered a chain of events that was to shatter the family.

Within a year, Uncle Peebles had met and married a beautiful young widow. My father did not react well to Carey being replaced and took it out on Peebles's new wife. They were no longer invited to stay at Cawdor and consequently neither were Boojum and Alexander. Emboldened by the exclusion of the Friesen family, Hugh did the same to his brother's family. James had divorced his wife Bridget and remarried, but Hugh had taken a dislike to his new wife as well. 'Why the hell do they remarry?' he would growl, and now James was welcome to stay only if he came alone. Slaine and Cara, the daughters from James's first marriage, were cut adrift too, and we saw them very sporadically. None of us even met Sarah and Lucy, the two daughters of his second marriage, until they were teenagers. Suddenly, from acting as the stage for our extended family gatherings, Cawdor was fenced off. No-one else had a house big enough to have everyone to stay, so our family connections began to unravel.

Cath protected us as best she could, but who was there to

protect her? Who were the men of the family who would stand up for her? There were none. Her father was so deaf that conversation was almost impossible. He did not have the smallest idea of what his son-in-law was up to. Her only brother, Bill, had the mind of a child. No-one took Drunkle Uncle seriously; 'Uncle' George, he of the sponging from Genesis to Deuteronomy, was far too toadying to consider challenging Hugh; Pa's younger brother James was hardly ever around; and, although he loved Cath, Uncle William at Altyre was too much of an ally and spree partner to fight her corner. Uncle Peebles was older and possessed of an innate authority, but he came north even less often than James did since the froideur over his remarriage. The uncomfortable truth was that there really was something different about how otherwise level-headed people viewed my father. His status gave him leeway, a *droit de merde*. What I once admired as a cool, laid-back approach to life among the adult men in our family looked more and more like a moral vacuum.

Business boomed, and as Cawdor got busier and more crowded it became harder to use it as a normal home during the months it was open. Whenever we took short cuts against the flow of the people, we found ourselves being touched gently on the arm by motherly tourists and asked if we were lost, or told off by those with traffic-flow issues: 'You're going the wrong way, pet.' Everything had to be kept meticulously tidy in the house, as if we weren't there, which was ironic, because the signs of our presence were a large part of what people said they enjoyed about

239

visiting. So many houses open to the public have room after room of anodyne orderliness and a dreary deadness. The visitors liked the fact that Cawdor was a real family home strewn with our books and photographs.

One summer holiday the numbers at Cawdor picked up to such an extent that we moved across the moor to stay at Drynachan. While there, Pa began expanding his collection of stuffed animals in glass cabinets that lined the walls of the sitting room. There was a snarling wildcat, a pair of ptarmigan in their white winter plumage and two oriental pheasants with long wedding-dress trains of scimitar-shaped feathers. Pa had just taken delivery of a golden eagle when I wandered into the room. He asked me what I thought of this latest acquisition. I went and had a closer look and, for want of anything better to say, asked him if he'd bought it at auction.

'No,' he said. 'I had it shot.'

I was appalled. Eagles were an incredibly rare sight.

'That's illegal!' I spluttered.

'Don't be so bloody bourgeois,' he snapped.

'What? But you wouldn't kill an osprey, would you?'

'They're endangered.'

'Which makes eagles vermin?'

'Oh, go boil your head,' he said.

I left the room in a rage and reported the incident to Emma. 'At least he's not making us eat it,' she replied with a shrug.

Towards the end of that summer Emma's first serious boyfriend came up from London to stay at Drynachan, but given the crepuscular direction in which Pa's mood was heading the day after Charlie's arrival, we decided it would be best to retreat to the Gordon Cummings' for supper. It was a lovely evening and we arrived back at Drynachan in the early hours. The keeper's dog gave a couple of warning barks as we drove past its kennel at the top of the drive. A few rabbits skittered away across the lawn as we approached the house and pulled up.

The first thing that struck an odd note was that the front door was ajar. It was possible that Pa was out walking his dog Sandy, but our headlights would have picked them out, and besides, my father hated us leaving the door open because the wind was apt to fling it shut with a mighty slam, or sheep would wander in, or a hundred thousand bugs and moths would arrive to conduct their fatal worship of the light bulbs. He was always shouting, 'Shut. The bloody. Door!' However pissed he might be, it was not like him to leave it open.

As we crossed the little yard in front of the house, we could see that the glass in the door was smashed. Our conversation came to an abrupt halt. We looked at each other and wavered, before Charlie quietly pushed the door wide and we stepped into the hall. It looked like there had been a burglary. Lamps, vases and chairs were tipped over, belongings lay everywhere and clothes were flung down the length of the staircase. When we got to the foot of the stairs, I realized that the mess was not indiscriminate: everything belonged to Ma. The chaos suggested noise, and lots of it, but the house was utterly silent. We followed a thin trail of blood along the carpet towards the sitting room. I could barely breathe; it had finally happened. I expected to find my mother lying dead on the floor in front of the fire, or slumped half on, half off the sofa, her hair covering her beautiful, battered face. None of us said anything. All I could hear was the banging of my pulse and the sound of air rushing in and out of my body.

We got to the sitting room and Charlie gingerly pushed the door open. My father was nursing what looked like a pint of whisky. He had his back to us and was staring out of a broken window pane at the star-spattered night. He did not turn his head when we came in. Charlie cleared his throat nervously. 'Are you all right, sir?' No reply. I saw that the back of Pa's trousers were ripped to the knee and was swept with relief: maybe the trail of blood was his and not hers.

We left him where he was and went looking for Ma. We took it in turns to peer round the doors into each room along the length of the long passage leading back to the stairs. In the hush, I suddenly realized that just because it was not her blood, it didn't mean that she had not been killed. Maybe he had throttled her. None of us dared call out in case we woke the Smalls.

We came across my mother upstairs. She had heard us coming and was making a frantic effort to tidy their bedroom before we found her. It was completely trashed.

'Are you all right?' Charlie asked.

She gave a quick nod, face turned to the wall.

'There's blood downstairs,' I said.

'It's Pa's, I think,' she said, trying to steady her voice amid heavy, stifled sobs, and answering as if we might be discussing a lost shoe. My father had been kicking in all the windows; he had gashed his leg on the glass. Ma moved around the room with difficulty, her neck and an arm held stiffly, as if in pain. We tried to help, but she ushered us out. 'No. Go to bed. Please.'

'What happened?'

'Nothing, really. Really. Nothing. Go to bed.'

She could not bear to be seen so wretched. Pa had wrenched her neck, dislocated her shoulder and given her an aikido chop under her nose that had cracked the roots of her front teeth. I was just so relieved that she was alive I felt almost happy.

Just when we thought our holiday could not get any more gruesome, it did, after a visit to a house on Loch Ness. Our host lived almost halfway along it, a fifty-mile drive for lunch. I always found the loch a horribly oppressive place, a long, deep slit in the land where the dark water is as deep as the steep hills soaring up on either shore are high. Because there were seven of us, we normally travelled separately. Pa boy-racered off in his Ferrari on his own; Ma hauled the rest of us. At the end of an afternoon of gut-straightening cocktails, Pa offered a lift to a girl who was one of our fellow guests. He set off before us, but arrived home two hours after us, tousled and smudged with lipstick. His attempt at some high-speed grooming as he approached the front door was ineffectual. It was obvious what had gone on.

Cheating on one's spouse is not the mark of a magnificent human being, but this girl was way, way off limits. She was our age; she'd been messing around with us at lunch, not him. She was at Emma's school and we knew her family really well. It had never felt as if the family had been more ruthlessly subjugated to his libido than when I saw him in his School Olga disarray. I felt ashamed, and not merely of Pa. It felt like there was enough shame to spill over all of us.

Emma had a far more robust attitude to Pa. In the small hours of one night, he buzzed her telephone and summoned her to his study. Cretinized by drink, he gave her a long, maudlin lecture about how all he wanted to do, all he really wanted to do with his life, was 'take the clothes off beautiful women'. She got up mid-polemic and left the room. 'Take a cold shower!' she called over her shoulder as she padded back upstairs, shrugging off the whole incident as a passing nuisance.

The next spring holidays Pa pitched up in my bedroom in the middle of the night. He shook me awake and told me to come to his bed. He was dressed in the heavy Tibetan robe that had belonged to Jack. For a groggy moment I could not pull away from the mittened fist of sleep to grasp what he was saying. When he repeated the order, I was panic-stricken; the werepig was in my room. All I wanted to do was say 'No!', but at sixteen I simply did not have the emotional vocabulary. The technicalities of a blunt rejection were quite beyond me. I had always done what he told me, and so I did this time. I trudged after him down the stairs, unhappier and lonelier than I had ever felt before.

My parents' bedroom had never been a place we went to

when we were ill or had nightmares. It was too long a trek in the pitch dark from any of our bedrooms. Our Christmas morning ritual was the solitary incursion into their privacy here. The room had last been decorated at a time when they fitted tapestries rather than carpets. The bedroom door was concealed behind a tapestry, so when it was shut there was an unbroken panorama of woven murals.

We reached my parents' four-poster. I could see that only one side of it was disturbed. I kept wondering where the hell my mother was. Had Bluebeard killed her this time? I perched on the furthest edge of the bed – my mother's side. Last time I had sat there it was to open my stocking; now Pa told me to lie under the covers. I got under the damask bedspread, but he told me to get between the sheets. 'I said, get *in*.' I did as I was told. He lurched round to his side of the bed, but as he reached forward to pull back the blankets he gave out a little slack-jawed groan; his eyes rolled back in his head and he collapsed across the bed, spark out. I wriggled away faster than an eel, sped over to the tapestry and fumbled clumsily for the hidden door latch. I raced up the spiral steps to the attic floor. Logic told me that he wasn't chasing me, but panic wouldn't believe it. Back in my room, I pulled jumpers off shelves and dresses off hangers to make a nest, pulled the door shut and slept in my cupboard for the remainder of the night.

It is not what happens to you but how you react that matters. I went over and over the scene in my head. I knew Emma would have handled herself better. She would have been able to see him off and be sleeping soundly five minutes later. For weeks afterwards I was terrified he would return, or go for Emma, without my having warned her because I was too freaked out to say anything to anybody. To this day, the incident remains enigmatic. I don't know what he intended. Maybe it was just a pre-dawn cuddle, but even that would have fallen far short of being welcome. Pa never mentioned it again and nor did I. Until my mother brought it up three years later.

Into this train-wreck of a home life came ploughing a new character. It turned out to be our future stepmother.

Summer at Drynachan had become a fixture for us, so Sheila de Rochambeau had rented the neighbouring castle of Dalcross. She invited my parents, Colin – who had just graduated from being a Small – Emma and me over to dinner. It was always a relief to go out because even though Pa got drunk, he could be charming and urbane in company. People invariably enjoyed Pa's witty anecdotes, but having listened to them on dozens of occasions it felt like we were quietly pedalling on a hamster wheel of his humour.

Unusually, on this night we were all together in one car. We barrelled the few miles across undulating farmland, past Kilravock Castle and through a bare-earthed beech wood where so many Highlanders had spent their last night alive before Culloden. Dalcross Castle is small and beautiful and the closest stronghold to the battlefield. It is reputed to be haunted by a boy soldier from that time. After the rout, dozens of the defeated Highlanders fled to Dalcross, but in the chaos of retreat the heavy front door was left unbarred. They only realized this when royalist soldiers raced into the courtyard after them, and the young boy rushed back to secure the bolts. They shot him as he ran down the stone staircase, leaving his spirit to try to complete the task in perpetuity. People who are sensitive to such things say that they can feel the ghost shoving past. With the boy dead and the door open, the Highlanders were rounded up, marched to a nearby barn and barricaded in, along with other wounded men who had crawled in there for sanctuary. Cumberland's men set the thatch alight, and thirty-two were burned alive. Whenever I visited Dalcross as a child, I would stand on the staircase nervously hoping to feel an ethereal draught as the boy passed clean through me.

We arrived in time for drinks before dinner and joined a party of about fifteen in the first-floor drawing room. Among them were faces we knew, like Sheila's twins Eric and Marc, with their matching scars now faded to white, but mostly the guests were strangers. There were a diminutive Greek and his girlfriend, and a tall woman with hennaed hair and formica-white skin. Her name was Angelika Lazansky.

When dinner was announced the party went into the dining room, where a buffet was being served. My father and Angelika took their food into another room and I did not see him again until we were having coffee. Pa had long blithely ignored my mother's feelings, but had always made some attempt at behaving properly in front of his children. But not this time. Ma did her best to relax everyone with a show of dignified composure, but a stilted air of embarrassment hung over all the guests for the entire evening. Her

247

attitude was that the only possible response to bad manners was a display of good ones; I wanted her to stand up, make a scene. But that was never my mother's style. I was furious with her for doing nothing, saying nothing. Of course, I was furious with the wrong person.

When we left, we left together, but it was obvious that Pa was annoyed that he had not come in a separate car. As we made our way down the haunted staircase, I prayed that the boy would be there to pitch him onto his face.

Chapter 14

By the time you swear you're his,
Shivering and sighing,
& he vows his passion is
Infinite, undying –
Lady, make a note of this:
One of you is lying.

Dorothy Parker

AS THEIR MARRIAGE IMPLODED IN SLO-MO, MY PARENTS had far too much to cope with on the domestic front to keep up with the details of five different school careers. I suddenly realized that not only had they taken their eyes off the ball, they hadn't even bought tickets to the game. Seizing the moment, I told them I planned to leave Cobham and would do my A levels in one year, at a crammer. It was great. They did not notice I was bunking off a year early without a single plan for the future.

I had no idea what I was good at or how to get a job; all I knew was that I sure as hell wasn't going to be showing people how to tie a life-jacket correctly as they flew above the world's landmasses or murmuring, 'Chicken or fish?' while dressed in a red tabard. It was holidays for ever – wasn't it? All I needed was to pass my driving test and gain full physical independence. When I passed, Pa's congratulations came in a letter with the usual advice for if and when I got a car, that I should look for one with good brakes: 'as your face is your fortune, it is important to keep it (and your neck) intact'. He went on to wonder if I could afford to run such a car, and concluded I should look for a 'rich lover'.

Before I fully achieved independence, the end came for Hugh and Cath. The combined loss of Edith, Wilma and Carey paled into insignificance compared to the moment when our mother finally left. In the midst of all her misery, a man came along and paid court to Cath, someone who saw her as a dreamy beauty who should be treated like a queen. The affair was over almost as soon as it had started, but Pa went wild. *He* was the philanderer, she was the long-suffering faithful one; it was an outrage. His anger towards her was brutal and sustained until at last she could take no more and moved out.

I do not remember how I learned of the *coup de grâce*; it was certainly not something that was announced by them as a united front. I think they both just hoped it would all segue smoothly from marriage to divorce without the need for query or comment. Because Hugh and Cath were so reluctant to speak to us about the upheaval, I felt tongue-tied and frightened that I would upset them by raising the subject. There were other girls at school whose parents had divorced, but we were all too young to articulate our shared distress in ways that were helpful. Mostly we just got into trouble with our course work and cried a lot. A typical conversation would go as follows:

'How were your holidays?'

'Bit rubbish really.'

'Why?'

'My parents split up.'

'Oh. Mine did that last year.'

'How was it?'

'Really awful. You?'

'Same.'

'I've got Science in a minute. See you.'

'See you.'

Ever since we had walked through the silent and smashed-up rooms at Drynachan, I had lived in dread that Pa would one day kill Ma. At least now I knew that would not happen; but neither would the fierce fantasy of a return to the happy family I remembered from Wales be fulfilled. We were emotionally adrift. I came to dread Ma's friends ringing to console her. I tried not to listen as she talked to her friends on the telephone, especially the litany of women who had been sharing our family life, but it seemed all the details I wanted to forget immediately were the things that stuck like cat prints in concrete. As far as my father was concerned, any serious discussion of our parents' separation was absolutely unwelcome. The only time he even mentioned it was two lines in a letter: 'Don't be glum or sad, nor waste your time brooding about Ma & me, etc.; it's a dull patch, and no fun, but it will pass into oblivion.' Emma seemed to shrug it all off in a world-weary way, and my three younger siblings seemed too young to have a conversation about it. We all carried on as five separate satellites, uncertain how to orbit separate moons. Communications with parental command had gone from the deafening static of the last few years to a cavernous silence. While my mouth stayed shut, my subconscious worked overtime with the arcane manifestations it was prone to. For a whole term I awoke, gasping in panic, as the same Cold War dream visited night after night. I was about to die. A nuclear bomb was about to fall on the school, but because nobody had told me I had not evacuated with the other girls.

Now that Cath no longer had to withstand the marital attrition, the reality of what she had been putting up with crashed down on her. She was wrenched away from her busy life as the hostess of Cawdor, and from all her friends in Scotland. Worst of all, she still loved Hugh. She hoped that one day they would be able to sit down and put the past behind them. I prayed that they would not; there was too much blood under the bridge already. Second worst of all was that despite her obvious hurt, Pa immediately bought himself a pied-à-terre a block away from her new home in London. His flat was, moreover, on the ground floor facing the street, so unless she wanted to make a fifteen-minute detour she had to face the possibility of bumping into him every time she left the house.

Even though we now had this strangely cluttered

London set-up, it was hard to know how Hugh's playboy lifestyle, unfettered by the encumbrance of a wife, was going to fit us in, or even if he had the desire to do so – and if he did, whether I would feel safe with him knowing that Cath was no longer in the wings. To my surprise and relief, he did not cut us adrift. Although he still never came to school, we flew up to Scotland regularly and saw him whenever he came to London. Hugh was always in a better mood when out on the prowl and far away from the mechanics of estate management. Now that he was single he was apt to draw us into his view of women.

As we walked down the street he would say, 'Great tits! Did you see them?'

'No.'

'She looked French. Terrible bra though.'

'Oh.' His enthusiasms made me squirm.

Instead of any heartfelt talks, we would go to exhibitions and movies, but never to the theatre, which he loathed and despised. Granted, the frisson that comes from witnessing genuine dramatic art is far rarer than reviews suggest, but Pa's rejection was total. I don't believe he ever saw a single production of *Macbeth*. It was an odd hole in his cultural life. He preferred to take us out to eat in one of his clubs, and was tickled when waiters ushered us to a discreet corner of the restaurant having mistaken Emma and me for Olga Nethersoles. I hated the idea of waiters thinking I was his underage lover and expressly called him 'Pa' as loudly and as often as possible. After an aeon spent over dinner he would shunt back his chair, prise himself upright and stand there, swaying like a palm tree. By this time several fags would be alight, one in his mouth, one in his hand and another smouldering in the ashtray. Arm in arm, we would stagger into the street where he would hail a cab with a deafening lost-dog-on-the-moor whistle using two fingers from each hand, like panpipes made flesh.

He could be wonderful, mischievous company, but as a parent he would only very occasionally proffer verbal advice. It rarely went further than seat belts and complaining that I didn't wear enough lipstick. Now that he no longer had Cath to whom to delegate the duller parental duties, he did his best to pass them on to his daughters. And we were to tell Colin to get on with his driving lessons or doctor's appointment, and to remind him he couldn't just come 'goofing up here on the spur of the vagueness & expecting the right petals to fall off the tree'.

To begin with, I was extremely nervous about spending time at Cawdor without Ma there. I was not *more* frightened of Pa coming to my bedroom now she was gone, because she was nowhere to be found on the previous occasion. What did frighten me was the idea of Pa losing his temper without her there as a buffer. But it was soon clear that Cawdor was a relaxed place to be for the first time in as long as I could remember. Pa had always been able to reinvent himself in his letters, and now that Ma had gone he had another stab at reinvention beyond the pen. His extramarital life, always hectic, now came out into the open. His temper was once more under control, and four girlfriends – Catherine Schell, Ginny Fass, Gay Close and Angelika – came to stay in the swift rotation of a boil wash. What amazed me, having been witness to his excesses for so

long, was that any of these women should want to go any-
where near him. As their visits became regularized, it
became apparent that Hugh did not know any of them well
enough to pull up the boulder of his personality and show
them the underside. We all benefited from that.

Catherine Schell was not only our mother's namesake, she
looked uncannily similar. She was like an echo of Ma – as
if Pa couldn't quite shake off what had fascinated him in
her and had found comfort in a replica. She had a gentle,
rather impenetrable character and her interest in tarot and
telepathy fascinated him; the Betty episode had convinced
him of his own occult sensibilities. He told us that she came
from a German aristocratic family who lived in Hungary.
Her father had been a successful diplomat, but the Nazis
confiscated their estates and they escaped to America. After
the war, her family moved to Munich, but by then
Catherine had forgotten her native tongue and she wound
up in England.

Catherine had played a love bunny called Tracy Draco in
the Bond film *On Her Majesty's Secret Service*, but she never
mentioned to us she was an actress. We had no idea what
she did until we turned on the television one evening
and she appeared wearing a spangly blue catsuit with
reptilian bumps across her forehead, playing a seductive
alien life force called Maya in *Space 1999*. She said that,
given her upbringing, it had been apt casting. 'I am an
alien. Wherever I go I can't feel that I really belong.' Long
after she had left our lives, we heard that she had retired
from acting and had gone off to run a guesthouse in

France. It seemed fitting that as someone who felt she was a foreigner in every country she had settled in a new one with the role of making fellow travellers welcome.

Gay Close was by far the youngest of the four. I was into making anagrams of everyone's names at the time so she became known as Easy Clog. She was in her early twenties, an open-faced, textbook beach blonde with a sunny, optimistic nature who was flattered to be spoiled by a rich older man. He described her in a letter as 'a dear person, totally devoid of bullshit'. Pa would whisper that she was an 'illy' – adopted – and he decided that her biological father was most probably an aristocrat. After Ma left, his interest in people's social standing grew more pronounced, and if they didn't have a title but he liked them, he tended to make one up for them.

Ginny Fass was a small, jolly woman – not an immediately obvious choice for Pa, but intelligent, maternal and a fine sommelier, something which impressed him immeasurably. Unusually for Pa, a friendship had developed before the affair began. Although Pa normally liked obviously glamorous women, in Ginny he had stumbled across something else. Her character bore comparisons to Aunt Carey. She would not put up with a jot of nonsense from him. She was happy to stand her ground when they disagreed, and she was the only one of the four who seemed to be sensitive to the fact that the family baggage trolley was piled high and that the children of his marriage might be feeling frail. When Fred and Laura came up to stay for their half-term, she was shocked when Hugh ordered them off to bed at the far end of the house and refused to accompany them. They were still young enough to dread the idea of a long corridor to a dark wing. When she pointed out that they were not dawdling because they were naughty, but because they were frightened, he ignored her, so she took them under her wing, tucked them into bed and told them that if they had any problems in the night they were welcome to come to her room. She slept in her own room rather than share Hugh's bed that night, in case they did. This kindness instantly won us all round. Her intelligence and innate goodness meant we all liked her tremendously, and for a long time it was a great relief to us that she seemed the most serious of all Hugh's girl-friends. He would occasionally say to us, 'I'm never going to get married again, but I can see Ginny as my long-term companion.' We never had the slightest inkling that he would marry Angelika.

Of all his girlfriends, Angelika was the only one with whom I felt thoroughly ill at ease. She would laugh, but her eyes never seemed to follow suit. My father appeared enchanted. But I felt that Angelika had no time for us girls at all, and what I took to be her disdain surfaced in odd places. When I came home sunburned after a hot weekend, she looked me over and then looked away saying, 'One should never, *ever* go in the sun without a hat, in the sense that it is simply – how should one put it? – so *plouc* [hick] to have a tan.'

We were never entirely sure whether Hugh's girlfriends knew about one another, but we were used to keeping our mouths shut and not asking questions. As it turned out, they didn't. Pa liked to cut things very fine, and thus Gay finally learned about Ginny when she arrived one day on a morning flight and found that Ginny was ill in bed at Cawdor and had not left, as intended, the night before. Pa sped to the airport, met Gay, gave her a brief explanation with promises of lavish apologies, and hustled her into a local hotel. 'You owe me big time,' she warned, and settled in to a day of room service.

The four women in my father's life neatly represented the corners of a playboy's dream. In its own eccentric way, it was a stable and cosy time. My father's ego was clearly stroked to the right degree. Even his relationship with Laura was improved. When she was ten, a friend of Ma's with a deaf child of her own had watched the way Laura failed to respond and suggested they get her hearing properly checked out. The hunch was right. She had no hearing in her right ear whatsoever. This was a huge breakthrough, because although nothing could be done, we all now knew which side to direct our voices to and, more importantly, Laura could warn strangers not to talk to her deaf side. In the way children do, she put aside all Pa's past taunts and was so doggedly affectionate that he quite forgot his old habits; besides, Cath, the real target of his attacks, had departed. In our new template of dysfunction, we were all shambling along rather happily.

The harem arrangement carried on for several years. We never asked Pa what was going on, we just accepted this new situation where we knew all the Olgas' real names. I don't know how it ended with Catherine, but Gay eventually went off with a younger man, and to our dismay, Ginny cooled and effected a partial withdrawal after Hugh flung a book at her head saying, 'The problem with you, Ginny, is that I can't destroy you.'

In London, punk had just rudely exploded into the national consciousness. For a nanosecond, it felt like an iconoclastic, shin-kicking movement with real political clout. But, no. Punk had swagger, but its manifesto was boringly nihilistic. Looking back, it is hard to recall the amount of naivety it had required to believe that society was going to be irrevocably shaken up on the strength of a sardonic reading of the national anthem by a bunch of cheeky boys looking like crowned cranes. The call of the herd was strong in my teenage bones, though, and for a moment I loved punk. It was thrilling and frightening, especially as its whole ethos was based on hating people like me.

I wasn't a proper punk. I never basted my hair with diluted sugar to produce stalagmites, or wore black lipstick, nor did I have any safety-pin piercings. Up until then my wardrobe was filled with all my mother's old fifties sunray skirts and satin stilettos; now I had PVC trousers and mohair jumpers that looked like a web spun by a spider the size of a guinea pig. Yet I was a ridiculous creature who knew all about Jacobite battles and a fifteenth-century woman called Muriel but nothing about The Ruts' tour dates. It would have been churlish not to be proud of Cawdor, yet our upbringing had made an anachronism of me. Of all the things drummed into us, the only ones with any application to the modern world were the importance of being polite to strangers, and a sketchy knowledge of trees. Even now, whenever I cross Hyde Park a list forms in my head as I pass each tree: hornbeam, plane, catalpa, ash, plane, ilex, false acacia, plane, walnut. I still get a twinge of anxiety if I pass one I cannot identify, and I can hear Hugh's voice: 'Come on, vole brain. Look at the seeds. See the bark. Think!' I go up to the trunk and stare at it, hoping that the solemnity of my approach will somehow impart its identity. It never works; all I can ever think of is 'TRRRREEESKIN!' There was nothing in punk that required my narrow historical expertise or my second-rate dendrology. After all the money spent on my education, it didn't feel as if I had any credentials at all.

After such a slow start, suddenly I was dating. My head was filled with boys, boys, boys. I trampled on other girls' toes and had mine trampled on and realized that sex was rarely pure and never simple. And if I should ever lack sufficient remorse for any bad behaviour, my older sister was always there to remind me of the precise quantities I should be experiencing. I could not translate my own stumbling experiences with the opposite sex into a more sympathetic understanding of my father's philandering. I never stopped longing for him to be impossibly noble and effortlessly wise. But what I wanted was unattainable. It was like hoping that Yassir Arafat would go to bed and wake up as Nelson Mandela.

Anyone who comes from a divorced family knows that it ruins Christmas: frosty wind makes moan. There was never any question of our parents showing a united front, although Ma would have done it for our sake; Pa preferred to keep her at arm's distance and not be reminded of his abuse. Normally, we spent Christmas with Ma, and New Year with Pa. We knew Pa had a choice of companions, whereas Ma was still a million miles away from getting involved with anyone else again. But after four Christmases in a row like this, we lost our heads and elected to swap the visits round. It turned into a bizarre disaster worthy of a novella.

Pa got drunk and wayward on Christmas Eve. Unbeknown to us, our mother's Christmas neatness with saved ribbon and folded paper had made the whole thing bearable for him. Seeing Cawdor so tidy when it was open to the public made him intolerant of any sort of untidiness, unless it was his. The shiny packages spreading out from the foot of the tree just looked like mess to him. After dinner, he gave the parcels a good kick, and then became adamant that we must open them forthwith. He wanted it all cleared away as soon as possible, or he would keep on kicking. We could tell he was in a dangerous mood so we opened everything. It was a hurried, tense affair, with Pa checking the labels and then throwing the parcels at us with more force than was strictly necessary. One present from my godmother was just shards of pink glass when I opened it, posing problems as to the gist of my thank-you letter.

We woke up the next morning to an irascible father and an unstructured day that stretched away before us and left us wondering what we could do to keep out of his way and fill the long hours. Church was out. Our family presence at Cawdor kirk had continued for a couple of years after my

261

grandfather's death, until one day Pa stomped out mid-sermon. My mother shrugged and signalled for us to stay put until the service was over. At lunch, Pa declared that he would never go again, because the new minister's sermons were 'too boring'. I wasn't sure what had made them more boring than all the others we had listened to, but his days of regular worship were over. Christmas Day turned into a shapeless day of boredom, and then Ma called. Her mother had died. Nature abhors a vacuum, and the emptiness of the day was now filled with guilt.

The following Christmas we reverted to the old plan of spending the New Year in the north – except this time Pa cancelled abruptly at the last minute. When I asked him why, he replied curtly that he had accepted 'a better invitation' in France, so with only days to go before New Year's Eve we all scrabbled to slot in with friends. Pa rang a week later, saying he was now back, and invited us all out to lunch in Soho. Emma had left for Kenya to stay with her new boyfriend, David Marrian. Only Colin and I were still in London, so we trudged off, still feeling slightly peeved over the way he had ditched us.

We met in one of those crowded Chinatown restaurants with windows obscured by flattened mahogany-coloured ducks hanging from butcher's hooks. Steam belched from the kitchen and the Chinese staff shouted what sounded like death threats at one another. When Hugh arrived, he was with Angelika. We made desultory conversation. Neither of us mentioned that his cancelling our New Year had been upsetting; that would have been talking about our feelings, and there was always an unspoken pressure to keep to the surface of things. Halfway through the meal my father heaved a buffalo sigh and said wearily, 'I've got something to tell you.'

Something about his tone made me guess immediately what it was. It must be about Sandy. After his old dog Wasp died when I was nine, my father had got another Labrador. He was named Sandy after a neighbouring laird. When the human Sandy was invited over to shoot, my father would delight in screaming 'Sandy! You bloody stupid arse! Fucking come here!' and observing the man's disquiet. Sandy the dog had once been able to sail over a five-bar gate, but he had grown deaf and arthritic; the last time I had seen him he had had great difficulty getting up. He must be dead. My father was about to break the news.

'Is it ... is Sa ... ?' But I couldn't bring myself to finish off the sentence. I stared at my plate and prepared myself for the blow.

Hugh cut across my dread. 'Angelika and I have got married.'

The information settled into every pore. So that's where he had been – just getting married. This news came with zero warning, without telling us, without inviting us. Just getting married. To Angelika. My plate engrossed me. I willed Colin to say something, but his plate had got him in its grip as well. Neither of us spoke. I had not had even the slightest inkling that this was coming, and later I learned that he had not even bothered to let Ginny, who was still on the scene, know either. Well, at least Sandy was still alive.

Eventually I said, 'Why didn't you tell us?'

My father said in a tight, irritable voice, 'I didn't need you lot lowering the tone. Now, who ordered the sizzling pork?'

And the subject was closed.

Even if both parents escape from a divorce with their hearts intact, children rarely do. Stepfamilies are, by definition, a product of loss. Things in our family got off to a famously bad start. Later, this famously bad start came to be regarded as a highlight. I tried to let Emma know, but she was out of touch for weeks. When she did get the news, her letter from Nairobi sounded far more composed than I had been.

> I got a letter from Ma after the New Year informing me about The Happy Event betwixt Pa & A. Ye Gods it's Bad News. I was so cross – I sat about for days thinking up nasty telegrams but in the end never sent one – we then went on safari for two weeks to the coast & when we got back Pa had sent a letter telling me all. Sometimes he's amazingly insensitive, he said that you'd been 'curiously miffed at not being told in advance'. What a nightmare. Pa's really so stupid sometimes. Hey ho.

Angelika did not have children of her own, but their place was filled by a pugnacious pack of squat Jack Russells. When they were puppies you could pick one out of the skirmish and then pull them all off the ground one by one as they gripped onto each other's legs like a string of fanged sausages. Angelika had a long rawhide whip that she used to separate them. Every time we came to Cawdor we hid it, but whenever we returned it was back in its place behind the door in the flower room. Dogs could be thrashed, but Hugh was the one who really needed a strong hand.

The urge of any new wife is to stamp her own personality on a home, and things began to change very fast. All the fruit and vegetables were grubbed out of the kitchen garden and replaced with a holly bush maze and a hideous fountain made by one of Angelika's friends. My mother's old bathroom was the first to get a makeover. When we arrived home for the Easter holiday, we were surprised to find a gleaming new lock on the outside of the door, like the loo in a boarding house. When I plucked up the courage to ask my father about the new lock, he gave me a tired look and said, 'You are forbidden to defile that bathroom further.' It was a wonder there was no doorbell, like the one Jack had by the courtyard door leading to his loo. It was a couple of years before the bathroom door was left unlocked one day and I peeked in. The old ivy tendril wallpaper had been replaced with salmon-pink, crushed suedette, and the cheval glass had gone to make way for a fitted mirror surrounded by panto bulbs.

Our mother was a banned subject. We never once managed to have a family discussion with Pa, let alone attempt to resolve our recent past. Angelika took up Ma's old habit of dressing in matching outfits with Hugh. She was a much more conservative dresser, so it was a cashmere jacket and the ubiquitous black polo-neck sweater rather than the floor-length velvet coats my mother used to wear. Issie Delves-Broughton, an observant stylist friend of ours, had noted the recurrence of this low-key uniform and one day came over for tea with twelve friends in tow, having instructed each of them to dress in a black polo-neck as a silent joke. To their delight, Angelika and Hugh did not disappoint. Fifteen people stood sipping champagne in the Tower Room looking like a guild of jazz critics, their hosts appearing to notice nothing strange at all.

We slowly worked out that we were expected to write thank-you letters for having us to stay; we were put in Coventry by Pa if we forgot. One time when I came home, instead of being put into my own attic bedroom I was told I would be sleeping in a guest bedroom at the far end of the house. Before I left to go south again, I decided to pop into my own bedroom for a moment. The door to my little staircase was locked, but there was another entrance to it on a lower floor so I went up that way. Behind my bed was a walk-in cupboard that stretched the length of the wall. A light came on automatically when the door opened. Someone had left it ajar. I walked across to shut it and could see that the cupboard no longer contained my things but was crammed with clothes, hats, shoes, scarves and costume jewellery – all Angelika's. My room had become her overspill wardrobe. I had to suppress an irrational urge to pour live yoghurt into every pocket. Cawdor had a dozen attics and eighteen other bedrooms, including two just beyond mine that had been unused since I was a child. I closed the cupboard and left the room.

It seemed pointless to speak out about my bedroom being annexed, but I wrote down how I felt in my diary. When I got back down to London, the diary was missing from my suitcase. My thank-you letter included a request for its return. It arrived in a small packet with a tiny note from my father that read *'dew dew . . .'* ('well, well . . .' in Welsh). So presumably he had taken and read it. There was no further communication for four months. A letter from Colin reassured me I was not missing much. Pa was making his life difficult too.

Cawdor is really grisly. I have invited Bill J to stay, which could mean Pa disinheriting me for having such awful friends. Pa is a little grumpy and has just this evening called me 'an arrogant sod' for changing the TV channel without asking, which seemed rather hypocritical. However, I can never retaliate because I usually burst into tears before I can get the words out in time – so I didn't bother.

Whatever feelings Angelika inspired in us as together we explored every cliché of the stepmother myth, it was clear that our father was smitten. She had a neck like a gerenuk, and we all knew he had a terrible weakness for them. He blamed all his former ills on an unhappy marriage, and put all his previous bad behaviour down to Cath's provocation. But however much the first flush of love with Angelika gave him hope, all he had done was slap a pile of icing on top of a fungus-filled cake. This belief, that with a new bride he was a changed man, meant that he avoided any confrontation with the werepig. So why would it go away? Angelika made an admirable attempt to control his drinking. To start with it was only on rare occasions that Hugh drank until he fell over, but his appetites remained essentially the same as before, only the behaviour became much more covert.

Meanwhile, the redecoration of Cawdor continued apace. To us who had lived in it for years, the place seemed dangerously close to becoming a museum rather than a home. In the drawing room, the sofas and chairs stood opposite one another in millimetre-perfect lines, like the foyer of a pompous Bavarian hotel. All the upholstery was uniformly navy blue and restuffed to within a feather of exploding. And the bathroom door lock was only the beginning. Hugh now clinked about the castle like a prison warder. Large metal rings the size of neck chokers dangled at his waist. The rings carried umpteen keys for drawers, cupboards, doors, gates – his heart. It was a look that had some comic potential.

While Angelika set her stamp on the decor, Pa was busy in the Tree Room, having just uncovered an old dungeon. The oldest walls at Cawdor varied in thickness between two and four feet, but the wall at the southern end of the Tree Room was curiously thicker. My grandfather had long suspected that there was a lost chamber, but when he had got a mason to drive a crowbar between the stone joints near the ceiling, they had found it solid. While the walls were being repointed, my father asked the mason to try again; this time they pushed the crowbar in lower down, and it penetrated a large space. A small passage was excavated. Inside was a bottle-shaped dungeon, called an oubliette, twelve feet long and half as wide with a tiny grilled window for light and ventilation. The only access, long since boarded over, had been through a trap door in the Tower Room above, meaning that the prisoner got dropped down the 'neck' and could only be released by being hoisted back out.

My father was in his element. After days spent in the Charter Room where all the family archives were stored, he eventually dug out two possible references to it. One was a letter from James III of Scotland, written in the fifteenth century, instructing the Earl of Huntly to persuade the then Thane of Cawdor to release William Rose of Kilravock from his 'prison'. (A few years after this, Muriel's father John was married off to the Rose daughter Isabel to heal this neighbourly rift.) His second find was some papers pertaining to one Callum Beg (Callum is a diminutive of Malcolm, and Beg means 'little' in Gaelic), a notorious local poacher who had been caught stealing a sheep – a crime that received the death penalty in the 1680s. He was brought to Sir Hugh Campbell and locked up with the ill-gotten sheep – another sign that there was some sort of prison arrangement within the castle walls. Just as Pa had a soft spot for Hamish Davidson, the mink liberator, Sir Hugh had one for Callum. He made sure his prisoner had a sharp knife and then conducted a long interview with the sheep's owner. In the meantime, Callum had time to butcher the animal and throw the pieces through the prison bars to the Thane's pack of hounds, which had been left conveniently in the courtyard outside the dungeon. With no sheep there was no evidence, and Callum walked free. Rapid recidivism led to Callum's capture by the Roses, and once again the neighbouring family got woven into the story. Sir Hugh galloped off to Kilravock and begged for Callum's life, but this time in vain. They hanged Callum and buried him in a field.

My father took me to the Tree Room to show me the box of relics he had found among the dirt and rubble at the bottom of the dungeon. There was a small comb made of bone, a thimble, several mouse skeletons and the leather sole of a tiny shoe. It seemed unlikely that a man like Callum Beg would keep a comb handy; in fact, every object pointed towards a woman's belongings, except for the tiny leather sole, which looked like it would fit a seven-year-old.

'They can't have thrown children into the dungeon, can they?' I asked.

'It's not a child's shoe,' my father said. 'I sent everything down to the V&A to see if they could put dates to anything. They have said it is definitely a lady's shoe.'

'It's so small.'

'Well, it shows you how wee people were.'

'But even so, why was a woman in the dungeon?'

'It was probably a wayward daughter, thrown in and forgotten about. They weren't called "oubliettes" for nothing.'

The idea of my ancestors imprisoning women was not an encouraging image. 'Not a lot has changed,' I joked. 'In those days they locked daughters in, and these days you lock daughters out.'

Hugh did not laugh, and making light of the situation did nothing to change it. If he accepted a distant dinner invitation while we were staying at Cawdor, he would order us to leave and check into a local hotel. We were not allowed to sleep the night alone in the house. I imagined it was in case we suddenly felt an urge to set light to the soft furnishings and spray the tapestries with fire accelerant. Hugh always expressed surprise when I opted to catch a train south rather than have dinner for one, and only the Golfview Hotel to burn down.

Our stepmother never talked about her past, but I gradually gleaned that she was born in Czechoslovakia, and her parents had fled to Africa during the war. She had grown up on a farm in Rhodesia.

At eighteen, Angelika escaped her dusty African backwater and moved to Paris. Once she had mastered the language she went into public relations. One of her best friends was Marie-Christine Reibnitz. I imagined that the two women had much in common, and both burned with an ambition born out of families that had been displaced by war. Marie-Christine was born in Czechoslovakia too. The Reibnitz family moved to Australia after the war, and later to a fruit farm in Mozambique. When we met at Dalcross, Angelika had only recently come across the Channel and had managed to swing a date with Prince Charles. Marie-Christine, meanwhile, tilted her sights further away from the throne and ended up as Princess Michael of Kent.

Chapter 15

There is no reason why good cannot triumph as often as
evil. The triumph of anything is a matter of organization.
If there are such things as angels, I hope that they are
organized along the lines of the Mafia.

Kurt Vonnegut, *The Sirens of Titan*

WHEN SHE LEFT CAWDOR, HUGH HAD GIVEN CATH THE
basics to furnish her new home, but after his remarriage
he made demands for their return. My mother obliged,
but put her foot down when the list extended to the
wedding presents that commemorated a marriage she had
not wanted to end. Hugh wanted back linen that had been
personalized with their initials entwined in red stitching on
the corner of every sheet; she refused. He wanted a pair of
diamond clips that Jack had given to his new daughter-in-
law, but unless Hugh was planning to wear the clips
himself, Cath did not see why she should hand them over.

She did agree to return the clips, but only to Colin's fiancée – whenever he got engaged – not to Angelika. Sometimes my mother would refuse to take the phone calls, in which case we got it in the neck instead. After Pa had yelled at me during yet another round of Chinese whispers, a letter came in which he apologized for trying to use me as a conduit for his conversations with Ma rather than doing it directly, saying he had been 'horrid and boring', occasionally going off 'Moh's Scale – the scale of hardness'.

Despite his fabled generosity, every now and again Hugh could be spectacularly cheap. Ma was shattered after these bullying sessions. She was in a terrible state generally for a long time, and it took her years to pick up the pieces of her confidence. It was very hard to live with her. We couldn't help. We just wanted to escape.

One rainy summer's day, Ma and I were heading down Eaton Square towards Waterloo station where I was to catch a train to stay the weekend with Mosh Gordon Cumming. I was holding a bunch of mimosa Ma had bought to give to a friend she planned to visit after dropping me off. We were driving along in a comfortable silence, listening to Villa-Lobos playing on her car stereo. I was watching a money spider lowering itself in little spurts down a gossamer strand hanging off her rearview mirror. We were not allowed to touch the cobwebs in her car, or pick at the moss that had formed on the rubber around the window frames; she was fiercely protective of the wildlife that was gaining a tiny foothold in the corners of her car.

'Liza.' My mother had a special clipped voice when

something embarrassing was being raised, especially if it was of a sexual nature.

'Yes?' Immediately on edge, and staring out of the passenger window wondering if we were about to tackle contraception or a similarly irksome topic.

'Has your father . . . has Pa . . . ever . . . made love to . . . you?'

Oh God. My gut fell like a crashing elevator as my thoughts flipped guiltily to the night Pa had come into my bedroom three years earlier.

'Please tell me. I won't be cross with you, darling,' she added softly, kindly.

'No!' I said, louder and angrier than I intended. The 'no' filled the car in a way that the 'no' had so singularly failed to do in my bedroom. It made me stop for a moment. And then, gabbling, 'How long have you thought that?'

She paused. 'I would say . . . about . . . three years.' I continued to look out of the window and told her about the night when Pa had woken me. She said, 'Oh good, I am relieved,' and the conversation moved on. I did not understand that she was trying to be gentle enough for me to tell her something terrible. I had nothing terrible to tell, other than a scary, confusing dawn visit, but why, I wondered, hadn't she asked before? Why hadn't she come to my rescue if she had misgivings at the time? And the travesty of the phrase 'made love' – did she imagine it would be something I might have desired? That it would have been anything else other than an incestuous rape? I was horrified. 'About three years' she had said. The accuracy of her suspicion split us apart with laser precision. My faith in

Ma as sane, honourable and utterly fair had never faltered, but until then I had not fully grasped to what extent her views had been bent out of whack by life with Pa. It took a decade for our relationship to repair after that short conversation we had while driving east down Eaton Square in a car smelling of mimosa.

Not for the first time I was cross with the wrong parent. Or rather, with the only one with whom I dared to be cross.

Emma and I had grown closer during our parents' long break-up. There was an unspoken pact that we would try our damnedest to act as padding for the Smalls, who were no longer so small. Colin's exams went well and he went up to Oxford; Fred and Laura were still at school and both eventually went to the University of East Anglia.

Emma and I, along with her Kenyan boyfriend David, moved into an attic flat in a Victorian redbrick house near World's End in Chelsea. I liked the area; it reminded me of listening to the shipping forecast on those long childhood car journeys from Wales to Scotland. 'Biscay . . . Finisterre . . . Sole . . . Fastnet . . . Lundy.'

'Where's Finisterre, Pa?'

'It's at the end of the world.'

Hugh hardly ever came to visit us there – too scruffy – but he showed a vague patrician interest in it. He wrote to me comparing our attempts to decorate it with Edward Lear, whose Croatian servant, when asked for a progress report on his new house, replied, 'him go on like one old tortoise'.

At nineteen, I fell in love. Christopher was the most handsome, awkward boy I had ever laid eyes on. He moved into our flat and our first year together was spent in a daze of head-over-heels bliss. The next three were spent reconstructing, wholly unconsciously, a pretty accurate replay of my parents' relationship. We were young and impatient so we telescoped it all into a fifth of the time. Mostly we reprised the demise.

Something that is seldom acknowledged is how incredibly common addiction is – maybe as high as one in three. When I was young in London, the role of drink was recast as heroin. Heroin was very edgy, very punk, and scores of my peers got into it. I loathed what it did to people: the nodding out, the scratching, the lies, the cracked voices and the needle-prick pupils. I wasn't born to be a junkie; I was a drinker; I came from a long line of drinking folk. I drank until I could drink no more and then stopped lest I invite the werepig into my waking dreams. I went off to New York to do a course at NYU, and on my return Christopher had started using heroin. Despite compelling evidence that our affair was in tatters, I did the same thing I had done with my father: I hung on and prayed for a miraculous improvement. I couldn't conceive of ending my relationship with my own father, and applied the same thinking to Christopher. My efforts to keep him away from heroin were futile, although I did discover that by far the best hiding place for a crash helmet is in the oven. Christopher eventually checked himself into rehab, but my first authorized visit was also my last. The advice of his counsellors was that if Christopher was going to start over it should be without any reminders of his past, and that included me.

Word reached Hugh that I was heartbroken by the perfunctory ending of our affair so he wrote me a letter that meant well, but it was clear he had not really been paying much attention at all. He tried to make me feel better by pointing out how tedious 'cocaine' made people because it caused delusion of 'genius', and saying he hoped 'Richard' would find the strength to 'discard his crutch'. Cocaine and heroin aren't that easily confused; one is a fluffer, the other a cosh. Cocaine is the drug of choice for hyper party-animals who want to get a whole lot happier. Heroin is for depressives who like to hover on a velvety cloud of death-like torpor. But what really jumped out of the letter was 'Richard'. Four years with Christopher and now he was Richard? If nothing else, the letter made me laugh out loud for the first time in weeks of post-romantic gloom.

When we were at home Angelika had a slightly better rapport with Emma than with me, and set about unilaterally trying to make a suitable 'match' for her. It was all a hopeless failure. She simply did not want someone else's choice, even if he was a) grand or b) rich. Hugh was still writing me letters fretting about cars and accidents and who I drove with: 'Your overdraft is certainly not your fortune, so your face may have to be its stand in.' It was meant well, but the message was rammed home with such metronomic regularity that it maddened me. His one gift to us girls would be to desperately steer us towards a rich husband; he was incapable of thinking in any other way.

He had absolutely no way of talking to us about jobs as he had never had one. In fact, a vanishingly small number of people in our circle of family friends seemed ever to have been employed.

After a couple of years, my relationship with Angelika became so tense that one weekend at Cawdor she approached me in private to air our difficulties. I opened my heart and tried to explain to her how I was sad that I could no longer think of our home as a home. She was equally honest. Instead of the stilted politeness that blighted every visit, we had been frank with each other for the first time. It felt like we had reached a watershed. I returned to London feeling uplifted, and for the first time hoped that we would reach some sort of understanding and that Cawdor could be a happy family home.

A month went by and I heard nothing from Pa. I thought little of it. My father often went silent for long periods. He could be extremely awkward on the telephone. Sometimes when he rang he would kick off the conversation with 'Well, whadda you want?' as if it was me who had made the call – and at a most inconvenient time for him. Six weeks went by, and still I thought nothing of it. They often went away without telling us.

Through the course of each year Hugh arranged his life so that he moved between three houses, the furthest house being about ten miles away from the other two, which were only a couple of miles apart. From late August to early November he and Angelika lived at Drynachan and hosted shooting parties. From November to April they lived at

Cawdor. When Cawdor opened up to the public for the summer months they moved to Auchindoune, a handsome house just beyond the Big Wood at the foot of the bonfire hill which belonged, through a series of trusts, to Colin. It was a good size for the son and heir to raise a family in due course, and to be on hand until the time came to take over Cawdor. But while Colin remained unmarried, Hugh made a unilateral decision to enjoy the usufruct of it. Whenever they moved they packed a pantechnicon's load of luggage that included pot plants, the silver lid for Angelika's marmite pot, the dog whip, champagne crates and all the other baronial bric à brac they could think of. This endless shuffling around this small, obtuse triangle caused them both a great deal of self-induced stress. As Hugh put it, 'Today is flitting to Auchindoune day, on which we lose 2 baskets, one corkscrew, all underwear, the temper (twice) and Faith.' Or, as Joseph Brodsky said, nobody is as bored as the rich, because money buys time, and time is repetitive. When they weren't traipsing between Cawdor, Drynachan and Auchindoune, they shuttled to Paris, where they had a smart Left Bank apartment. For their stopovers in London he bought a flat in Belgravia, a much grander place than his old pied-à-terre. I went to the London flat twice. The Paris apartment was off limits.

September arrived. It was my twenty-first birthday. Among the cards on the doormat lay an envelope written in my father's elegant italic script. He often forgot our birthdays, so I was thrilled that this time he had not. I even wondered if he had remembered the thousand-pound bet not to ride horses he had wagered me a decade earlier – a naive hope: when I did finally remind him, he denied all knowledge of it. I saved his letter until last as they were always a delight and any funny snippets must be read aloud to Emma. I noticed for the first time that the intertwined Cs that headed his writing paper had now sprouted a crown. The letter read: 'What I shall give you for your birthday is exactly what you deserve – nothing.' It turned out he had been fuming about my conversation with Angelika; he said that I should realize 'honesty is not blatant tactlessness', and that I had abused his love. We were back to square one. What I had thought had been a helpful conversation turned out to have been a diplomatic disaster.

After this, it was off to Coventry again until after Christmas, when Pa wrote to patch things up. I went up to stay again, but I realized that I must stick to superficialities. In fact, superficiality had become the order of the day. Cawdor stopped being a place that was a hub of the local social life. Our relations had not been welcome for a long time, and now most old friends and neighbours got frozen out too. A big surprise was the end of Hugh's friendship with Patrick Lichfield. Even more surprising was the reason: Patrick had been caught straying, and his wife had left him. He was devastated and looked to his old friend for support, but Hugh was not just unsympathetic, he was highly censorious. If Patrick was an unexpected departure, then the severing of his link with William Gordon Cumming was incomprehensible. William had divorced Cath's sister E so there was no longer any conflict of loyalties. The two men had been like brothers and had used each other's houses as second homes since their teens, yet for the last two years of his life Hugh refused even to speak to William.

The few who remained friends from his first marriage were a posy of art dealers who flattered Hugh by slavishly dressing in his jazz critic style. And there was a stream of new European friends spending their time, it seemed, comparing notes over where they went boar hunting. Whenever my father wrote about it, it sounded deadly to me, all that cold and wet, but as usual he turned it into a joke: 'a curious sport ... and mildly dangerous because wounded pigs and excited Frogs are not reliable'. And when the house guests had finished talking about boars, they moved on to the partridge shooting in southern Spain; whose yacht, and whose chalet; who was there, who, who, who, and how rich? The wives, who appeared to me as groomed as show ponies, wore tastefully neutral tones in cashmere and clacked with jewels. I thought they were brittle, dull and self-referential. One lunchtime I heard statements like, 'One simply must see the Alhambra at dawn in November to understand fully the resonations. Last time we went, our party included [King] Juan Carlos [of Spain]. He was very *simpatico* and truly erudite.' To an outsider these were conversational culs-de-sac; but I thought that between themselves, it was an elaborate game of verbal bridge designed to elicit envy and admiration. To play, you had to meet any boast with a parallel boast, but to win it seemed to me you had to trump with a showstopper. Something like, 'Ah, Juan Carlos! He dropped in on us only last week. He is so spontaneous like that. I said I forbade him to leave without taking a crate of our divine new pressing of olive oil and sleeping with my grandmother.' The only other way to win was to bring in a note of lofty censure. 'Isn't it so humiliating the way that every social climber throws herself at Juan Carlos? One can tell who they are because they all make him pose outside their houses so they can display the photographs in every room.' You could almost hear the thwack of silver against walnut as the picture frames were banged face down in half a dozen minds. On that occasion the atmosphere around the dining-room table bristled with airs but precious few graces. Once upon a time Hugh would have beaten a rude and hasty retreat from people like this. Not now.

Chapter 16

I'm off to the concrete sub-surface bombproof shelter,
where I hope to hold out after the general collapse of life,
as we know it.

Philip K. Dick, 'War with the Fnools'

OVER THE NEXT FEW YEARS ALL THE CAMPBELL OFFSPRING,
with the exception of Fred, moved abroad. Colin went off
to study architecture in New York, where he stayed for
seven years, commuting back when duties rose above
desire. Laura overlapped with him there for four years. I
went to live in Kenya, and some time later Emma moved
there too. It was not a premeditated exodus, but a life
without the obligation to see our father and his wife so
regularly was much easier. Fred, by contrast, soldiered on
and visited Hugh frequently. Despite the fact that he was
now at university, large areas of their relationship had
remained static since the days when he was a barrel-shaped

'Box' who only ever said 'unhunhuh'. Hugh generally regarded him as the congenial family clown. Pa could not see that Fred was never going to be suave in his mould; he was one of life's innocents. Doctors say that a chronic tickle is more torment than an ache. It was all very well to be laughed at when in high spirits, but Hugh's refusal to recognize any of Fred's depths began to look like a kind of open-ended persecution. Fred, out of all of us, was the most serious. He was assiduously green in all aspects of his life, long before it caught on with a wider public. He hand-washed his clothes in his bathwater. He rode a bike and took trains rather than burn up fossil fuels. Letters from him arrived on old household bills. He recycled everything he possibly could.

After graduating from UEA, Fred enrolled to read architecture at Edinburgh. While there, a girlfriend he adored ended their affair. He was crushed. Student friends urged him to visit a church where a charismatic priest was attracting huge congregations. Fred went along, and when the preacher told the assembled crowd that if there was anyone ready to embrace the Lord they should come up to the altar, he found himself overcome with emotion and going up to receive Christ into his life. Initially I was baffled by his rebirth as a Christian, but as soon as I gave it a second of thought it looked like a perfectly logical solution for the predicament he was in. With a broken heart and a father who was capricious in his affections, he had found in God an unconditionally loving authority who was never drunk or hungover. He wasn't actually there, but because of that he was always present. His conversion to Christianity gave Fred solace, but it gave Hugh more ammunition to mock. When Fred wrote from India telling him of his intention to be baptized when Ma came out to visit him, his response in a letter to me was 'You could have knocked me down with an earthmover. I hope the mother doesn't drop him in the aisle.'

There was once a tradition in titled families that second sons went into the Church. It was an acceptable way to earn a living outside commerce, which was not. The custom was long defunct, but in Fred it had revived, not as an alternative career, but to keep him sane.

My mother had had family connections with East Africa since her Uncle Doug moved out there after the First World War. He lived in a higgledy-piggledy sprawl of a house crowned with billows of bougainvillea and honeysuckle on a cattle ranch near Mount Kenya. Ma and Aunt E travelled out to visit their uncle and aunt every couple of years, and on the occasion when Emma accompanied them she had met David Marrian. When, after a couple of years, they got engaged, they decided to marry in Kenya. There was no way on earth Emma could or would marry at Cawdor. Angelika and Ma still had not 'met' since Dalcross and Emma could not bear for it to happen at her wedding. She was pretty confident that Pa, who had never yet shown any signs of an obligation towards time-honoured acts of paternal support, would not come.

In the weeks before their wedding David took us on safari to the Mara, a landscape that achieves naturally what Capability Brown did through long-term planning and careful planting. The only place that had ever given me that same sense of stately emptiness was Scotland. But this was warm. At home, a post-lunch trudge-about was often damp and sometimes dull. Africa opened its gigantic mouth and sank its teeth deep into my brain, into the ancient lizard part where the phone is off the hook to reason and will power. I fell completely in love with it and was very envious of Colin, who blithely tagged along on David and Emma's honeymoon before setting off to travel back to Europe overland. The trip took him two months, during which time Hugh pestered him frequently. In a letter Colin wrote:

My life is not without excitement – I am going to the Sudan tomorrow – in fact, there was a bit of melodrama – the day I got my visa Pa sent a cable saying that I had to be back in the UK by March 31st to sign some document. It was probably one of his ploys because Emma rang to say I'd gone to the back of beyond already, to which he replied he was going to contact the border guards, the embassy & James Bond to get me back.

When I went back out to Kenya for the second time, it was not with any intention of staying, but to keep Emma company when she went out to see David, who had flown out from England on his own a month earlier. He was working on a commission to paint a large mural in a hotel on Lake Naivasha. Hearing of our plans to join him, a friend, Desmond MacCarthy, asked to tag along on his way to visit a childhood friend. After a week in Naivasha, we flew with Desmond in an old Dakota plane to the Lamu archipelago, a dozen small islands nuzzled into the Indian Ocean coastline under stepping-stone clouds paving a vast blue sky where vultures circled improbably high on invisible thermals. Dhows waited to ferry us all across the deep channel that separated the airstrip from the main island. The jetty had a large section missing about halfway along, making it impossible to reach the dhows by that route. We picked our way down onto the exposed coral, seaweed slicks and mussel-encrusted cement posts while hefting suitcases and trying to keep our balance. The majority of the Dakota's passengers were bleeding discreetly by the time we reached the boats.

We landed at the village of Shela and followed Desmond up and down narrow sandy alleys until, with a cry of triumph, he banged on the heavy, studded door of a house sandwiched between a madrasah (school) and the village mosque. He turned the big ring handle and pushed the door ajar. 'Wilbur!' he called, and then louder, 'Wilbur! WILLIE!' We walked into a small courtyard with a well in the corner and jasmine growing up the walls. There was no response, nothing moved, and then there was an imperceptible noise. 'Shh!' said Desmond sharply, and we all stood still. There it was again: a small groan. We followed Desmond's pointing finger to the first-floor veranda, where there was a writing desk with a mess of books, papers, ink bottles and paintbrush jars, and among it all the top half of a naked man, sound asleep. A powerful pair of freckled shoulders heaved gently up and down and a great tangle of curly blond hair hid the face.

Willie woke with a start. 'Desmond!' he croaked. 'How lovely.' He got up from the desk, tightened his sarong around him and came rushing down the steps to greet us.

'Sorry we disturbed your siesta, Wilbur,' said Desmond.

'Certainly not,' Willie replied, 'I was meditating. Now, tea. I'll ask Wilson to make us a pot. Wilson! We have visitors; can you bring chai, please? And Wilson, bring some gentian violet too. They're covered in jetty wounds.'

A young man in royal blue shirt and matching shorts came skipping into the room waving a bottle of gentian violet and beaming ecstatically. He took each of our hands in turn and shook them ardently before skipping off again, singing. 'Wilson is terminally sunny,' Willie said as he swept a tangle of fishing paraphernalia off the table and into a basket. 'Now, come and sit.'

The beauty of the country, the excitement of having reached the coast, the heat, this house, this sleeping lion-man – and three days later Willie happened to mention that his lucky number, like mine, was twenty-four. On such diaphanous threads, I fell head over heels. If he had been left-handed, it probably would not have taken so long. After a fortnight Desmond returned to England. I stayed on. Five months later, I was still there. I knew Emma would pass messages on, but it took me a month to get in touch with my mother because the situation centred on a man, and these sorts of conversations were always very tricky to have with her. After two months I thought I owed Hugh an explanation too, but I was not sure what to say. In the end I just sent him a postcard saying, 'With love from the Bolter x'.

Was I running away? Sure was. There was no crisis, but I felt uncertain as to where my life in England was headed. It sure made it easier to jump when home life was stifling; malignant. Without warning, I had been shown a totally different world, and it felt like something worth grabbing on to.

I had spent two months travelling around Egypt and got all the aggravation of being a Western woman in an Islamic culture, so living in a Muslim enclave was not on any of my wish lists. But now I was wedged between a madrasah, where children chanted the Koran by rote all day, and the village's main minaret, where the loudspeaker was cranked so high that we could hear the imam's wristwatch ticking before he began to call the faithful to prayer every dawn in a husky vibrato. Moreover, having been perfectly satisfied that the first fish I had caught with Hugh on the Findhorn would also be the last, I suddenly found myself living with a fisherman.

Kenya had the same degree of enchantment for both of us; the only difference was that for Willie, the beautiful part was the bit covered in water. My first love had been addicted to heroin, and now my second was addicted to fishing. It might not be what I had predicted for my love life, but it definitely seemed like an improvement. Everything revolved around fish. Nils, a tall Dane with permanently bloodshot eyes from the glare of the sun off the waves, was one of the most fanatical. He spoke of feeling physically different when the plankton count intensified. 'That's not so surprising, considering you're half-man half-fish,' I said, teasing. He gave me an intent look, as if I had accidentally penetrated the very essence of his being, and after a long time he nodded slowly and muttered, 'I like to think so.'

It is a myth that the English have a monopoly on discussing the weather. The rain was ignored, but Shela residents talked endlessly about the winds. There was Kusi, a south-eastern wind; Kaskazi, a north-eastern wind; Matalai, a gentle sea breeze; Omandi, a gentle land breeze; and Marhibu, its stormy form. And finally, there was Haiwa, a heavenly zephyr that put all the sailors into such a good mood that they shouted 'Haiwaaaa!' at each other as their dhows passed. Those who weren't fishermen were engineers – the equivalent of vets for the fishermen's boats. They congregated every day on the local hotel balcony to squint into the horizon and discuss the arcane minutiae of boron-coated spigots, buckler plates and Bimini knots. I realized it helped to be deeply in love to tolerate such relentless, lone-themed conversations.

After seven months I flew home, tied up all the loose ends of my life, and returned to Lamu. I saw Hugh twice. The first time we met at a Japanese restaurant. 'How tanned you are,' Angelika said, and disappeared behind her menu. I started off excitedly describing my new life. 'Honestly, Pa, there is one boat captain who is the exact spit of the mine boss in *Butch Cassidy and the Sundance Kid*. I met his wife so now we know what sweet Betsy from Pike looks like . . .' I wanted to tell them more, but as my father's eyes glazed over with boredom I faltered, slowed down and eventually stopped talking altogether. I sat through the rest of lunch watching Angelika pop pieces of sushi into Hugh's mouth and listening to them bicker about what dates would be the least inconvenient for their chef's summer holidays.

The second time I saw Hugh was just before I flew back out to Kenya. He rang and we arranged to meet at the Royal Academy. When I arrived, I was amazed to find him on his own. Angelika had gone to visit her mother in Munich. I asked him what had brought him down to London this time. 'We've just been visiting Angelika's sister in Kent,' he replied. Angelika had a *sister*? Living in my least favourite county? We had known her for nearly ten years and she had never once mentioned to me that she had a sister, let alone one living in the same country. I asked him what she was like. 'Ten years older, married to a farmer, provincial, not nearly as good-looking as Angelika. Her name is Mechtilde' – he said this exaggeratedly, gurgling spit in his throat – 'which speaks volumes.'

After a pause he went on, 'But her daughter . . . now she . . . was . . . a different matter.'

'Sorry, Pa, I was miles away. Whose daughter?'

'Mechtilde's daughter. Much more like Angelika; amazingly sexy girl. Really stunning.'

As he talked, he looked flushed and agitated. My stomach gave a little heave.

'How old is she, Pa?'

'Dunno. Late teens.'

'She's your *niece*, you know.'

'She's my niece that I *don't* know, actually,' he threw

back sharply, and then said, 'I've had quite enough of French Impressionists for one day; let's have lunch.' And we walked round the corner to his favourite oyster bar.

We were a little early and the place was busy, so we sat in an alcove by the bar until our table was ready. I was quietly thrilled by the idea of having my father to myself for an entire meal, but the conversation about Mechtilde's daughter had got my hackles up, and when a woman dressed in tight trousers and a chunky belt asked if she could squeeze in beside us, it was a relief. My father ordered a bottle of champagne, and as we made our way through it Hugh invited her to join us for lunch. She said she was from Jersey; I don't remember her name. As they shared a menu, Hugh and the woman were flirting with each other so much I suddenly began to wonder whether her arrival at our table had been contrived. Certainly the friends she said she was meeting never showed up and never got another mention. Even if her arrival was spontaneous, she was mutating into another Olga Nethersole with astounding speed.

Once we had eaten, I had had enough and hoped that she would leave. Jersey Olga had different plans and insisted we go on to a drinking club she knew about. My father agreed immediately and they walked off down Piccadilly and into Shepherd's Market with me traipsing behind feeling like a gooseberry. Jersey Olga pressed a bell on an unmarked door. While we waited to be let in, she took a cigarette off my father. He held out his lighter and I watched as the flame circled the tip of her cigarette in wobbly ellipses. Eventually Jersey Olga took his hand in both of hers and steadied it long enough to achieve their shared objective.

A buzzer let us in and she led us up a narrow staircase to a musty second-floor room with drawn blinds, a small bar and velour banquettes. It was empty aside from a tired-looking barman with an extravagant comb-over and a pair of men sitting opposite each other at a table in the far corner who appeared to have fallen asleep. Either that or they were playing a very intense game of dominoes. My father sat drinking brandy. Jersey Olga ordered a foamy coconut and curaçao cocktail. When it arrived, my father grimaced and said it looked revolting. 'Oooo nooo, it's yummy,' she said, putting on an ickle-wickle girl's voice, popping a maraschino cherry between her lips and, with a pantomime wink, very slowly drawing it into her mouth. My father smiled as if it was Christmas, but from where I was sitting it looked like Halloween. Every time Jersey Olga threw back her head and laughed, her red-nailed hand went to his thigh and his hand kept it there. There was a moment when he asked me a question and touched my knee, and we sat there in a louche little daisy chain.

During the course of this afternoon, two things became abundantly clear. First, Hugh was back to his philandering. The way he told it, any past cheating was all down to being unhappy in his first marriage. His interest in Jersey Olga certainly made it look as if he was returning to his wandering ways. Second, however squeamish I had felt about his infidelities as we grew up, I had been under the impression that he strayed with alluring, sophisticated or at least interesting women. Jersey Olga was none of those things; she was brassy and coarse and had a laugh like a peacock. His bragging about personal freedom that afternoon with Jersey Olga seemed less swaggering than sad and hollow. I had recently read an interview with the writer James Ellroy who said that the last intelligible words his father had spoken to him before dying were, 'Try to pick up every waitress who serves you.' If I had been a son, Hugh would have given me similar guidance.

When Jersey Olga dipped her finger into her glass and pushed it into Hugh's mouth, I said my goodbyes and left them to it.

We decided to buy the house on Lamu, which until then Willie had been renting. In a country that does not have a written history, folklore substitutes, and Shela House came with its own small saga. An old Kenya settler named Kay Wilson had bought three plots. On one, she built the house; on the second, she made a walled garden; and the third she left as open land, where she sank a well. Later, when she enlarged the house onto the third plot, she built a courtyard that enclosed the well. The villagers were furious. Fresh water is scarce on Lamu and there was an understanding that all wells were public property. A delegation of villagers pushed their way into her house to dispute her decision, but instead of engaging in any sort of dialogue, she stood on her veranda dressed in a nightdress and sang an endless medley of nursery rhymes, until the exasperated villagers left. When she died, Kay requested her ashes to be scattered under the lime tree she had planted in the garden. A group of mourners and curious villagers gathered around to witness the ceremony, and after a few thoughtful words, Kay's urn was upended. As the ashes pattered on the ground, a dozen scruffy chickens dashed forward to peck at her earthly remains. The locals saw this as definitive proof that she was a mganga (witch), and long after she died it was rumoured that she had buried human bones inside a statue, a badly proportioned nymph in a toga that still stood in an alcove in the courtyard, as some sort of eerie sentinel to guard the well. It reminded me of the Fyvie curse:

Ane in the ladie's bower.

This was an incredibly happy period of my life, even though it involved fishing almost every day. We had no telephone, or rather we did, but it had been stolen – not the handset; the actual number had been sold by a bent telephone engineer. Try as we might we could not get through the red tape to buy another, but it was no loss. It was good to be far away from home and communicating only by letter. Hugh did not write often, but when he did he did not sound happy. One postscript written with a 'heavy duty' hangover while Angelika was away complained, 'I wish I weren't so dependent on a lady,' and expressed the wish that I didn't live so far away. 'Tonight I feel low,' he wrote.

One weekend, while Willie was away in a fishing competition, Wilson and I set to work on our back yard. We pruned the bougainvillea, whitewashed the walls, and Wilson dug in a new post to extend the washing line. When

Willie came home, I showed him our handiwork.

'Where did you get that line from?' he said, grabbing our new washing line and having a careful look.

'There were a couple of coils in the bottom of one of the dresser drawers. Why?'

'It's not washing line. It's detonator cord left over from a salvage job I did on a reef wreck. I'm going to have to take it down. I'll find some regular cord.'

Half-man half-fish Nils had won the tournament, and that night all the fishermen piled into our house to celebrate. No sooner had the subject of the detcord come up than the men felt bound to put it to use, immediately. Kay Wilson's old statue was the focus of their attentions. They clambered into the alcove, wrapped it in cord, lit the end and stood back. There was a polite but dissatisfying 'pop'; the statue remained unscathed. Willie ran to the dresser drawer and found a second, longer coil. This time there was a deafening blast; bottles and glasses smashed, cushion feathers filled the air and a hail of plaster and masonry coated every surface. Wilson rushed into the room to see a bunch of swaying men ashen with dust. The clear-up job was complicated by extreme drunkenness. After ten minutes they gave up and headed out to play midnight golf in the dunes, with a set of ancient clubs left in a storeroom. There wasn't a golf course within two hundred miles of Lamu, so the men invented a game in which each of them took a handful of balls, wrote the dates on them, climbed the highest dune and smacked them off into the distance. They then raced off in search of them, with minimum success; the real enjoyment of the game was coming upon a ball with a date from six months before. Anyone out on the dunes that night would have seen what looked like a quartet of renegade statues absconding from their plinths and cavorting in the moonlight.

The next morning I came downstairs to find Wilson in the courtyard with a broom. He had filled a basket with some of the larger pieces of rubble. 'Look,' he said, and handed me what had been the upper arm of the statue. At the broken end, where it had been severed from the torso, was a large bone running down its centre. 'There are more like it in the basket.'

'That is quite horrible,' I said, dropping it.

'It's a good thing the statue is destroyed. You must not be frightened; the spell was not for you. I shall get a mganga to come and clean the house of spirits. The coast is full of witchcraft and curses.'

'Don't worry,' I said, 'it's just the same where I come from.'

*

A year later, Willie and I got married. My face was not my fortune. I had always pictured my wedding at Cawdor kirk, but we got married in Kenya for exactly the same reason as Emma had. Despite Cath's willingness to meet them as a couple, Hugh would not budge to put the relationship on to a friendlier footing.

In the months after our wedding we moved away from Shela House, not because we were spooked by the statue, but because we fell in love with Kiwaiyu, a remote island further up the archipelago, away from the constant fishing talk and the red-eyed mechanics washed up on the mahogany reef of the hotel's bar. We built a long mangrove-pole jetty for the boats and dug out a staircase in the steep sandy cliff that led to a grove of thorn trees. Our living area was a clearing under the trees with some Swahili furniture and a bed with a mosquito net. We went fishing almost every day to catch supper, kept a few chickens for their eggs and bought crabs and octopus off the local fishermen. From time to time a lion swam across the channel and culled the local goat population; but otherwise, there were no big predators there. We roamed the island without any of the watchfulness needed on the mainland. At the northern end there were rock pools, some caves lived in by porcupines, others by a large colony of bats. Our beach was five miles of pristine white sand stretching away into the shimmering distance to the southern tip, and a few hundred yards offshore was a beautiful coral garden. The centre of the island had rolling hills covered in seagrass and low succulents, just like a tropical version of the warren at Stackpole, but with smaller, wind-wizened trees. On the landward side, impenetrable mangrove swamps stretched for miles in every direction.

Two wells sustained the tiny population with water that was brackish enough to give our morning coffee a salty tang. We fished to live, and Willie lived to fish. Every day we would be out at sea, hauling in tuna, travelly and, if we were unlucky, dorado, which Willie despised because its meat deteriorated so quickly in the heat. In the time it took us to get back to shore it had turned to oceanic kapok. There was no fridge, no generator, no electricity. When the sun went down, we lived by lanterns, and when we wanted a hot shower we lit a fire under a large Benghazi boiler and hoisted up a bucket with a showerhead welded to its bottom.

There were no roads within fifty miles. Kiwaiyu was not under any flight path, so the only things to see in the sky were bee-eaters, fish eagles, clouds and a billion sequin stars. On clear nights, not only did the moon cast its reflection across the creek waters, but Venus too. It was heaven, aside for the hankering for news of the wider world. The *Spectator* magazine arrived by dhow, months after being sent, and I would fall upon it hoovering up every column, even the television reviews. Our post was sporadic, but I had a family of keen letter writers and I loved sitting in the hammock reading all the correspondence from my family at their different points across the globe. Hugh's letters shrank to a trickle and were all the more precious for their scarcity. He sounded happier, but with Pa it was totally impossible to tell if his words bore a true reflection of his life. In one letter he reported that they had been plagued by high winds, which had brought down power cables, leading to 'a small but excellent firework display, and silencing the telly to Lady C's discomposure'.

I got pregnant, and a few months before our daughter was born we built a thatched shack where she and I could shelter from the sun. Storm's birth changed everything. She was a breech, both her hips were dislocated and she had to be strapped into a Pavlik harness that ran over her shoulders, round her chest and down her legs to little stirrups for her feet. Storm had to be in it twenty-four hours a day, and the good Doctor Pavlik had not designed it with equatorial humidity in mind. From living a totally outdoor life, suddenly I was confined indoors from sun-up until dusk with a tiny white baby. After three years of island life, we gradually reached the conclusion that maybe this was the time to leave and go somewhere else. We headed back to Willie's home in Norfolk.

Willie's parents wanted, understandably, to meet their fellow in-laws. My mother came and met them, but my father remained elusive. It was hard explaining to them that it wasn't that Hugh didn't want to meet them, he just did not adhere to normal social niceties – they were for 'other people'.

'I'm sure he'd come if we lived in a stately home too,' Willie's father said grumpily.

'No, no! God, no, it's nothing like that.'

But he had a point. I wondered whether Hugh would have come if they had.

I thought I might be able to solve the impasse at Storm's christening, although yet again we were faced with mother–stepmother awkwardness. I thought, 'What the hell, christenings are happy and brief and no-one has to stay. If we can all cope with the initial awkwardness, it will never be as bad again.' My father sent a note in reply to my invitation. 'It is not very likely that we will attend a christening in Norfolk next month,' it began. And then he changed the subject to Alexander the Great. For a moment I thought about explaining that I wasn't just inviting them off the cuff to a random christening of any old baby, but to that of his first granddaughter. Then I dismissed the thought. My parents-in-law were hurt and puzzled. They never did meet him.

I got pregnant again, but the work Willie had hoped for in Norfolk never materialized and our marriage suffered under the stress of having two babies and no breadwinner. It was becoming obvious that Willie functioned far better in the wilds than in his home country, so six months after our son was born we were packed and ready to leave for Sumba. Willie was in his element again, although I found the going tough. In Kenya, even though our friends were scattered over hundreds of miles we knew they were there. On Sumba, we did not have a single friend, and while Willie was out at sea my days were slightly lonely, chasing butterflies with two toddlers as my assistants.

Chapter 17

The trouble with closets is that they make skeletons terribly restless.

HUGH'S DEATH IN THE SUMMER OF 1993 BROUGHT US BACK from Indonesia. Cath met us at the airport. She brimmed with quiet sadness about missing Hugh's funeral. I ordered a wreath, left Willie with our babies and flew up to Scotland. The flight path took us over Cawdor, and the thought of the plane dipping its wings as it brought our father home made my eyes leak tears. We also flew over Kilravock, half hidden by tall beech trees, and lastly Dalcross, each castle with its specific significance in the course of our family history. I was cross-eyed with jet lag, but Colin looked after me and drove me to the graveside.

Since I had heard the news of Pa's death, the sadness had been interspersed with adrenalin-fuelled highs, sensations that were almost as physical as they were emotional. Aside from

Ma, there was no-one left above me on the family tree and it felt as if I had been shoved into the topmost branches. In my mind's eye, this family tree was not a stout oak such as you might see on the page of a genealogy book, it was a spindly poplar that bent and shivered. Hugh's death brought with it the sensation that we were all now, inescapably, adult, and yet, with the loss of a parent, I had never felt more child-like.

A few days later in London, White's Club in St James's celebrated its three hundredth anniversary. It was the party for which Pa had used up all his dying energies trying to ascertain if the Percys of Alnwick had answered their invitation, and it had now become his wake. The original guest list had not been compiled for such an event, so it was an odd bunch marking his death. The family seemed to be existing in a rarefied state of loss, and I remember little about the dinner other than seeing Margaret Thatcher looking like a Roman candle in a gold dress, holding court on an upstairs balcony and sitting next to an old Lovat Fraser friend who had been my only punk friend north of the Grampians. White's is normally men only, but they had bent over backwards to accommodate that alien creature, woman, and had set aside several of the gents' toilets where they had piled every shelf with enough boxes of Tampax to stock a chain of pharmacies.

The service was on 6 September, the day he would have turned sixty-one.

The shock of missing his funeral had left me craving a solemn, ceremonial goodbye. I wanted to hear his old friends telling stories about him, summing up his life and charting the highs without the lows. As the day of the memorial drew closer, however, it was becoming disconcertingly clear that the service was not going to follow the normal order. People started dropping out and Colin could find no-one who would give an address. None of us felt able to do it. William Gordon Cumming or Patrick Lichfield would have been perfect candidates, but as Hugh had rendered them erstwhile, it did not seem appropriate. The more we looked, the more Hugh's life seemed full of people he had either cut off a long time before, or had only been friends with for a short time, and on the most superficial level. Colin made call after call, but could find no-one. When I suggested that maybe he should do it, Colin said he just could not face it. The service went ahead without any homilies.

I had clean forgotten that, because Hugh had converted to Catholicism, the whole ceremony was going to be, well, Catholic. The fact that it took place in a gothic horror off Manchester Square wouldn't have mattered, but it was full of priests who had never even met Hugh. They spoke of him loitering with angels at the Pearly Gates awaiting the nod from St Michael. It sounded highly unlikely. These were the sorts of sentiments that would have had Hugh rolling his eyes and stifling his irreverence with a handkerchief rammed into his mouth. If Hugh was indeed at the Pearly Gates, I could only imagine him bumming a fag off St Michael. Towards the end of the service, the head priest invited the congregation up to the altar for communion, then gave a dry little cough and added, 'For those of you who are not Catholic, it is preferable that you please stay seated during this act of worship.' The whole service had been a series of pious, everyman brushstrokes, and the only chance to share in the ritual was subject to segregation. Angelika stood up to take her place at the head of the queue. I didn't have the nerve to gatecrash. By now I was thinking, 'Did I wax my legs for this?'

As the Catholics shuffled up for their transubstantiated snack, I was surprised to see Louis Grieg, a friend from Scotland, waiting in line. I knew he was a devout Christian, but had never realized he had converted to Catholicism.

When the service was over I saw him in the porch and said, 'When did you convert?'

'What?'

'I didn't know you had become a Catholic.'

'Oh! I haven't, but I wasn't going to pay any attention to that bollocks about not joining in.'

That one remark was far more in the spirit of Hugh than anything else that had gone on, and it made me laugh. I wished I had done the same, instead of leaving with a sense of complete alienation and the feeling that the memorial had failed on every level. The fact that this mood was universal made it even more depressing. The congregation spilled out onto the church steps and the general talk was what a rum, incongruous affair it had been; how little, if anything, of Hugh had been conveyed. In life he had had such a dominant character; in death he was reduced to a chimera.

Angelika had booked a private dining room in a hotel next door to the church for a memorial lunch. I stopped to talk to Uncle James who was with his two eldest daughters, Cara and a tearful Slaine.

'Shall we go ahead and get a drink?' I said.

'We're not coming,' James replied. 'I think we're going

to try out a little Chinese place off Marylebone High Street that Peebles told us about.' He squeezed my hand, gave me a kiss and wandered off, sandwiched between his daughters, their arms about him.

I stared after them, until they had vanished round a corner. I was aghast. Instead of being a lynchpin at the lunch, I had to conclude that this gentle, loving man, our uncle, Hugh's only brother, was not on the guest list. Lunch was a trial. I did not know half the people and had no energy for any get-to-know-you conversations.

The memorial had been the antithesis of what I had hoped for, and now, more than ever, all I really wanted to do was spend a few days with my brothers and sisters in a place that meant something to Pa, a place we all loved. The more I thought about it, the more a visit to Drynachan seemed to be the answer. I asked Colin if we could arrange a weekend up there. 'I don't know . . .' He sounded vague. A couple of days later we all met up for supper at Laura's flat and I tried again, hoping I would be able to persuade the others that it was a good idea.

'Please, it would mean so much . . .'

'It's not that simple,' Colin said suddenly.

'What difficulty could there be?'

'I don't think Angelika will agree to it.'

'But what could upset her about us going there?' Colin looked uncertain, so I took a deep breath. 'Pa is dead. Drynachan belongs to you now. Angelika doesn't live there. Surely you can go whenever you like?'

'No.'

'What do you mean, "no"?'

'I mean it's complicated.'

'What do you mean, "complicated"?'

'Pa has left virtually everything to Angelika. I've all but been cut out of the will.'

The will reading had been a couple of weeks after Hugh's death. None of us, other than Colin and Angelika, had gone, or had even known it was taking place. Since then, Colin had kept the revelations to himself, too shocked and ashamed to tell anyone. Heirs in the primogeniture system get disinherited only in extremis; if they are so wholly irresponsible, so dissolute or so mad that the consensus is that they will put the future of the whole family in jeopardy. Colin did not have the first idea what he had done, so the contents of the will came out of the blue. Not only had Hugh leaned down and pulled a gigantic rug from beneath his son, he had stigmatized him too.

As they left the solicitor's office, Colin had said to Angelika, 'Why didn't Pa tell me?'

'You never asked,' she had replied.

We sat around the table stunned. Colin was extremely uncomfortable. If he had been able to, he would probably have remained silent on the subject for ever, just like our great-grandmother Joan had done over the shame of her syphilitic husband. What weighed most heavily upon Colin was that when he became the 26th Thane, Cawdor was lost to the family. No wonder he had felt unable to read a homily about Hugh in church. My mourning came to a shuddering halt. 'Oh Pa,' I mumbled. 'You total cunt.'

Hugh had neither earned nor bought Cawdor. It had

taken no talent to receive all this extraordinary privilege other than being born the correct sex. These possessions were entrusted to his care, but Cawdor was not *his*. Not only had he shafted his own son in the will rewrite, he had shafted the previous twenty-four generations. This stony treasure had survived six hundred years of wild Scottish history, including a crucial battle fought on its doorstep, yet it took only one drunken rake to piss it away. Hugh's life achievements amounted to a list of perfidies: demolishing Stackpole; selling Golden Grove and all the Welsh land; brutalizing his first wife; rebuffing his extended family; discarding friendships like used tissues; indulging in fabulously injudicious sexual adventures; destroying his health; and then revealing his most wretched act only after his final exit. We would never know what he had so urgently wanted to tell Colin as he lay dying in hospital.

There was a further chilling discovery. Hugh had not changed his will in a fit of steroid-fuelled rage during his final decline, he had done it seven years into his second marriage and then spun a web of lies, constantly interrupting Colin's attempts to get his architectural career started by demanding his presence 'to learn how to run the place' when he had already secretly signed over Cawdor to his wife.

Like a lot of sons, Colin had rebelled against many of his father's ways. He didn't drink much and he had never smoked; he had the beginnings of a career; he had one girl-friend at a time; he was a pretty steady guy. He loved his father. To be fair, Colin did have one really irritating fault: he was a useless timekeeper and missed a lot of planes.

Maybe that was his crime. But throughout our childhoods Hugh never missed a chance to stress that, twentieth century or not, we were all subordinate to the institute of primogeniture. Emma, Laura and I had been laboriously groomed to expect nothing. As girls we were outside the grand scheme of keeping everything intact for the heir, blah de blah de blah. We had heard it ad nauseam, so the indigestible irony for us girls was that while Pa had insisted that his daughters remain disenfranchised, he had broken the archaic tradition he had championed by handing every-thing over to a woman.

I had never realized before that there is clearly an art to writing a will. For a man who had so much, Hugh's will was an amazingly curtailed document, only one page long. Its effect was to tie Angelika and Colin together in a way that seemed almost consciously designed for maximum friction. Cawdor belonged to Angelika along with any 'Welsh' furniture from Stackpole, which included most of the portraits of our forebears, yet the 'Scottish' furniture belonged to Colin, thanks to a trust that had thwarted any desire of Pa's to hand that over to her too. At Drynachan, it was the reverse: the house belonged to Colin, but the furni-ture was left to Angelika. In a stroke, Hugh had effectively torn the estate apart. Not surprisingly Colin felt that his behaviour was under scrutiny and feared that failure to comply with her wishes would ensure that Cawdor never, ever returned to the family.

Two good things happened to Colin. Firstly, he married Isabella, an Irish beauty and his long-term girlfriend whose loyalty and level-headedness was unwavering. She was a good businesswoman, and despite the distraction of having three babies in hectic succession she was instrumental in helping him return to viability those parts of the estate entrusted to him and therefore outside the reach of the will. The second good thing was Uncle William. Horrified by what his former best friend had done, William stepped in and gave Colin emotional and practical support that lasted until his death.

Though the punishment had fallen on Colin, the rejection hit us all. Why had Hugh done it? What were his motives? During the first year, we were confused and out of kilter with one another.

I went up to Drynachan filled with questions that were almost too painful to ask. After lunch on my first day there, Angelika met me in the sitting room and said, 'I have been giving certain matters my serious consideration.' She paused. 'It must be a little bit sad for you girls, in the sense that you have not been given anything of your father's, yes?' This empathy made me ever so slightly unsure. I said nothing. 'I am prepared to give you something of your father's,' she continued. 'I have already done the same for your sisters. You can take one of his fountain pens.'

'Thank you.' I was not sure if I should voice my immediate reaction – but what the hell. 'I have a problem with Pa's pens. He was right-handed and I am left, so we wear our nibs down at different angles. I won't be able to use it. Would it be OK to have something else instead?'

She walked out of the room. I took that to mean no.

The desire to understand Hugh's motives for disinheriting Colin haunted me. Questions circled tediously, the mental equivalent of grinding my teeth. The big picture was out of focus and the small things irritated – like why, on my last visit to Cawdor before his death, had Pa bothered to rant about Ma coming back to live in the north when he had made Angelika the chatelaine? The curiosity was two-way, and while we were frustrated in all our attempts to determine the underlying cause of Hugh's decision, it seemed that our stepmother was equally keen to know about us. Any mail sent to me at Cawdor would be forwarded, having been opened first and sellotaped back down. It took some time, but eventually all my mail avoided Cawdor and the only letters that ever arrived for me there were those of a postal stalker called Gary, a man who lived in a secure mental hospital somewhere in the Wirral. Gary was a complete stranger to me, but three or four times a year he wrote me rambling letters that recalled the wonderful times we had had together in Holland Park along with a couple of Siamese cats. I was grateful that his letters went to Cawdor rather than his knowing where I lived in London, but nevertheless I was irritated by the thought that his letters might be scrutinized before they reached me. I preferred to keep my lunatic private. Eventually, in a flash of inspiration, I wrote a letter berating Angelika for opening my mail, then I sealed it in an envelope, addressed it to myself and sent it to Cawdor. Having opened it, she forwarded it to Colin saying, 'As you know I open everything that comes in my mailbag without looking at who it is addressed to,' and that she thought I 'needed psychiatric help'. Perhaps that was why Gary was drawn to me.

*

The fountain-pen day was the last time I was invited to stay with my stepmother. We all continued to visit Scotland a couple of times a year, taking it in turns to stay with Colin. If we wanted to go home, it was easier to buy visitors' tickets along with everybody else. From time to time we bumped into our stepmother there. Once, Emma and I were with our children when we came upon her in the drawing room giving a personal tour to a party from Scottish Heritage. Angelika did not notice us as we joined the back of the group and swept an arm past our family portraits saying, 'And these, over here . . . these are all the generals.' It was not clear to which of the many portraits she was referring, but it was nice to hear that all the boys had got promotions. Pryse hadn't even been a soldier last time I passed his frame. She ushered the group into another room, but I stayed behind to gaze at the Pa-in-drag portrait. We spotted Angelika again as she waved her guests off and we went over to say hello. In a flash of mischief we asked her if she could take a photograph of us. We handed her a camera and stood in front of the portcullis, grinning gormlessly and giving the thumbs up, enjoying the irony of her stepchildren and step-grandchildren as tourists in their family home.

Colin lived by the Findhorn in a small farmhouse which he enlarged to accommodate his growing family. It turned out that Hugh had run the estate into the ground. The farms had been poorly managed and great blocks of forestry had been neglected to the point where the woods were impenetrable. The plantations had never been thinned, and as the trees grew they had become so tightly crammed together that they had to be clear-felled before maturity, thus wasting much of the original investment. Uncle William helped Colin turn Drynachan from being a sparsely populated grouse moor into a profitable partridge shoot that provided funds to help repair other parts of the estate.

Drynachan was problematic though. Angelika insisted on getting the use of it in the middle of the shooting season, regardless of the headache of re-housing the paying guns elsewhere. Sometimes, Colin had eight men crammed into his house, to make way for our stepmother. Whenever they clashed over this, Angelika's stock response was to threaten to remove all the furniture. Colin finally decided enough was enough. He hired a fleet of pantechnicons and carried out the threat for her, delivering a lodge-full of furniture to her other house, Auchindoune. Through all of this, Colin managed to keep the family together. My marriage had collapsed within months of Hugh's death. Having lost the two central men from my life, and having become a single parent of toddlers, I was a mess. Colin was unceasingly empathetic and supportive.

Although Angelika lived at Cawdor during the off-season, while it was open the castle was run as a tiny company with her and Colin as its two directors. When Colin queried some of her business decisions, she resigned her directorship and went off to New York. The company articles stated that, 'if at all possible', one of the directors 'should live at Cawdor through the winter months', so Colin, as the sole remaining director, moved his family in. Even though he knew the move was doomed, he was elated. He rang us all up and said, 'You'd better get a move on if you want to come and stay because Angelika is going to use all her energies to get me out.'

It was strange to go back to Cawdor. For the first time since Hugh's death, we wandered through the corridors behind the visitors' route. The main guest bedroom had new hangings on the four-poster bed; a riot of flounces in various shades of peach, decorated with Princess Michael of Kent in mind, and a Christmas card from her still stood on the mantelpiece in late spring. The guest loo was still lined with pictures of us as children, wearing kilts, holding dogs, dressed for aikido, but it was upsetting to find that rooms not on public display were now in squalid disarray, and at the top of the tower there was a huge, unattended leak. Cawdor had become very sad for us.

As Colin predicted, Angelika rushed to court. She petitioned that the furniture, which had survived the wear and tear of half a dozen generations, would suffer from being used by her step-grandchildren. The judge bowed to her appeal and ruled that Colin and Isabella could stay, but their children could not. The final score from that skirmish was: Inanimate Objects – 1, Current Thane – 0.

Whenever I ran into any of Hugh's old friends, I quizzed them for clues about his state of mind when he rewrote his will. Patrick Lichfield was as baffled as any of us. Hugh had acted as Patrick's trustee and had been instrumental in organizing his family affairs to safeguard the estate for Patrick's son. I went to stay with Guy Roxburghe, one of our family trustees, to find out what he thought. His answer was that Angelika was very good at running the castle shop. Other trustees repeated this explanation. So, running a shop that sold oven gloves and cardboard cut-out Cawdors through which all visitors got siphoned on their way to the exit trumped the rightful inheritor. Perhaps Buckingham Palace will go to Camilla Parker Bowles because of her superlative ways with souvenirs. Other old friends made suggestions that 'he must have done it as a tax dodge'.

'Then why would he keep that secret?' I would ask.

'Well, it will be entailed, so it reverts back after death.'

'It's not entailed. Angelika could leave it to Robert Mugabe.'

'She's bound to move out in a few years. After all, she's a widow rattling around on her own in a house with, how many bedrooms?'

'About eighteen.'

'Exactly. Cawdor's always been a family house. Colin's got, how many children?'

'Three, and another on the way.'

'Well then, she's bound to move. What about London?'

'She sold their flat. She prefers to stay at Kensington Palace with Marie-Christine Kent. Anyway, she spends all her time in Paris.'

'She could buy something nice there.'

'She already has.'

'Well then. There's Auchindoune as well, so she's got plenty of places to go, hasn't she?'

'Yes but—'

'It'll come right. You'll see.'

'Hmm.'

*

Anyone who has lost a parent knows that when one dies it does not mean the end of the relationship. They live on in your head, and as I tried to come to terms with all that had happened it sometimes felt like Hugh's character conflicts were so bizarrely acute that instead of building up a picture they busted it wide apart. He was a tree lover who neglected his beloved woodlands. He held lifelong anti-Catholic views, but became one on his deathbed. He was a control freak with the capacity to fall totally under the influence of another, and his heroes were Jimmy Dunbar, who humiliated his heir, Hamish the mink vandal, and the Wolf of Badenoch. Obsessed by continuity, he decided the rules did not apply to him. He had displayed the family motto 'Be Mindful' on his belt buckles, but had never taken the words to heart. He worked hard to protect the inheritance of other people's sons, but spurned his own. He was a philanderer who censured straying friends. He seemed to me to have behaved recklessly in his second marriage, but Colin was left to untangle the mess. It was hard to analyse such chaos when his unravelling had to be seen across the span of his whole life.

Hugh was a sensitive little boy and his nervousness was exacerbated by a neurotic mother. Extravagant adult fears on open display are as contagious as ebola to children, and Wilma's steady determination throughout the war years was that if the end was not nigh today, it would be to-morrow. His mother was a far from reassuring figure; that role was filled by Hugh's nanny, Miss Dunkerley. When Hugh was about seven years old, however, she took to 'fooling around' with him – something he described as a heady mix of panic and excitement. One evening, when my grandfather Jack was back at Cawdor on shore leave, Miss Dunkerley had taken Hugh into her bed as usual and was molesting him when the door creaked open. Jack Cawdor had come to join her. Miss Dunkerley leapt out of bed and managed to defer his visit with some whispered excuses and promises while Hugh lay hidden under the pile of rumpled covers, heart hammering with the thrill. Miss Dunkerley's attentions and this scene in particular were crucial in shaping my father's worldview.

From an early age he had been disabused of any notion that parents are faithfully paired, like swans. Not only had he been witness to nocturnal family deceits, he had also scored a dubious victory over his Oedipal rival. If this gave him a reckless sexual confidence, it came with an inability to assess who was off limits. Hugh's fixation with nannies resurfaced when we were growing up. Our beloved cook Edith's room was one of the few exclusion zones when he was tipsily tiptoeing around at night.

When Hugh was in his early teens, Jack's drinking and inability to express himself turned to violence. When he broke Wilma's toe, he showed his son that physical abuse was an option, and as his parents' marriage creaked, Hugh identified with the abuser rather than the abused. Wilma's attempts to get Hugh's sympathy were rebuffed so thoroughly that he effectively severed any affectionate ties with his mother.

An inability to articulate his own timidity allowed Hugh's inferiority complex to flourish in the shady recesses of his thoughts. When I listened to the stories of the ass and the tree, Muriel and John the French repellent, they were just that, family stories. To Hugh, being born the heir made the same stories cautionary tales of what he had to live up to. These seeds germinated into a desperate reverence for people with a steely core. First he found, or perhaps was found by, Thatch, and later Angelika. The other way he dealt with his fears was with alcohol, but his drinking spun out of control. His addictions went unaddressed and got worse and worse. It was as if too much money kept him muddled.

When I was going through a box of all my old letters, I happened across a crumpled checklist written when I was about thirteen, in a juvenile attempt to work out what ailed him. It read like one of Aunt Carey's cherry-stone rhymes:

> Manic-depressive
> Schizophrenic
> Psychopath
> Bastard

'Manic-depressive' was crossed out. My reason for eliminating it was that while he did have moments of mania and wild profligacy, he was not a depressive, showing some melancholy tetchiness only when he was hungover. 'Schizophrenic' was also crossed out. I dismissed that theory after asking him if he ever heard voices in his head. He laughed and said that I had gone mad.

I had compiled the list after watching a documentary about psychopaths. It had left me wondering. A professor with a lisp that was unfortunate for the number of times he had to mention the word 'psychopaths' said that only one per cent of them went on to be murderers. By this time I certainly believed my father was capable of killing someone. The professor went on to say that 'psychopaths love power and often gain ascendancy in corporations, politics or within family systems during periods of turmoil. When necessary, the psychopath will be extremely charming and seductive, but it is only ever motivated by self-interest. They are without empathy or conscience; like a piranha in a goldfish bowl they cannot turn into a goldfish. There is never going to be an epiphany.' I liked the bit about the piranha, but I knew in my heart that my father *was* capable of an epiphany. I knew he had the capacity to empathize. He even had a conscience, although it was a little underused. 'Psychopath' had therefore been crossed out too, with a small 'phew' written in brackets. In my earnest teenage way, I was trying too hard to pathologize. Hugh was just a common-or-garden drunk, yo-yoing between hangovers and drunkenness, sinking further and further into the quicksand.

In the end, I had put a tick against 'bastard'. Of course that was wrong too. Another truth emerged when I found a letter he had written the year before he died, in which he blamed his recent absent-mindedness on the sleeping pills 'which I have taken for years and which have just been banned', while rejoicing in the fact that he now had 'a cast-iron excuse' for the memory blanks we had all been aware of for years. I had taken no account of it before, but rereading it made me ask his friends slightly different questions.

The sleeping pills, it turned out, were the upshot of a hefty cocaine habit. I was amazed – not that he was a cokehead, but that I had missed it when it was so blindingly obvious. Hugh was always up until the early hours, forever leaving the room only to return mopping his nose with a large spotted handkerchief, forever having wild mood swings. Coke extends the capacity for drink and delays the falling-over stage, but it seemed a miserably sad state of affairs that Hugh took it night after night on his own. No wonder we all felt so out of step. I also understood why Hugh had got his drugs muddled up in his letter to me about my boyfriend 'Richard'. He had written that 'cocaine' made one 'more boring than a drunk because it has the effect of making you believe you are a genius'. He was inadvertently counselling himself.

The last person anyone expects to find in the next-door cubicle in a nightclub is a parent, but it was much less frightening to think that the balance of his mind had been tipped by drugs rather than the sober, internal tics I had listed against mental disorders as a teenager. Coke was not the whole answer, but it went some way towards an understanding of the crazy paranoid behaviour, the women, his lack of judgement, the hexes, the violence. Hugh was like a child. He adored the luxuries Cawdor gave him, but loathed the burden of being the Thane. He could only really express himself and feel free in his letters. Writing gave him real joy. In his letters he could be his best self, and whenever I reread them the bad memories diminish and I can believe he loved us all. Although away from the page expressions of emotion often made him wince, I do think he loved us all very much, poor man. Maybe, just maybe, somewhere in that crazy head of his he thought he was doing Colin a favour. As a child hiding within the man, he might have found it hard to imagine that his son would be able to cope with the responsibilities Cawdor entailed, and resolved to free him from the chains of primogeniture. As Shakespeare put it

> To throw away the dearest thing he owed,
> As 'twere a careless trifle.

Acknowledgements

I would like to thank Marianne Velmans, Jonny Geller, Jo Micklem, Patrick Janson-Smith, Daniel Balado, Deborah Adams and Doug Keen for their support and faith. My love and thanks to Miles Bredin, Milla Guinness, Raffaella Barker, Natasha Fairweather, Kathleen Tessaro, Gilly Greenwood, Kate Morris, Debbie Susman, Jill Robinson and Aly Flind for all the reading, listening and encouragement.

I would also like to thank Mad Harper, Joseph Farrell, Mairead Lewin, Sarah Stitt, Catherine Fairweather, Simon Tiffin, Ruth Burnett, Clarissa Pilkington and Louise Guinness for their loving friendship.

My love to Emma, Colin, Fred and Laura with whom I shared a mad, bad and often beautiful childhood, and especially to my mother, who, while being a very private person, let me write about things that were very painful for her. A more courageous, kind and dignified woman would be hard to find.

My love, as ever, to Storm and Atticus, my wonderful children, who were so patient with me as I burned supper after supper while trying to write. And who both know full well that I am only going to write another book to cover up for the fact I can't actually cook.

And lastly in memory of a father, who, but for his failure to escape the vice-like grip of a pernicious disease, would have been a truly spectacular human being.

The sadness is that while my father was a brilliant letter writer, and on paper was able to express his kindest, funniest and most generous self, I have been unable to quote extensively from any of the letters he wrote to me as a child because of the laws of copyright and the contents of his will. To protect a few minor characters, I have changed some names.